ALCATRAZ SCREW

120

D0835113

Alcatraz Screw

My Years as a Guard in America's Most Notorious Prison

George H. Gregory

University of Missouri Press

Columbia and London

Library of Congress Cataloging-in-Publication Data

Gregory, George H., 1913–1996
      Alcatraz screw : my years as a guard in America's
   most notorious prison / George H. Gregory.
         p.   cm.
      Includes index.
      ISBN 0-8262-1396-0 (alk. paper)
      1. Gregory, George H., 1913–1996.   2. Inmate
   guards—California—Alcatraz Island—Biography.
   3. Prisons—California—Alcatraz Island.   4. United
   States Penitentiary, Alcatraz Island, California.   I. Title.
   HV9475.C2 G74   2002
   365'.92—dc21
                                    2002023839

Designer: Kristie Lee
Typesetter: The Composing Room of Michigan, Inc.
Printer and binder: The Maple-Vail Book Manufacturing Group
Typefaces: Adobe Garamond and Frutiger Ultra Black

I dedicate this book to my wife,
Velma, and her computer.
Without them, this book would
not have been written.

Contents

Acknowledgments
by Velma Avant Gregory

Following my husband's death on October 7, 1996, I continued efforts to find a publisher for his manuscript. I would like to thank the people who gave me advice, encouragement, and support throughout the process.

A special thanks goes to John W. Roberts for his suggestions on footnotes to clarify prison terminology, his help in establishing the chronology of events, and especially for writing a masterful introduction for the book. His experience as chief archivist for the Federal Bureau of Prisons makes him uniquely qualified for his contributions.

Rebeka Brady assisted greatly in preparing the manuscript. With her background in public relations and marketing, she supplied an objective point of view that was essential in many aspects of the preparation.

Encouragement from Dori Gores was exceptionally meaningful because of her profession—she is a book editor and former publisher. It was through her advice that I found a publisher.

Others to whom I wish to express my gratitude: Jolene Babyak, for help with details about Robert Stroud and so much more; Johnnie Brunner; Willis Denome; Anne Diestel, who made available a number of the photographs and documents used in the book; Nora Harris of Harris Indexing Service, for indexing the book; Frank Heaney, who was a correctional officer on Alcatraz; George H. Gregory III, for advice and support; Zella Kotala, for proofreading; and Susan Little, for a first editing of the manuscript.

I also wish to thank the people at the University of Missouri Press: Clair Willcox, acquisitions editor; Jane Lago, managing editor; Beverly Jarrett, director and editor-in-chief; and Gary Kass, editor. I am deeply grateful to them for patiently answering my numerous questions and guiding me through the process of preparing the manuscript for publication.

Introduction

by John W. Roberts

Few subjects have been the focus of more misinformation than the former
U.S. Penitentiary at Alcatraz. The imposing white prison perched upon a rocky
island in San Francisco Bay is well-known as a location for gangster movies, as a
staple of popular lore, and as a tourist attraction. But the inside story of life on
The Rock remains as elusive as it was during Alcatraz's scant twenty-nine years
as a federal prison.

Ironically, it was the U.S. Department of Justice that helped pave the way for
the emergence of myths about the island prison. During the penitentiary's early
years, the Justice Department mandated that its operations be cloaked by a policy of official silence. Prison administrators therefore seldom responded to the
wild tales of abuse that soon emerged, and which gave Alcatraz its gruesome reputation.

In more cynical times, that policy might have been interpreted as a sinister
cover-up, but the department's intention was quite mundane. Many of the inmates incarcerated at Alcatraz enjoyed the sort of fame normally reserved for
movie stars. Being sent to the most secure prison in the country could burnish
their celebrity image to a high gloss. Al Capone, Machine Gun Kelly, Doc Barker, and Robert "Birdman" Stroud were too famous as it was, reasoned the Justice
Department, without further enhancing their role-model status for young toughs
by allowing the public to stay up-to-date about their lives on The Rock. At Alcatraz, they could be cut down to size *inside* the walls by denying them the sort
of privileges they had previously enjoyed in other prisons and by treating them
like any other inmate. And they could be cut down to size *outside* the walls by
stifling publicity about them. Or so the department thought.*

John W. Roberts is the senior archivist of the National Park Service and was formerly the chief
of archives for the Federal Bureau of Prisons. The opinions expressed in this introduction are those
of the author and do not necessarily represent the positions of the National Park Service or the
Federal Bureau of Prisons.

*David A. Ward, "Alcatraz and Marion: Confinement in Super Maximum Custody," in John W.
Roberts, ed., *Escaping Prison Myths: Selected Topics in the History of Federal Corrections* (Washing-

The veil of silence inadvertently created an information vacuum—a vacuum that was filled quickly by former inmates with axes to grind and by reporters with newspapers to sell. As outrageous stories about Alcatraz as America's version of Devil's Island proliferated, the Justice Department realized its mistake and began bringing judges, political figures, reporters, and even stars of gangster movies onto the island in an attempt to show opinion-makers that the facility was nothing like its increasingly notorious image. But it was too late. The mystique of Alcatraz, inaccurate as it was, had become part of American culture.

The lurid tales of brutality at Alcatraz are so familiar they may be considered clichés. They are also so outlandish they may be considered fabrications.

A 1994 motion picture, *Murder in the First,* took the legend about as far as it could go. It depicted an actual inmate, Henri Young, who, according to the movie, had never committed a violent act before being sent to Alcatraz on a minor first offense in the 1930s, but who was driven to homicidal insanity by the unspeakable conditions on the island. The film went on to show an aging and out-of-touch warden who was responsible for running three prisons simultaneously and was so seldom on the island that he had no alternative but to relinquish control of Alcatraz to an associate warden, a sociopath prone to committing atrocities against the inmates—such as confining Young to a dark, subterranean dungeon for years and severing his Achilles tendons as punishment for an escape attempt. The movie concluded with the brutalized Young bravely triumphing over the prison in the only way he could, by committing suicide.

In fact, Young, far from being a minor first offender, was a career criminal with an extensive prison record who had robbed banks, taken hostages, and committed at least one murder before ever going to Alcatraz. The actual warden at Alcatraz at the time of Young's incarceration had *previously* run other prisons but was never warden of more than one prison at a time, and, contrary to the film's depiction of him as an infrequent visitor to Alcatraz, he lived on the island in a home just a few yards from the cell house and was there virtually every day of his fourteen-year tenure. The evil associate warden was entirely fictitious. Young was confined to his cell for several months following an escape attempt, but the movie's depiction of him languishing underground for years had no basis in fact. And instead of committing suicide, Young spent several years in other federal prisons following his murder of a fellow inmate (under circumstances completely different from those shown in the film), after which he was transferred to a state prison in Washington to serve a sentence for an earlier murder conviction.

---

ton: American University Press, 1994), 81–82, 86–88; Paul W. Keve, *Prisons and the American Conscience: A History of U.S. Federal Corrections* (Carbondale: Southern Illinois Press, 1991), 178–82.

In the 1960s he escaped from that prison and was recaptured, and in the 1970s he was paroled—only to jump parole and disappear. As far as anyone knew, he was still alive at the time *Murder in the First* was released.

Inventive as it was, *Murder in the First* reinforced widespread misconceptions about Alcatraz. The myths about Alcatraz were so pervasive and seemingly credible that even the venerable *New York Times* was initially taken in by the empty claim that the film was based on a true story. Later, after becoming acquainted with the facts of the Henri Young case, the *Times* published a correction (see *New York Times,* March 3, 1994, page C15, and April 6, 1994, page A2.)

Yet even after one pares away the myths, the sensationalism, and the fiction about Alcatraz, the story of the prison remains a compelling chapter in American history. Alcatraz housed some of America's most dangerous convicts and played a critical role in the evolution of American prisons.

The U.S. Penitentiary at Alcatraz opened on August 11, 1934. The island had been the site of an army fort and then a military prison for seventy-five years before it was renovated and retrofitted to house those considered to be the country's greatest public enemies. It represented the federal government's response to the epidemic of murders, gangland massacres, kidnappings, and bank robberies that had dominated the headlines for more than a decade and left the nation reeling. It was more secure than any other civilian prison and was intended to instill a greater sense of dread among the inmate population.

But the Justice Department's fledgling Bureau of Prisons (BOP), which had begun operations only five years earlier, was never entirely comfortable with the idea of Alcatraz. The new prison seemed more in keeping with the "lock 'em up and throw away the key" philosophy of the BOP's Justice Department rival, the Federal Bureau of Investigation, and its director, J. Edgar Hoover. The draconian image of Alcatraz was at odds with the more reform-oriented and professional approach to corrections being championed by BOP Director Sanford Bates and Assistant Director James V. Bennett.

Bates and Bennett quickly found a way to incorporate Alcatraz into their new approach, which emphasized the related concepts of inmate classification and diversified housing. Before the 1920s, the vast majority of adult male felons were housed in one type of prison—the traditional, maximum-security penitentiary. In keeping with the latest thinking in the corrections field, the BOP instituted a range of prisons with different security levels: low-security camps, medium-security correctional institutions, maximum-security penitentiaries, and such specialized facilities as prison hospitals, detention centers for suspects awaiting trial, youth reformatories, and a campus-like prison for women. Inmates could then be classified according to the seriousness of their crimes, the number of years they would have to serve, their requirements for medical treatment or other programs, and their propensity for violence or escape, and assigned to the prisons that were best suited for handling them.

The new approach carried at least three benefits. First, because the most secure prisons were also the most expensive to operate, it reduced costs by reserving space in maximum-security penitentiaries exclusively for inmates who were truly dangerous and required that level of security. Second, it gave the BOP an important disciplinary tool: Inmates who were violent, attempted to escape, or committed other infractions could be moved up the classification ladder to prisons that were more secure and less desirable. Similarly, the possibility of transfer down the classification ladder to prisons that were less restrictive could serve as an incentive to encourage inmates to avoid misconduct. Third, separating violent and intractable inmates from the rest of the inmate population made it possible to ensure the safety of staff and inmates alike, to maintain a more "normalized" environment in minimum- and medium-security prisons, and to offer the sort of educational and work-related programs that were fundamental to the vision of Bates and Bennett.

Under this plan, Alcatraz became more than simply a high-profile dumping ground for celebrity inmates. It became the apex of a graduated system of classification and diversified housing. It was the ultimate sanction that helped make the rest of the system work. It offered a greater measure of security than even the traditional maximum-security penitentiaries, thereby becoming the first of what in later parlance would be called a "supermaximum" facility. And in so doing, it took the pressure off the rest of the prison system by isolating the 1 or 2 percent of the inmate population that were the most disruptive and uncontrollable. Like all the prisons at each of the security levels, it played a precise and distinct role that contributed to the overall efficiency of the system.

Despite finding a legitimate role for Alcatraz, the BOP remained dissatisfied with the facility. Its location was always highly unsatisfactory to the bureau. Situated in the middle of picturesque San Francisco Bay, the prison was in full view of San Francisco to the south, Marin County to the north, and Alameda County to the east. It could be gaped at for a nickel a throw by tourists peering through high-powered telescopes installed along Fisherman's Wharf. Its image appeared on postcards and other memorabilia, and it came to symbolize the Bay Area no less prominently than the Golden Gate Bridge, Chinatown, and the cable cars. Oceangoing freighters, cruise ships, tourist boats, pleasure craft, and ferries were continually passing within only a few hundred yards of Alcatraz, and the prison seemed to invite constant scrutiny. The bureau considered this fishbowl environment to be the source of unnecessary tension and unfair criticism.

Moreover, operating costs for Alcatraz were always extremely high. Food, fuel, fresh water, and other supplies needed to maintain a small city consisting not only of the inmates but also of staff and their families had to be barged to the island at great expense. Most inmates at Alcatraz were transferred there from BOP facilities in the east and midwest, leading to enormous travel costs. And by the 1950s, renovation of the aging buildings had become so expensive that it would have been more cost-effective to tear them down and erect new structures.

As early as 1939, only five years after Alcatraz was activated, James Bennett (who had succeeded Bates as BOP director) began campaigning to replace the facility with one designed specifically for supermaximum-custody operations and located in the midwest—far from tourists but closer to other BOP facilities. Twenty years later, the bureau finally secured an appropriation to design and build a state-of-the-art prison in Marion, Illinois, which, after its activation in 1963 and a shake-down period of two or three years when it housed youthful offenders, became the new Alcatraz.* Almost as soon as Marion was authorized, Alcatraz began gearing down. Gradually, staff and inmates alike were transferred to Leavenworth, Atlanta, and other federal prisons, until the last group of inmates was taken off the island on March 21, 1963, and Alcatraz was officially deactivated.

The federal agency responsible for maintaining government real estate took control of the deserted prison but was unable to decide what to do with the property. One night in 1969, a group of Native American activists surprised the elderly government caretaker and his wife by invading the island as part of a political protest. The occupation generated a blast of publicity at first but it quickly lost its cachet, and the government waited out the last bored stragglers who finally vacated the island two years later. In 1972, Congress made Alcatraz a national park, turning the site into a natural-history preserve that included an extremely popular museum dedicated to the prison's history.

With a million or more visitors crowding onto the island every year, the image of Alcatraz endured. Everybody had an opinion about the old prison, it seemed, and most of them expressed their opinions. Filmmakers continued to grind out melodramas that were more fiction than truth, but which encapsulated the public perception of Alcatraz as a brutal, Bastille-like dungeon. Top prison administrators, such as longtime Alcatraz Warden James Johnston, former BOP Assistant Director Fred Wilkinson, and retired BOP Director James Bennett, wrote about Alcatraz in their memoirs. Former inmates from Alvin "Creepy" Karpis to Morton Sobell weighed in with their own side of the story. Journalists

---

*Ward, "Alcatraz and Marion," 88–89; Keve, *Prisons and the American Conscience,* 187.

and historians wrote books about the prison. Even the children of Alcatraz staff members, now grown, turned out publications.*

In fact, about the only people who were not saying much were the staff members themselves. With a few exceptions,** the correctional officers responsible for day-to-day prison operations, who walked the tiers and the catwalks, supervised the inmates, broke up fights, searched for contraband, investigated infractions, and put their lives on the line every day, have been silent.

Until now.

George H. Gregory was a correctional officer with the Federal Bureau of Prisons for twenty years, fifteen of which were spent at Alcatraz. His memoirs present an unusual and important perspective on staff–inmate relations, interaction between staff and management, the implementation of official policy, and the evolution of prison philosophies at Alcatraz.

Gregory was a product of the American heartland. Born in South Dakota in 1913 and raised in Minnesota, he was an avid camper who made Eagle Scout, a powerful football player, and a gifted writer who was reporting for his hometown Duluth newspaper while still in high school. When the Depression forced him to interrupt his studies at the University of Minnesota and Duluth Junior College, he entered the field of social work and coached immigrant children at settlement houses in Minnesota.

*For examples of books by prison administrators, see Sanford Bates, *Prisons and Beyond* (1936; reprint, Freeport, N.Y.: Books for Libraries Press, 1971); James V. Bennett, *I Chose Prison* (New York: Knopf, 1970); Fred Wilkinson, *The Realities of Crime and Punishment: A Prison Administrator's Testament* (Springfield, Mo.: Mycroft Press, 1972); and James A. Johnston, *Alcatraz Island and the Men Who Live There* (New York: Scribner's, 1949). Books by former Alcatraz inmates include Morton Sobell, *On Doing Time* (New York: Scribner's, 1974); Alvin Karpis (as told to Robert Livesay), *On The Rock: Twenty-Five Years in Alcatraz* (New York: Beaufort Books, 1980); Leon "Whitey" Thompson, *Last Train to Alcatraz* (Railroad Flat, Calif.: Winter Books, 1988) and (with Helen Thompson) *Alcatraz Merry-Go-Round* (Fiddleton, Calif.: Winter Books, 1990); Nathan Glenn Williams, *From Alcatraz to the White House* (Seattle: Willjoy Publishing, 1991); and James Quillen, *Alcatraz from Inside* (San Francisco: Golden Gate National Park Association, 1991). For examples of books by authors who grew up on Alcatraz as the children of staff members, see Don Hurley, *Alcatraz Island Memories* (Sonoma, Calif.: Fog Bell Enterprises, 1987) and *Alcatraz Island: Maximum Security* (Sonoma, Calif.: Fog Bell Enterprises, 1989); and Jolene Babyak, *Eyewitness on Alcatraz: True Stories of Families Who Lived on The Rock* (Berkeley, Calif.: Ariel Vamp Press, 1988) and *Birdman: The Many Faces of Robert Stroud* (Berkeley, Calif.: Ariel Vamp Press, 1994). Among the numerous scholars and journalists who have written about Alcatraz are David A. Ward, Paul W. Keve, Thomas Gaddis, Bruce J. Campbell, Pierre Odier, Clark Howard, John Kobler, John J. DiIulio, and James P. Delgado.

**Frank J. Heaney, an officer at Alcatraz in the early 1950s, coauthored a book about his experiences there (Frank J. Heaney and Guy Machado, *Inside the Walls of Alcatraz* [Palo Alto: Bull Publishing Co., 1987]). Philip Bergen, a longtime captain at Alcatraz, contributed to a book about the famous 1946 escape attempt, as did former inmate Clarence Carnes (Don DeNevi, Philip Bergen, and Clarence Carnes, *Alcatraz '46: The Anatomy of a Classic Prison Tragedy* [San Rafael, Calif.: Leswing Press, 1974]).

In 1940, Gregory began his BOP career as a trainee at the U.S. Penitentiary at Leavenworth, Kansas. Upon completion of his training, he returned to Minnesota for his first regular assignment, as a correctional officer at the Federal Correctional Institution in Sandstone.

Despite his exemption from the draft as a correctional officer, Gregory volunteered for the U.S. Marine Corps during World War II. He went on to earn the Purple Heart during the landings at Iwo Jima, sustaining a nearly fatal wound when a sniper's bullet ripped through both of his lungs. After the war and a prolonged recovery at a military hospital in Chicago, Gregory returned to his wife and three young sons in Sandstone and resumed his career at the federal prison.

The BOP transferred Gregory to Alcatraz in 1947, after it closed down the Sandstone facility. He remained there for the rest of his career. When Gregory got there, Alcatraz was home to approximately 260 inmates. It was also home to nearly all of the hundred or so staff members, who lived on the island with their families. The warden, the associate warden, and the physician lived in large houses; the captain and other ranking officers in cottages; and most of the rest of the staff in apartment buildings. Gregory, having been divorced shortly before his transfer, moved into the Bachelor Officer Quarters.

Gregory quickly immersed himself in the close-knit Alcatraz community, where the off-duty lives of staff members and their families revolved around a social club, a bowling alley, and the old military parade ground, which had evolved into a children's play area. Eventually, Gregory remarried. And he also resumed his studies.

By working the morning watch at Alcatraz—midnight to 8 a.m.—Gregory had his days free, and was able to enroll in the San Francisco College of Chiropractic. After earning his degree and obtaining his license, he opened an office on Market Street in downtown San Francisco and maintained a successful practice there for several years.

In April 1962, less than a year before the BOP closed Alcatraz, Gregory was badly injured in an accident on the prison's dock. Unable to return to work following extended medical leave, Gregory retired from the BOP. He and his third wife, Velma, moved to Marin County, just north of San Francisco, where he became active in charities and civic organizations. Soon, the couple were spending each summer at a lakefront cabin in northern Minnesota, where Gregory was able to visit with his sons and to renew old friendships.

Gregory also found time to write and study. He wrote about his wartime experiences and about his work for the BOP, and he was an avid reader of histories, religious texts, and philosophical works. During the last years of his life, he tackled his last big project—his memoirs, *Alcatraz Screw*. After many rewrites, he completed the manuscript shortly before his death, on October 7, 1996. Velma then took on the demanding tasks of preparing the manuscript for publication and finding a publisher for her late husband's book. The appearance of *Alcatraz Screw* culminates years of effort by George Gregory and Velma Gregory alike.

George Gregory arrived at Alcatraz during a critical juncture in the institution's history. Only a year earlier, two officers and three inmates had been killed in the island prison's most violent upheaval—an escape attempt gone awry, known as the Alcatraz Blastout. Then, one year after Gregory's arrival, the first warden at Alcatraz—the legendary James "Salt Water" Johnston—retired.

Over the next decade and a half, Gregory participated in or witnessed many important events in the history of Alcatraz and important trends in the practice of corrections. The early 1950s was a time of unrest in prisons throughout the United States. The national inmate population expanded greatly after World War II, at the same time that inmate work assignments dwindled because of a reduction in defense contracts for prison factories and a general economic downturn. The result was a dangerous increase in inmate idleness, which helped give rise to several serious prison disturbances. Alcatraz was a comparatively small prison (almost always fewer than three hundred inmates as opposed to the thousands that were confined in large penitentiaries) and it maintained both a fairly steady inmate work program and high standards of discipline. Yet it still felt many of these nationwide pressures—especially as the increasing number of disruptive inmates in other facilities meant an increasing number of inmate transfers to The Rock.

Meanwhile, philosophies of prison management were changing. Building on the theories of "individualized treatment" that had taken hold in corrections circles in the 1930s, prison administrators were moving toward an increased emphasis on rehabilitation that culminated with the so-called medical model that characterized American corrections in the 1960s. And, although the administrative decisions and court rulings that considerably expanded inmate rights lay twenty years in the future, restrictions on inmates at Alcatraz and elsewhere were already being loosened in the 1950s—thereby requiring Gregory and other officers to learn new procedures and objectives.

Gregory was one of the few officers who worked at Alcatraz during the administrations of all four of its wardens: Johnston (1934–1948); Edwin Swope (1948–1955); Paul Madigan (1955–1961); and Olin Blackwell (1961–1963). He was present for several daring escape attempts—including the still unsolved disappearance of the Anglin brothers and Frank Morris. And he was there at the end, as Alcatraz began the process of shutting down.

In short, he saw it all—and he remembered it all. In *Alcatraz Screw,* George Gregory tells a unique story about a unique prison.

Author's Note

Alcatraz Screw tells what it was like to be a correctional officer at the U.S. Penitentiary at Alcatraz from 1947 to 1963. The incidents in this book really happened, and represent the substance of my experiences as I remember them. I have made an effort to present them in a readable story form, not necessarily in chronological order. Many fictitious names are used to protect the guilty as well as the innocent.

I wish to thank Lawrence "Larry" Carpenter for his valuable advice. Larry is an expert in the field of penology. On retiring from the Federal Bureau of Prisons, he received a presidential appointment to the Federal Parole Board. He is called on frequently to advise states and counties on incarceration procedures.

My thanks also to Ernie Yates, a Los Angeles attorney, for his good advice during the writing of my memoirs. Ernie understands the criminal mind.

I am also grateful to Beth Ashley; Jolene Babyak; Barbara Brauer; Greg Coiner of Art Works; George H. Gregory III; the staffs of Golden Gate National Recreation Area and San Francisco Maritime National Historical Park; John W. Roberts, former chief archivist of the Federal Bureau of Prisons, and Anne Diestel, archivist specialist; and Barbara Ruzicka.

1

Destination: Alcatraz

"U.S. Penitentiary, Alcatraz," said the voice on the other end of the line.

"This is George Gregory. I've just arrived from Sandstone," I said.

"Yeah, got your name here as one of the guys transferring in. Where are you?"

"I'm in San Francisco at the Ferry Building."

"Take a cab to Pier Four at Fort Mason. You'll have time to get the last boat coming over tonight."

After driving a few blocks in silence, the cabdriver asked rather timidly, "Are you a guard out there on Alcatraz?"

"I will be. I'm a screw."

"You're a what?"

"A prison screw."

"Never heard you guys called that before."

"It's an old term that refers to the locking system in some prisons. You insert a big, long key into the lock of a cell door and screw it in until the door is secured."

"I don't envy you. From all I hear, that can be a rough place."

It was the middle of November 1947, late on a Saturday night. A cold drizzle was falling.

"This is it," the driver said as he drove out to the end of the pier. He helped me put my footlocker and seabag in the waiting room. I paid him and as he got back in his cab, he said dubiously, "Should I wish you good luck?"

"So wish me good luck," I said. I stood for a minute looking out at "The Rock," which was just barely visible in the fog. For the first time, I felt a grim chill—a feeling that I would experience regularly throughout my tenure on Alcatraz.

13

Several people were already in the waiting room and others trickled in to catch the last boat of the evening to Alcatraz. Since the only reason for being in the room was to go to Alcatraz, there was an immediate connection among us. We exchanged gossip about mutual acquaintances and I was given a lot of advice. One fellow told me very seriously not to unpack my seabag because Alcatraz was sure to close soon.

I was straining to see Alcatraz through the fog when the prison boat, the *Warden Johnston,* loomed up out of the mist and bumped gently into the dock. Two of my new friends grabbed my footlocker and headed for the gangplank. I picked up my seabag and followed.

At the bottom of the gangplank I was met by the boat officer, who said, "Are you Gregory?"

"Yes, I'm George Gregory," I said, and showed him my identification card.

"We've been expecting you. Come aboard."

Most of the passengers went inside the cabin to avoid the cold mist. But in my excitement to see, feel, and hear everything, I stayed outside at the railing. Jim Keller, whom I had known at Leavenworth, joined me and we shivered together.

Out in front of us a huge ship was plowing its way toward the open sea. The *Warden Johnston* kept going right on toward it. I looked around nervously toward the operator as we headed straight for the prow of the big ship and asked, "Are we going to hit that ship?"

"No, we're not going to hit it," Keller laughed. By this time some of the other men had come out to join us.

"How does the operator see in this fog?" I asked as we rocked in the wake of the outgoing ship.

"What fog?" was the reply, along with laughter from all.

"This is nothing," said a gray-headed gentleman. "One time the fog was so thick the boat operator could not find the boat slip. He couldn't see the island until he was right on it. We didn't have radar on the boat then. He would get close enough to see the island but would not be in the right position to dock. So he would go back out, turn, and try again.

"We finally got everybody down on the dock with anything that could make noise. When we heard the boat coming close, we made as much noise as we could. We hollered, beat dishpans and oil drums, blew whistles, and rang bells until we finally guided the boat into the slip. It sure scared the passengers, but it got them in safely."

Once on the island, I was directed to the dock office, where I met Lieutenant

Johnson, dock-in-charge. The lieutenant rather unenthusiastically coached me in the "signing-in" procedure.

When I laid down the pen he said dolefully, "George Gregory, huh? I suppose you're new to the service like most of the rest we've been getting lately."

"Seven years, sir, with a couple of years out for the war."

The lieutenant's eyebrows went up. "Seven years? Thank God for little favors. We can sure use some experience around here."

Suddenly I realized how very tired I was, tired to the point of exhaustion. I didn't want any more chatting.

"I understand you have a great BOQ here. After five days on the train I could sure use a good night's sleep," I said through a deep yawn.

The lieutenant gave me a brief glance of sympathetic understanding and pointed down the dock—south from the office and on the same level. "They call it the Mule Barn," he said. "That's where most of the unmarried guards live. There are several vacant rooms. Take whichever one you want."

The Mule Barn. What a name! The story was that it had been a mule barn when the army used the island.

I pushed open the door and walked down the hall until I found what appeared to be an empty room. Turning on the light, I jerked back. It just couldn't be!

What a filthy, dirty room—a stained mattress on the bed, newspapers all over the floor, everything coated with thick dust, and no towels or bedding anywhere in sight.

I looked into another room. It was the same.

Alcatraz has great bachelor officers' quarters, I had been told. I had expected a neat, clean room all made up and ready for me to rest my weary bones.

Feeling outrage and insult, I dropped my belongings in the hall, slammed out of the building, and headed back to the dock office with a roar. "Lieutenant!"

The lieutenant was relaxing in a captain's chair, reading the financial page. When he looked up at me, his face showed serious disapproval.

"Lieutenant!" At the second roar, the lieutenant's look of disapproval turned into an angry scowl.

"What kind of a place is this? Those damned rooms aren't *fit* for a mule. They're not even fit for rats. I want a decent place to sleep and I want it right now!"

The lieutenant got up and looked as though he were going to give it to me with both barrels. Then he softened up a bit.

"Now, mister, you just calm down. I'll be expecting an apology when you get squared away. I don't know anything about those quarters. I'm a married man and haven't had any occasion to be in the Mule Barn. Now what can I do to help you?"

Only slightly mollified, I said, "That place is stinking dirty. No blankets, sheets . . ."

"Bedding and a towel I can get for you. Sit down and I'll be right back." He drove off in a pickup and was back in a few minutes with blankets, sheets, towels, and even a couple of pieces of used soap.

I grunted a thank-you and walked away. The lieutenant called after me, "By the way, you're due up top for the eight o'clock shift. Got an alarm clock?"

"On Sunday?"

"Yes," was the terse reply.

As I walked back to the Mule Barn, watching the spooky billowing and puffing of the fog in the path of the floodlights and listening to the eerie, loud squalls of the foghorns, I thought, Gad, I haven't even stood my first roll call but I've already got a lieutenant mad at me.

I made up my bed and flopped on it, as lousy as it was.

It had taken a few months, but here I was at the U.S. Penitentiary, Alcatraz. During the May 1946 riot at Alcatraz, I was on a list of three Sandstone officers slated to come out to The Rock, as Alcatraz was called. As the main method of travel at that time was by rail, prison officials decided to "wait and see" before sending officers from the Midwest to the West Coast. The riot ended before it became necessary to send us.

But the abrupt closure of Sandstone Federal Prison, about eighteen months after the Alcatraz riot, necessitated the transfer of officers as well as prisoners to other institutions. Three of us were sent to Alcatraz. It was noised about that I was sent to Alcatraz because I was tough on convicts. Suffice it to say, we went wherever we were assigned.

In spite of the filthy room and the foghorns, I soon fell asleep.

2

The Beginning of
an Adventure

The next morning I was up early. After a shower in a none-too-clean shower room and a feeble attempt at getting the travel wrinkles out of my uniform, I walked up the long steep hill to "up top."

From the Mule Barn, the most southerly building on the dock, I walked along the water's edge toward the Dock Tower. The drizzle of the night before had stopped, but it was still overcast and cold. The wind blew through the Golden Gate from the Pacific Ocean, causing whitecaps on the bay. The wind also delivered the fresh smell of clean salt air to my appreciative nostrils.

I looked up at the officer in the Dock Tower as I passed, threw a perfunctory salute in his direction, and went on my way. I wasn't sure of what that way was, but there didn't seem to be any other route to the top of the rock. I went through an underpass and up a switchback road, past occasional brick retaining walls. Many of the plants lining the roadside and clinging to the hill were geraniums, some of which were in bloom. Nasturtiums and ice plants also grew in profusion.

There were terraced areas where vegetables were growing and more trees than one would expect to see on an island that had no natural soil. Dirt for growing plants had been barged over from the mainland, and shark meat was used for fertilizer.

Walking up the road, gawking at everything around me, I slipped and almost fell. I had stepped on a deep green, slimy, wormlike animal about four or five inches long with antennae—a slug, but a kind I had never seen before. I kept trying to get the thing off my shoe all the rest of the way up the hill.

In moments when there was a lull in the wind, I realized how quiet it was. The seagulls seemed content to sit huddled into their feathers. Some ships were moving silently in the bay. I could see land all around except to the west, where there was only the Golden Gate Bridge and the ocean beyond.

This sightseeing trip brought me to the main entrance and the beginning of my third assignment in the Federal Prison Service. In my eagerness to see the inside of Alcatraz, I decided to make a study of the view from the top at a later time.

I turned and looked at the entrance. The name U.S. Penitentiary didn't seem to match the impressive emblem: a bald eagle with wings spread as if ready to fly away, with lush horns-of-plenty on either side.

My eagerness was tempered with apprehension as I walked through the door and found myself in a foyer with halls leading off to the right and left. Directly in front of me was a barred gate with a double barred gate beyond it.* I stood there taking in the surroundings, the sounds, and the institutional odors. Alcatraz was painted battleship gray outside and inside. The Federal Prison System must surely have an exclusive on this color of paint. I don't suppose it ever drove anybody crazy, but I doubt it ever cheered up anybody, either.

I wasn't in any hurry. There had to be somebody eyeballing me from somewhere and sooner or later he would tell me what to do next.

Then someone hollered, "Are you Gregory?"

"Yes, sir, I'm George Gregory."

That was the only question or verification of me on my entry into Alcatraz. Alcatraz officers were such a small, close-knit group that the arrival of a new officer was prepared for well in advance by way of the very efficient grapevine. Those on duty that Sunday morning would have heard all the gossip concerning me and my arrival.

Looking in the direction of the voice, I saw the officer who had addressed me. He was inside an office that had big windows—bulletproof glass, no doubt. That would be the armory or control center. Kind of a small one.

Talking through an open section of the window, the officer said, "Turn to your right, Mr. Gregory, go straight ahead, and you will find Mr. Miller's office. He's the associate warden."

I walked past a couple of desks and saw a man standing in an office looking at some papers.

"Mr. Miller? George Gregory reporting for duty, sir."

---

*In prison parlance, "gate" generally refers to a main entrance to a building or section of a building that has security responsibilities. In most instances there are two gates. The holding area between them is called a "sally port." Only one of the gates is opened at a time. People wait in the sally port while the first gate is secured and the second one is opened.

He looked at me and said, "Take off that hat," in a voice more contemptuous than I felt necessary. After all, I was wearing a Stetson, which was the uniform hat at my previous assignment in Sandstone, Minnesota. Miller took the hat. And that was the last I ever saw of it. Had I known this, I would have kept it, saying I had to turn it in at Sandstone, or some other excuse.

Miller rummaged around in a gray metal locker and found a cap in my size. He handed it to me along with a badge. "This is what we wear here," he said. Alcatraz officers wore the police-type cap.

"Go on in the cell house and go to work," he growled.

I hesitated because I had thought this would be, more or less, a ceremonial reporting for duty with the rest of the day to get myself oriented. But the rumble from the associate warden left no room for doubt—I was expected to work.

Jamming my new cap on my head, I turned to leave, realizing immediately that I didn't even know where the cell house was. I was damned if I'd ask, though.

But, as I retraced my steps to the main entrance, the officer's voice came again from the armory and my indignation gave way to curiosity as I was directed through the security system that separated the country's most ingenious escape artists and most violent federal and state prisoners from the rest of society.* With one exception, the gates were constructed of gray steel bars, allowing clear visibility of the person wishing entry. However, the last gate to be dealt with before entering the cell house was made of thick steel with a bulletproof window.

I thought to myself, Hope I'm never late or have to leave in a hurry.

The gates were controlled by some kind of coordination between the armory and the gate officers, who had keys. I was silently moved along—as one gate closed behind me, another one opened in front of me. A much more complicated system than at Sandstone.

Finally I stood inside the cell house. I looked and listened. The visitors' room was right up front. There were three blocks of cells with three tiers each. Tall windows along the walls and a skylight above a main aisle lighted the cell house even on this overcast day.

I heard echoing sounds of grating steel as cell doors were opened, the reverberation of the final bang as they were closed, and the voices of convicts as they talked with each other from cell to cell. I moved a few feet to my left, to the entry of a main aisle with occupied cells on either side. Here I waited. Being experienced in prisons, I knew not to go barging down that aisle without a proper staff escort.

---

*The Bureau of Prisons approved the transfer of state prisoners when there was space for them in the federal system.

A convict pressed his face against the bars of his cell so as to get a better look at me.

"Hey, we got a new screw," he reported.

Other faces appeared at the cells' bars. The general response was a rather indifferent, "How long do you suppose he'll stay?"

"He's pretty big. He might last a while," someone said. A ripple of chuckles came from the cells.

I watched as officers moved up and down stairs from one tier to another, opening and closing cells by way of lock boxes at the end of each tier. Some officers nodded to me, more in curiosity than in greeting.

I was beginning to think, What a joint, when a fast-stepping officer came over and in a commanding voice said, "Open up cell six."

"Don't know your locking system," I said politely.

"You don't? Where did you come from?"

"I came from Leavenworth and Sandstone."

"Hmm." And he opened the cell himself.

Then an officer on a higher tier called down, "You from Leavensworth?"

"Yes." I noticed the "s" in the name and thought he must be a native of Leavenworth or else stayed there a long time. The people I met there always said "Leavensworth." I wondered how they spelled it.

He came down from the tier. "My name is Stucker. I worked at Leavensworth a long time ago. How are things back there?"

"Hi, I'm Gregory. I went from Leavenworth to Sandstone."

"Did you go through training at Leavensworth?"

"Yes, I did."

"That was a good hard four months they gave us. Those guys don't let a man go until they know he's a prison officer."

"Yeah. It's easier to work with someone who's had the same training as you. You always know what to expect from them."

"I know what you mean. Some of the situations that develop around here, you don't have time to tell an officer what to do. He'd better know. We still have several officers who trained down there."

"That's good," I said gratefully.

"I wish I could have stayed at Leavensworth."

"I felt the same way. Everything was well organized for a smooth operation."

"This is a good place to work, too," Stucker said with a good-natured chuckle. "C'mon. I'll start your breaking in. The locking system is really simple."

I learned how to lock and unlock the cells one at a time and how to control a whole tier at one time. The control panel had a list of the convicts and the number of the cell each occupied.

Stucker said, "Down there is the West End. That's the command post for much of the prison activity, at least during the day. And this aisle we're in is Broadway. Quite a few of our first cons came from New York. They so named it, and it stuck." The floor of the aisle was waxed and polished concrete. It gave off mirrorlike reflections.

While we were talking, the main gate opened and Mr. Miller came in and walked right past us, on down Broadway. I raised an eyebrow.

"He's okay," said Stucker firmly. "When he comes into the cell house it usually means he's going to hold court.* Let's go down there."

Stucker and I followed in the wake of Mr. Miller. The chatter of the convicts stopped as the men pressed their faces against the cell bars to watch the progress of the associate warden down Broadway, turning their heads as he passed to watch him until he was out of sight. The cell house became very quiet. I began to sense the power of this man. At Leavenworth and Sandstone, I had heard stories about Miller's being tough but fair with convicts and officers.

The associate warden was in charge of most of the activities on Alcatraz. He supervised both officers and convicts, held disciplinary court for the convicts, listened to their requests, and heard the complaints of any officer who dared complain. Miller accepted all these responsibilities with authority.

Down at the West End, Miller sat at a table and several officers stood around talking with him. Both sitting and standing, he gave the impression of being taller than he really was. He laughed frequently as he talked with the officers. His wide-mouthed, noisy laugh was almost boyish. But between the laughs he showed steady, hard eyes and a grim mouth set above a broad, strong-willed chin. Every time Miller opened his mouth to speak, the officers quieted immediately. I began to believe what I had heard about this man—he certainly had a commanding personality. Seeing the mutual respect between the associate warden and his officers caused me to change the negative thoughts I had had about him.

I was standing a little apart from the group at the table in a military at-ease posture, silently observing, when I became aware of noises that sounded suspiciously like grunting and groaning coming from around the corner of B Block. Being curious, I walked over to see what was going on.

Through an open cell door, I saw an officer and a convict struggling. It ap-

---

*"Court" refers to the disciplinary committee hearings that were conducted by the associate warden. An officer could refer a convict to the disciplinary court for any infraction of the rules.

peared the convict was trying to stick the officer's head down the toilet and was having some success. I entered, caught the convict by the arm, and righted the grappling pair.

"Okay," said the officer, looking rather sheepish, "let's get him out of here."

Outside the cell, I looked at the convict while keeping a firm hold on him. Wide, weird eyes; pale, sweaty face; slack jaw . . . Drugs? At Alcatraz?

Miller saw us. "Arnold," he said disgustedly, "you again? Might as well get him right upstairs to the hospital."

I had an armlock on one side of the convict and the officer I had saved from the toilet-dunking was on the opposite side. In this way we went through the gate from the West End into the dining hall and then took a sharp left to a locked door at the bottom of a steep flight of stairs. Another officer unlocked the door and we started up the concrete stairs with Miller right behind us. Arnold began screaming and hollering that I was hurting his arm. I knew I wasn't hurting the guy, but did have him in the right position to apply more pressure if needed.

"Let him go," Miller said.

I let go. Arnold jerked his other arm loose and, quickly turning, hit Miller pretty hard right in the chest. The associate warden would have fallen down the steep concrete stairs had I not grabbed him.

Regaining his balance, Miller shouted furiously, "Arnold, you stupid ass! Drag him up the stairs and if he lets out a whimper, work him over!"

The other officer and I caught Arnold's flailing arms and with Mr. Miller's not very gentle help we got him up the stairs and through the last gate into the hospital. We were stretching him out on an examining table when Miller said, "Don't be so damned easy on him," and slammed him down hard on the table.

When Arnold could get his breath he said, "Meathead, someday, you big bastard, I'm gonna cut your balls off."

"Yeah," said Miller, "and before you get that chance Mr. Miller will long be retired and gone fishing. And where will Arnold still be? Right here on The Rock doing even more time if he doesn't straighten up. So shut up."

At this point the doctor came in. He said, "You again, Arnold? How about some morphine and ipecac?" and gave him an injection. "Can we get him into a restraining cell?"

"Sure. Let's go," said Miller, grabbing Arnold by the collar.

Walking back down the stairs after taking care of Arnold, Miller and the other officer were laughing and joking as if having convicts on drugs was just "business as usual." I was puzzled and ached to ask questions. I knew I had a lot to learn about Alcatraz and its occupants, but I had not expected an education in drugs. I certainly was going to keep my eyes and ears at full alert.

The thought of drugs brought to my mind an incident, however irrelevant, that occurred at the railroad gate at Leavenworth. Trains went right into the prison pulling freight cars loaded with supplies. Convicts unloaded the cargo.

A young officer caught a convict returning from a day of work in the freight-yard with a Bull Durham tobacco sack full of marijuana. He put the convict on report and waited to be complimented by the captain.* Instead of a compliment, he got a reprimand. The captain said he should have reported it secretly. Then the convict could have been watched so they could find out where he was getting the "weed," how he was curing it, and with whom he was sharing it or to whom he was selling it.

Maybe this wasn't irrelevant at all. Where did Arnold get his drugs? What else was involved? *Who* else was involved? I had an uneasy feeling that I was at the beginning of a very unpleasant learning experience.

Back in the cell house, Miller looked at me with some interest. "You handle people pretty well, young man."

"Thank you, sir."

Again standing a little apart and studying the goings-on, I became aware that I was ravenously hungry. I looked at my watch: ten-thirty. That late? No wonder I'm hungry, I thought. I've got to eat.

I approached an officer who seemed to be some kind of traffic director, opening doors, shaking down convicts, and so on.

"Pardon me, sir, but could you tell me what I have to do to get something to eat around here?"

"Brown is my name. When is your lunch hour?" he asked, looking a bit surprised.

"Haven't the faintest idea."

"Well, what does your job card say?"

"I haven't been assigned to a post yet. It's my first day here."

"Well, officers' lunch is starting right now. Go into the officers' mess and they'll take care of you."

"And where is the officers' mess?"

Brown pulled open a big bulletproof glass door to let several officers through. "Just follow the crowd right on into the dining hall."

In the officers' mess, I selected a table and sat down.

"Sit over here. What time is your lunch hour?" I looked up to see the speaker, who was a convict—surly and craggy-faced, with hard, arrogant eyes—staring

---

*Putting a convict "on report" meant writing up an infraction of a rule, which resulted in the convict being called before the disciplinary committee.

coldly at me. I stared back and the convict gave in first. Shrugging his shoulders and clearing his throat, he turned and hastened out of the room. Looking around the room, I caught several curious gazes directed toward me.

Approaching my table was what I knew to be a steward. He was short, sweaty, and wearing whites that didn't fit very well. Some of the best prison stewards came from positions in major restaurants and top hotels—they ran a neat, clean, orderly kitchen and put out good meals. On occasion, a military-trained steward forgot that convicts were not privates to be ordered around. Others tried to get along with the convicts by letting them do as they pleased.

"Trying to give Pikolof a bad time, huh? Trying to get by without a meal ticket? 'Tain't your lunch hour. Who are you, anyway?" Along with his questions, which were asked as if he were a real tough honcho, the steward was trying to fashion his saggy face into something menacing.

Now all eyes were riveted on me. I thought, Another frustrated character trying to throw his weight around. I think I'll play with this guy.

"Did you say Pikolof?" I said pulling out my notebook.

"Yes, I said Pikolof."

"Would you spell it, please?"

"Spell it? What do you mean, spell it?"

"Well then, what's his number?"

"Spell his name? What's his number? Say, who the hell are you, anyhow?"

"The name is Gregory and those dirty whites of yours tell me we have spaghetti for lunch. So, cooky, why don't you just get that Pikolof character in here with a big plate of it because I'm hungry." Starting to get up, I continued, "And you better apologize right now for accusing me of trying to cheat you out of a thirty-five-cent meal ticket or your nose is going to look just like your spaghetti sauce!"

The steward made one last effort to look tough as I was getting my six-foot-four frame out of the chair, then he turned and fled.

"I'll tell Mr. Miller about this," were his parting words.

There was a moment or two of silence in the officers' mess and then one of the officers shouted, "Russky!" When Pikolof came slowly into the room, the officer said, "Why don't you quit this bullshit and feed this officer? He's new. Give him time and he'll learn you're the big boss around here."

The Cossack gave me an almost respectful look as he went for the spaghetti.

I sat down and noticed that the officers were now smiling in a friendly and amused way. The one who had handled Pikolof waved to me and said, "Not to worry. Just part of this place."

I ate the spaghetti along with plenty of homemade bread and butter. It tasted better than it looked. I finished the meal with a dish of homemade ice cream and leaned back in my chair to enjoy a cigarette.

The ongoing activity of the dining hall claimed my attention. Officers were entering, eating, and leaving. The Cossack was serving the ice cream. He dipped into the container with a large spoon and raked the ice cream into a dish with the forefinger of his left hand. As he reached for another dip of ice cream, he licked his finger. As I watched the repetition of this act, I became slightly nauseated. It was a long time before I ate ice cream in the officers' mess again.

Back in the cell house I took up my stand, still maintaining a bit of distance from the activity. An officer came up to me and said, "Your name Gregory?"

"Yes, sir, George Gregory."

"I'm Bunch Tompkins. Heard about your transferring out here. Heard you're a Marine."

"Yes, World War II."

"Yeah? What division?"

"Fifth."

"Did you hit Iwo?"

"Yes, I hit it and it hit me."

"Yeah, I know what you mean. I was with the Second on Saipan. I was a regular back in the China days. You heard of the Fourth Regiment in China?"

"Sure did. You're one of those Asiatic Marines, huh?"

"It was good duty. Look, if you need any help around here, let me know. I haven't been here too long, but I know the routine pretty well. By the way, there's a good club, Marines' Memorial Club, over in San Francisco. You might want to join it. It's just for Marines and doesn't cost anything. No dues. Take your discharge papers and you're in like Flynn. Drinks are pretty cheap and they have dances. If I were single, I'd go with you."

"Thanks, I'll remember that."

"Just hang around, be patient, and sooner or later you'll fit into the routine here. We're going to have dinner pretty quick. We usually start Sunday dinner a little early because we have movies in the afternoon. You'll probably see a movie today. See you later."

"Thanks for the advice, Tompkins."

"Bunch."

"Okay, Bunch." I thought as he ambled away that I sure would be glad to have his support. Even if his muscles were collecting some fat, I figured I would still rather have him on my side.

Shortly thereafter, I observed my first feeding of the convicts at Alcatraz. A lieutenant standing at the dining hall door blew his whistle and called, "Open 'em up!"

Officers at each end of each tier in the two occupied cell blocks, B and C, pulled in unison on the levers that opened all the cells. A crash of noise, and immediately every tier was full of convicts. They began filing down from the tiers, merging into two lines as they went into the dining hall.

I thought, All of the convicts allowed out at the same time? Just doesn't seem right. What if there were a riot, with all these convicts out at once and only a comparatively few officers? Seems like asking for trouble—fistfights, knifings, contraband being passed from one con to another . . . It just doesn't seem like good custody.

Even with the less volatile populations of Sandstone and Leavenworth, the convicts were released from their dormitories or cells one unit at a time. There was continuous movement of the line without crowding, waiting, or having to pause on the stairs from the tiers.

I shrugged my shoulders and said to myself, Let's not criticize yet. Just observe.

Again, I settled into an at-ease posture to watch the activities around me. The officer at the door occasionally stopped a convict and asked him to button the top button on his coveralls. I began to realize that Alcatraz had a peculiar dress code. The daily uniform was a blue shirt and gray pants made of cotton. On Sunday, the convicts wore blue wool shirts and pants. For meals, they had to change into light gray coveralls that had a close-buttoned neck. They were required to keep the top button fastened until they were seated at the table. Then they could unbutton the top button. This rule irritated both convicts and officers.

Through the steel-reinforced glass door, I could see an officer behind the steam table supervising the serving. Officers were also posted in various parts of the dining hall—a total of eight. There were several officers outside the dining hall, just standing around, chatting informally. The bulletproof glass door was locked after all the convicts had filed into the dining hall.

I was watching the general setup for serving a meal when I noticed the officer in charge of the door trying to get my attention.

As I approached he said, "You're the new man, aren't you?"

"Yes."

"Parant likes for us to stand right in front of the door."

"Parant?" I asked.

"Lieutenant Lyle Parant, acting captain. Wants to be captain real bad. Better walk easy around him."

Parant sounded like he could be difficult. Maybe I'd better ask Bunch about him, I thought.

"Well, as I was saying, he wants us in front of the door. That way, if we have to stop a fight it doesn't take long to get in there. If he thinks you're not alert and not watching the cons, well, he's liable to give you a little hell in a loud way. Really seems to get his jollies from it."

"Like this?" I grinned as I stood with my nose against the bars of the door, staring in at the cons.

"Look, friend, this guy Parant is no laughing matter."

"Sorry," I said wiping the grin off and sticking out my hand. "George Gregory."

"Claude Stevens. Glad to have you aboard. And if you can't get a board, get a shingle."

I groaned as if in deep pain. In the years to come, Stevens's silly little sayings and jokes would often lighten the chronic tension for the officers of Alcatraz.

A minute or so later, Stevens gave a high sign again. "See that fellow? Machine Gun Kelly. J. Edgar Hoover says he is a very dangerous criminal."

Translated, that seemed to mean Machine Gun Kelly was not all that dangerous. He had the stately and distinguished bearing of a successful banker. In spite of his gray hair, Kelly looked quite young. He liked the name Machine Gun Kelly, which had been given to him by the press. The convicts changed it to Slingshot Kelly in a gently joshing mood. Most of them liked Kelly and took his sometimes ridiculous stories in good humor. He did tell a good story.

The many different assignments I was to hold at Alcatraz gave me the opportunity to get acquainted with various convicts, and I often talked with Kelly. He loved to reminisce. Much of what he said was probably true. But as Alvin "Creepy" Karpis, who was also a member of the Barker Gang, once said, "You know, he talks about what he did in one caper like it happened in another. I was on some of those capers but I don't remember seeing *him* there."

One story Kelly told that I am sure is true, having heard it from other sources as well, was about something that happened at Alcatraz several years before my time. The convicts were on strike for better food. They went to work and obeyed all the rules, but would not eat.

At that time there was a Lieutenant Culver, known to the convicts as the Black Knight. He was respected as much as any officer ever was respected by the convicts. The incident happened after a few days of the strike, when the strikers were all getting pretty hungry.

As Kelly told it, "The Black Knight came up in front of my cell one evening with a big, thick sandwich. He had purposely made it with lots of stuff that would give off strong aromas to tempt me. I could smell the salami, onion, and garlic. As he held the sandwich right in front of my face, he said, 'Want it? You can have it. No? You don't want it?' Then the Black Knight took a big bite of the sandwich, spit it out, and slammed the sandwich down on the floor right in front of my cell and said, 'This is a lousy sandwich.' That made me mad.

"I said, 'Why, you sonofabitch, when I was on the streets I carried around twice as much money as you make in a year. I wore silk shirts and always had a big, new car.'

"And the Black Knight said, 'Yeah? Well, tonight I am going over to North Beach and have a big Italian dinner with all the trimmings plus a big carafe of wine, and then I am going to spend the night with a real cute girl. And you know what, Kelly? You will be here behind those bars and I won't even be thinking about you.'"

Kelly ended his story by saying, "You know, Boss,* I think that was when I really realized that I was in prison."

I was looking obediently into the dining hall when two big black guys jumped up from their table and started flailing away at each other. Stevens unlocked the door. Several of us rushed in. I got an armlock on one of the fighters and pulled him away. Just as I did, an officer grabbed the convict by the other arm and tried to push and shove him around.

"That's all right, I've got him," I said as I guided the convict toward the door. Once a fight is broken up, the participants usually settle down and go along without resistance as this convict was doing. In fact, most convicts who engage in a fight where officers can see them want it broken up fast, especially the one who is losing. But the other officer kept coming along and pulling on the convict.

"It's okay," I said, a little impatiently. "I've got him." Finally the officer let go of the convict and slunk off into the cell house.

As I steered the convict through the dining hall gate, another officer approached and said, "I'll take him now. All right, Biff, you know where the Hole is."

The rest of the meal went along without further incident. That afternoon, I helped hand-search the convicts as they went up into the auditorium for the movie.

That being finished, the lieutenant on duty said, "Mr. Gregory, you are not going to learn much going to the movie. I'm sure you know that routine. Why don't you wander around the cell house, shake down a few cells, shoot the bull and blow smoke with Tompkins and Stevens? You might learn a bit from those two."

It was a pleasant and educational afternoon, and the time sped by. I shook down a few cells. There was an incredible amount of junk in some of the cells. A number of magazines and books, more blankets than the standard four, extra

---

*"Boss" was a term sometimes used by convicts to address junior and senior officers for whom they had respect. Appropriate titles such as lieutenant, captain, or warden were used when addressing officers of those ranks.

clothing, musical instruments, baseball gloves, and dominoes made up most of the contraband. I was a bit curious about the large number of little bottles, packages, and small envelopes full of seemingly useless kinds of patented medicine. Probably cells of addicts. Not knowing the convicts yet and not knowing about any special rules Alcatraz might have, I left all the junk. I disturbed the cells as little as possible but did look for major types of contraband such as knives or tools—anything that could be a weapon or a cutting tool. Didn't find any.

Convicts were allowed only specified items in their cells—anything else was considered contraband. Four packs of cigarettes were issued weekly. Any more than four packs found in a cell was contraband. They would have been acquired illegally, probably by gambling. Books or magazines that had not been checked out from the prison library or approved for ordering had to have come from the outside—also illegal. How they got inside was the question. Extra clothing was considered contraband. It usually indicated that a laundry worker was indebted to the con with the extra clothing.

For reasons of cleanliness (and hopefully rodent-free cells), convicts were not allowed to take food from the dining hall. One convict managed to catch some mice and make pets of them. He kept them in his shirt and took them wherever he went—including the dining hall, where he fed them. He covertly dropped food inside his shirt when the officers weren't looking in his direction.

Seemingly harmless items such as pens, pencils, and paintbrushes could become lethal weapons when sharpened. Any tool or instrument that could possibly be used as a weapon or in an escape attempt for cutting bars or fences was contraband.

Down at the West End, Stevens showed me the shakedown record book. I entered the date, the numbers of the cells I had searched, and my initials. Convicts knew their cells would be searched, but they did not know when. There was no set pattern or schedule for shakedowns.

I learned from Bunch that his official title was cell house officer-in-charge or cell house officer number one. And that's what he was. Bunch was in charge of everything that went on in the cell house and was answerable only to the daytime lieutenant.

I also found out there was a very strict law concerning smoking in the cell house. Warden Johnston had a thing against smoking and he forbade it in various parts of the institution. This applied not just to the convicts but to the officers as well. I found this a bit trying because I was a pretty heavy smoker.

The supper feeding of the convicts was much the same as the dinner feeding. I observed the final lockup of the day and the convict count.

It was odd how both officers and convicts felt more secure at this time—the officers because all the convicts were locked in their cells for the night, and the convicts because they were now safe from other convicts.

During the day when convicts were out of their cells, officers were ever watchful. Since your hands were the only weapons you had, you didn't walk or stand around with them in your pockets.* You kept your hands free of objects whenever possible. You learned to walk wide around the corner of a cell block. Someone not exactly interested in your good health could be waiting for you around any corner. You learned to sit facing the entry to a room or office so as not to be surprised by an unexpected visitor. You stayed aware of others in a room or walking in an aisle with you. After lockup, you still walked in the middle of the aisle, out of the reach of any arm or missile that might come through the bars.

You could be flattened by your best friend if you walked up behind him unexpectedly and slapped him on the back in greeting. This was true for both officers and convicts.

The convicts were also forever watchful. *Their* hands were free whenever possible. *They* turned frequently when walking down an aisle to make sure an unfriendly person was not approaching. The young, good-looking men were always watching out for a big wolf or stud. Convicts did their best to be within the vision of an officer. Should you happen to notice a convict going into a secluded area, you became alert, because he wasn't doing this for any good reason. It could be for a homosexual rendezvous, for a place to hide while waiting to catch another convict or guard unaware, or for a place to drop contraband, such as a knife, for another convict.

The very walls of the institution seemed to breathe a sigh of relief as the last cell doors banged shut for the night. After the stand-up count, as in all formal counts in the institution, the Control Center officer rang a bell, signifying to everyone that the count was okay. The day shift was now free to go off duty.

As I turned to leave, someone tapped me on the shoulder. I looked around and the officer seeking my attention said, "My name is Burger, Sidney Burger. Going in to supper? Mind if I join you?"

---

*The officers manning the gun galleries were armed, but the officers who worked in other positions in the cell house were not.

3

The Mule Barn

Supper wasn't much: stewed beans (but I liked beans and these were pretty good) along with homemade bread and butter, sliced onions, and pickles. Dessert was cake, which was also good, made in the institution bakery with thick, rich, chocolate frosting. Not exactly what I would have ordered in a restaurant, but it was all right. I could get along with it.

Burger was a genial type who smiled readily and talked easily. He must have just made the height requirement, but he was muscular. He also lived in the bachelors' quarters, and as we walked down the hill after supper, he filled me in on a few mundane facts about Alcatraz.

In the Mule Barn, Burger stopped in front of an open door and said, "Meet Mr. Kestler."

Kestler was stark naked and had the silhouette of a Kewpie doll. Even his round, rosy face gave that impression. He was fat but had plenty of muscle. He stood in the center of the room, holding a broom by the tip of the handle between his thumb and forefinger.

Before I could respond to the introduction, Kestler said, "Can you do this?" and lifted the broom from the floor straight up to a horizontal position, held it there a moment, and then slowly let it down.

"Well, no, I don't think I can do that."

"Go ahead and try it, Greg. Just for fun," said Burger.

I took the broom and noticed that it was much heavier than an ordinary one. It had a long, thick handle of solid wood and had a coarse type of straw. I put the end of the handle between my thumb and forefinger and tried to lift it. I couldn't even get it off the floor in spite of the fact that I was not exactly a weakling. I looked at Kestler's big strong hands and marveled that anyone could develop such powerful fingers.

"Sure hope you're good-natured," I said wryly.

Burger laughed. "Beany, this is George Gregory. He just moved in last night. Why don't you come down to my place in a little while, and we'll have some coffee."

"Gregory, want to buy a radio?" Beany asked.

"No, I don't want to buy a radio."

We went down the hall to my room. Looking in, Burger asked, "Do you like this room?"

"What are you, some kind of a nut? Nobody could like this dirty room."

"Well, I've got something that is a lot better, but it's going to cost you some money."

"What do you mean, 'cost money'? I'm paying rent for this already."

"Yeah, but you'll have to do a few things yourself to make it livable. There's a room that is already fixed up, but you'll have to pay for it. Here, I'll show you."

Burger took me to another room and unlocked it. This room had the same layout as mine but was neat and clean, with a bed made up nicely, a bookcase, a rocking chair, and a small table with a coffeemaker and a few knickknacks.

"A guy named Winchell had this room but he transferred out last week. Lucky devil. He got to go back to Leavenworth. You can have this room if you want it. But he wants twenty-five dollars for the furnishings he bought."

I was about to object—I resented paying for furnishings when I'd been promised room and board at a reasonable rate. But I knew there was no point trying to argue with the government about it. I could choose the dirty room or this one.

"Okay, Burger, I'll take it. But I'm a little short of cash right now. I've got a whole stack of checks, personal checks for the most part from people back in Sandstone who owed me money. I haven't had a chance to cash them yet."

"Do you want to get them cashed?"

"Yeah, but I don't know a soul out here to verify them."

"Let me see them." Burger looked at them carefully. "Just endorse them over to me. I'll take care of them."

"What? Hey, that's over and above. I would sure appreciate it, but . . . "

"I'll have the money for you tomorrow. Need any now?"

This was the start of a very good and permanent friendship. Throughout the years, Burger proved to be a bit eccentric occasionally but always ready with a loan or good advice—and he could often think up an alibi when one was badly needed.

"By the way, Burger, I want to ask you a question."

"Shoot," he said, sitting on the bed in my new room.

"There was a guy by the name of Leonard at Sandstone, who came from here. He was telling me what a wonderful BOQ you had here at Alcatraz and what delicious food was served in the officers' mess."

"I've heard of him. He was here before the war, right?"

"Yes, he was."

"Things have changed. We have a new personnel director who is also the warden's secretary, and he apparently has pretty strong ties with the bureau. He is determined to save every nickel or dime he can to make himself look good. Anything officers are supposed to get, he tries not to give. You just about have to threaten him physically to get what you are entitled to by law. The training program has been shortened so much that it's of little value. That's the story."

Could this be a harbinger of the future? Changes were being made in the training program at Sandstone. But to make the same changes at Alcatraz seemed much more serious.

Having untrained officers underfoot was a strain on the busy, trained, and experienced officers. Their innocence and ignorance and, in many cases, their "don't give a damn" attitude could put a number of people in danger. Without training these officers in the weaponry used in the prison, we were all in danger. In one case, an experienced Alcatraz officer noticed that a new officer in the gun gallery kept looking at and fiddling with his weapon—an M1a carbine. Finally, the experienced officer asked what he was doing. The untrained officer responded that he was trying to figure out how it worked.

I reflected on my own entry into the prison service. It was the fall of 1939 and the Depression was still on. Gordon "Gordy" Miniclier, a friend of mine who didn't meet the height requirement, gave me an application. One of the questions on the lengthy form was, "Do you drink: not at all, moderately, or excessively?" Gordy argued that I should say "not at all." Our drinking in those days usually consisted of four or five of us sharing a bottle once in a while. Otherwise it was a one-drink stop in a bar when we had the price of a drink. After much consideration, I answered "moderately."

During the personal interview, I was asked, "Have you ever been in Laverne, Wisconsin?"

"No, I can't recall ever going there."

"Yes, you *were* there!" the investigator almost shouted in a most accusatory tone. "You went into the Badger Bar and Grill and had two drinks of whiskey on April 12, 1938."

"Now look, if you are trying to find out if I drink booze, just ask me," I bristled. "I've stopped in any number of bars and had a drink. I guess the one you mentioned is on the highway between Madison and Duluth. I went on a fishing trip with some friends over that way one time."

The investigator stood, extended his hand, and with a big smile said, "Mr. Gregory, that's what we wanted to know. We wanted to know if you would lie about it."

I didn't entertain much hope of getting a job with the prison service. But I took the written test along with about two hundred other men in Duluth. Examinations were being given across the country.

In the fall of 1940, I was notified that I had been accepted for the training program at Leavenworth, Kansas. I was in a class of seventeen. All of us had been to college. Most were college graduates. The intensive training occurred over a period of four months. Then each of us was assigned to a post under the supervision of an experienced officer. We worked six days a week and spent the seventh day on the rifle range.

After the regular eight-hour shift, our training continued on into the night. We had physical training sessions with intense concentration on defensive and come-along judo holds. The goal was to control the convict with as little physical harm as possible. We studied the judo holds and put in a lot of time practicing them on each other until we were fast and precise in our moves. Safety and security were continually emphasized in every aspect of the training. Interdependency was stressed—if one officer didn't do his job, other officers or convicts could be in danger.

We learned how to shake down a convict and a cell, subdue and restrain a convict, and how to work with another officer in safely opening the cell of an out-of-control convict. We collected many stories on the shenanigans pulled by convicts. We read books on penology and wrote reports. We listened to lectures on the overall operation of the Federal Prison System, including the chain of command. Our instructor gave us another type of lecture when we got uppity about our papers being graded by a captain who had not graduated from high school. It went something like this: "It might interest you to know that the captain keeps up with current books and articles on penology by looking up in the dictionary every word he doesn't know. And, for your information, he might not be able to spell 'schizophrenic' but he sure as hell knows one when he sees one. He is a top prison officer. College-trained people don't have a monopoly on brains." We were humbled and impressed.

We stood inspection every morning to see that we were properly attired for the day: pressed uniform, clean shirt, spotless tie, shoes shined, clean shaven, hair neatly cut and combed. When the ratings came out, I got a mediocre rating on "personal appearance." I felt my rating should have been much higher than that, so I went in to see the captain.

His cold gray eyes made me wish I hadn't confronted him with my complaint. After a moment, he opened his desk and pulled out a little black book of rules and regulations. Locating the section on personal appearance, he read it to me. According to the rule book, personal appearance not only meant how one looked but included behavior as well, on and off the job: participation in community activities such as Boy Scouts and Parent Teacher Associations was mentioned. The captain added that very few officers ever attain a top rating on personal appearance.

When I left the captain's office, I had a new definition of personal appearance and an indelible and respectful impression of the captain.

Even after all this training, an officer was considered to be on probation for at least a year, and the probation period could be extended. Written tests were part of the annual performance rating of all officers. Yes, things had changed a lot in the seven years following my entry into the prison service in 1940.

In my clean room, I settled down to read the newspaper I had picked up at the Alcatraz Store.* Suddenly a feeling of depression hit me very hard. The transition from excitement, noise, people, and action to a quiet, plain, uninteresting, and lonely room . . . the radio. Back to Beany.

"Okay, Beany, how much for the radio?" Beany picked up a radio from the bottom of a closet.

"How much, Beany?"

Beany went into deep thought. "Twenty bucks."

"Twenty bucks? Are you kidding? I can buy five of those for twenty bucks."

"Yeah, but you can't buy five of them right now, can you?"

"No, that's right. Tell you what I'll do. I'll give you a five."

"Ten."

"Seven-fifty."

"Sold."

So I took my battery-operated prize to my room and spent the evening listening to a variety of stations. It helped.

*The Alcatraz Store was a combination convenience store and post office and was for the use of officers and staff only.

4

An Alcatraz Screw
at Work

On my second day at Alcatraz, I was up early again. I had showered and was shaving when Sidney Burger stuck his head into the shower room and said, "Stop by on your way back."

I smelled the hot coffee when I was still several strides away from Burger's room. What a pleasant surprise—coffee, doughnuts, and orange juice!

"Help yourself, Gregory. And it'll be your turn to buy next week."

"Hey! This is above and beyond. Count me in, anytime."

"Beats going up top."

I fell in line for my first roll call at Alcatraz, wondering if my name would be called. It was and I hollered, "Yo."

Roll call was in the quad between the front of the main prison building and the lighthouse—this location was probably a carryover from the military days. The primary purpose of this activity seemed to be for the lieutenant to determine whether he had a full roster of officers fit to handle the next eight-hour shift. No time was given to inspection of attire, as opposed to Leavenworth, where you stood inspection and could be fired for standing roll call in less than a clean, pressed, and polished uniform. At Sandstone, roll call was very informal; we gathered in the squad room where the lieutenant checked us off on the roster.

After the roll call, the lieutenant on duty said, "Go on into the cell house, Mr. Gregory, and stand by. We'll find something for you to do."

In the cell house, Bunch was busy, as the cell house officer always was. "Can you operate these lock boxes now?" he asked me.

"Yes, sir, I can."

"Okay, I want Kone and Langston out. You'll find their names on the card in the box. Bring them down and stand them right over there by the wall. I'll get to them when I can."

After a time, Bunch came by and said, "Come on with me," motioning to the two convicts.

That is the way it went for me all day long. I helped with the feeding in TU—the Treatment Unit—where the convicts were fed in their cells. This meant keeping a close watch on the convict orderly to make sure each tray was delivered with full rations.

TU was a new cell block. It replaced what was known as D Block, from which there had been several escape attempts. Six of the cells had solid steel doors in addition to the barred doors. When the steel doors were closed, these cells were very dark. They were called "Hole cells," and hence the name the Hole, a term used interchangeably with TU. The six Hole cells were used for short-term punishment.

Being celled in TU meant losing the privileges of working, eating in the dining hall, using the recreation yard with other inmates, seeing a movie on Sunday afternoons, and earning good time.* Some in TU were not allowed to leave their cells except to go to the shower at the end of the tier. Perhaps the most notorious of these convicts was Robert Stroud, the so-called Birdman of Alcatraz. An administrative decision made by an assistant attorney general required that Stroud be confined in segregation for the rest of his life.

Stroud had killed a guard at Leavenworth and was given a death sentence. An appeal resulted in a second trial that changed his sentence to life in prison. The death penalty was the verdict of a third trial. Stroud was to continue serving his sentence in the U.S. Penitentiary at Leavenworth where he was to be placed in solitary confinement until his execution. Later, when the death sentence was commuted to life in prison, the order for segregation was not changed.

When I wasn't doing anything else, I would stroll around the cell house observing anything and everything. On one of these strolls I decided, just for a change of scene, to walk up on the second tier from the East End of the cell house. Just as I came around the corner, a convict rushed out of a cell with another one chasing right after him.

I hollered at them to stop and took after them. They got down to about the

*"Good time" was accumulated for good conduct and amounted to a reduction of a convict's sentence.

middle of the cell block when an officer from the other end, hearing the commotion, came up to help. We took the convicts down to the West End.

"What now?" Bunch asked.

I told him what I had seen.

"Which cell was it?"

"It was the first cell on the second tier," I said.

Bunch looked at one of the convicts and said, "That's your cell, Crawford."

Crawford was a little man, thin, fragile, and kind of nondescript. "Yes, sir, it's my cell."

"And you, Smith, what were you doing in Crawford's cell? As if I need ask."

Smith, a tall, strong, black man, said, "I wasn't in his cell. I just happened to come around the corner and saw the man running. I thought maybe there was something wrong, so I started running too." Smith tried to affect a look of innocence.

Bunch looked disgustedly at Smith and said to me, "Take him to the Hole."

"Why, Mr. Tompkins? I didn't do nothing," Smith said, trying to control his anger.

"No, just trying to commit murder, that's all you were doing."

"No, sir, I wouldn't hurt little Crawford, you know that."

"What I know is that you are going to the Hole. Take him out of here."

I took Smith by the arm. As we walked away toward TU, I heard Bunch say to Crawford, "Little man, we are trying to protect you, but if you keep messing with these big studs and leading them on, one of these days we'll be scraping you off the deck."

A few years later, Crawford was transferred from Alcatraz to another institution. Some time afterward, word came back to The Rock that he had been brutally beaten to death.

At the time of this news, I was in charge of TU and Smith was again one of the occupants. As I walked by Smith's cell one day, he said, "Mr. Gregory, did you hear about that little Crawford?"

"Yeah, I heard about him."

"Do you know why I was trying to get him that day?"

"You still remember that?"

"I sure do, that guy cheated on me."

"Oh? Cheated on you?"

"Well, you know how it is. I give him a blow job and he was supposed to let me punk him. But when he saw how big I was," Smith said, with a proud smile, "it scared him something awful and he took off like a rabbit at sundown."

The look I directed toward Smith was scornful as I said, "You could have crippled that little man."

"Not near as bad a crippling as it would have been if I had caught that little motherfucker," said Smith, laughing grimly. "Smitty don't like people cheating on him."

Smith was later transferred to another prison where he met his match. In one of the many little hideaways in the yard, he was found brutally beaten. In spite of the ruthless battering, which resulted in a crushed skull, Smith lived. But the last I heard, he was a hopeless invalid.

When I thought of these convicts, I felt exasperated and sad. What to do with them? Actually, quite a few of the Alcatraz convicts were of this type. They seldom made any ripples—just passed through life as a number and eventually disappeared. Never known, never remembered. It seemed such a waste.

It was Tuesday and Burger had the day off. He had gone over to the city the night before. No orange juice, doughnuts, and coffee. So I went up top for breakfast, which consisted of a bowl of cornflakes and a big, fresh sweet roll. "Blue john" was served with the cereal. The convicts working in the kitchen stole the cream from the top of the nonhomogenized milk. The result was a thin, bluish-colored milk called blue john.

It was my third day as an Alcatraz screw. At roll call, I was assigned to the cell house again. I ascended to my favorite perch, up on the second tier and right on the corner so I could lean back against the railing and observe all the comings and goings during the movement of convicts. I could also see the West End. Looking down on Bunch, I thought, He sure does deserve his nickname. Burger said the name "Bunch" had been given to Tompkins because he looked just like a bunch of muscles.

After the convicts left for work call, I chose some cells to search. This was the usual chore for idle moments in the cell house. I was up on the second tier in B Block searching a cell that was stuffed with magazines, books, partially filled medicine bottles, and extra clothing. Everything had a layer of dust.

I went over to the storage area in A Block, got a packing box, and proceeded to load up all the contraband in the cell. It so happened that the occupant was a hall janitor and was watching me search his cell. When I started loading the box, he came up and whined about how this was his property and I had no right to be in his cell. Eddor, a convict who was down on the flats,* started egging on the

---

*"The flats" were the wide aisles on the first floor between the cell blocks.

cell occupant. The occupant could see I was not happy about all this talk and quieted down because he didn't want me to write a report on him. Eddor didn't have the benefit of my facial expression to guide him, so he kept on nagging. I wondered what I should do about this interference from the flats.

I had just come from Sandstone, where the new policy of being nice to convicts was getting into full swing. We officers read it as, Don't bother the convicts, and especially don't bother the supervising officers with problems you might be having with convicts. In short, no one wanted to be charged with enforcing reasonable discipline.

All of this made me hesitant about how to handle Eddor. My first thought was to go down, nudge him against the bars a bit, and tell him I could fix it so he couldn't talk at all if he wanted me to. But not knowing just how far I could go, I went to see Mr. Miller.

"Do you mean to say that little pissant gave you some back talk? Bring him down and I will talk to him." Miller was sitting at the table in the West End where he held court. I brought Eddor to stand in front of him.

"Mr. Gregory tells me you have been using your smart mouth again." Turning to me, he spoke with increasing loudness. "Mr. Gregory, you take this sorry loudmouth into TU and you whip him upside the head until he can't stand it anymore and then throw him in the Hole."

This surprised me, to put it mildly. It was doubtful this scene would have happened in any other federal prison at that time. I took the stunned Eddor by the arm and guided him into TU. By the time we got there, he was really scared. I turned to face my charge, who seemed to have shrunk physically on the trip from the cell house. He didn't know what I was going to do. Truth is, I didn't know what I was going to do either.

Grabbing Eddor by the front of his shirt, I pushed him against the wall, and speaking loudly enough to be overheard by most of the TU occupants, I said, "Now look, friend, I'm new here, but I'm not new to the prison service. I'm not going to let you or anyone else get away with talking to me the way you did."

TU was quiet as I shoved Eddor into a cell. I was sure my message had been heard. I slammed the door shut and walked away.

I was looking down on Broadway when I saw the convict mechanic and his "girlfriend." How did I know it was his "girlfriend"? Just one of those things you learn to know, to sense. They were going to the kitchen. I remembered I had seen the two of them going to the kitchen just about the same time the day before.

Back down on the flats, I asked Bunch, "Something wrong in the kitchen? I saw the convict mechanic going back there."

"Go on back and see, but don't let it shake you too much," Bunch said with a sardonic smile.

In the kitchen there were several small grills that were used to cook hamburgers, bacon, and the like. The mechanic, Peter Evans, and his "girlfriend" were standing by one of the grills. Evans had a spatula in his hand and, believe it or not, on the grill were two nice, neat-looking, little steaks. Apparently I didn't hide my look of disapproval in time, because Evans looked up at me with a mirthless smile and hard blue eyes, as if to say, Make something of it if you want to, bub, but you will be a loser.

I wondered how often the convict main line* was served steaks—maybe on an infrequent holiday. And an officer? I'd be very surprised if officers were ever served steaks, I thought.

Back in the cell house I said to Bunch, "Well, I went, I saw, but I don't savvy."

"Special privilege, boy, special privilege. You're going to see quite a bit of it around here, it's just the way they run it. Doesn't seem to be doing too bad."

Later on in the day when Bunch had a break, he looked at his watch and said, "Come on, Greg, let's go have lunch."

Sitting in the officers' mess, Bunch told me the story of Peter Evans. It was in another prison some years ago that Evans and some other men lured a convict into a secluded part of the institution for the purpose of ending his stool-pigeon days. And they did. When found, the stool pigeon appeared to be sleeping—but one doesn't sleep with a broom handle protruding from one's rectum. It must have been a horrible death.

The associate warden at the prison, enraged that one of his informers had been so treated, did everything he could to get a confession out of Evans. Failing, he sent Evans and a couple of the others to The Rock.

Two railroad cars had been specially designed for the Federal Prison System to use in the transfer of convicts from one institution to another. Still hoping to get Evans to come clean, the associate warden came along and promised him immunity and whatever else he could think of to get him to turn state's evidence. But Evans never confessed. While on The Rock, he became a good convict with privileges and freedom of movement unusual for an Alcatraz resident. Many years later he received a parole and was last seen walking the streets in a Midwestern city, a free man.

Bunch ended the story. "It could be that he's become one of Mr. Miller's top informers. I'll tell you this, Greg, there are certain things here you just don't ques-

---

*The main population, convicts housed in blocks B and C, made up the main line in the dining hall. Convicts in the hospital and TU were served meals in their cells.

tion. Mr. Miller runs a one-man show and I think it's a good show. But he certainly doesn't want anyone telling him what to do and what not to do. So just go along with it, Mac. You don't have to like it, but as long as you're here, you have to live with it."

Mr. Miller made an appearance in the cell house. I went down the stairs from my observation point on the second gallery to get closer to the action. When Miller got settled at the desk, he looked at Bunch and said, "Get Joe Monde out here."

Bunch nodded to me and said, "He's in TU. Go get him."

In TU, I introduced myself to Officer Lewis, the officer on duty, and said, "I've come to get Joe. Mr. Miller wants to see him."

"Joe Monde?" A look of anguish and annoyance appeared on the hard-eyed officer's face as he got up from his desk.

"What's the matter?" I asked, "Is he a tough one?"

"Yeah, and he's playing crazy. He thinks he might work a transfer. Since the 'bluebird man' made it out of here with a crazy act, we've got others practicing their acting skills trying to get to Springfield or wherever."

"The bluebird man?"

"Yeah, he tried to convince us that he had bluebirds. In his cell, following him around, talking to him . . . and he even talked to them. He developed a pretty nice chirp, too.

"And believe it or not, his act worked on a naive psychiatrist. After being shipped out to the Springfield Medical Center, he wrote Mr. Miller, saying, 'I may be crazy, Meathead, but I'm down here eating candy bars. Please send me my bluebirds. I miss them.' A phony, but he got away with it."

(There was no post exchange or canteen at Alcatraz for the convicts. In other federal institutions, convicts were allowed to buy candy, fruit, cigarettes, certain recreational equipment, books, magazines, and newspapers from the prison canteen. At Alcatraz they could only order approved books and magazines, musical instruments, and recreational equipment. There were no snacks, smoking materials, or newspapers to be purchased. In addition to the four packs of ready-made cigarettes they were issued each week, the convicts could have all the bulk tobacco and cigarette papers they wanted.)

"Joe can be pretty rough when he wants to be. I'll open the door just a little bit. Just enough to let him out. Watch him," Lewis said.

"I'm ready."

Monde was lying on his bunk. Just as Lewis opened the door, he jumped off the sack and hit the door, sliding it back, and took a hefty swing at me, hitting me on the shoulder. Lewis quickly slammed the door into Joe. I followed that up by hitting Joe with my unhurt shoulder, knocking him against the sharp edge of the cell door with as much force as I could. Joe started sinking to his knees as though he were unconscious. Knowing he hadn't been hit that hard, I grabbed him by his black curly hair, pulled his head over, and sharply smacked it against my knee.

"Oooh, for God's sake, oooh," Joe groaned, "No more! What do you want to do, kill me?"

Putting my favorite come-along hold on the now screaming con, I said, "Mr. Miller wants to see you, Joe, and I have been delegated to take you to him. Now, how do you want to go? You want it nice and easy? Or you want to hurt? Shall we drag you down the steps?"

"I'll take it easy, you got me." Now groaning quietly, he looked at me and said, "You goddamned Marine, I've been hearing about you."

"Never mind the Marine stuff, I'm just a prison screw to you, and Mr. Miller wants to see you."

Joe Monde stood just a little back from the desk in front of Mr. Miller and eyed him with a suspicious and wary look, his small, hard, black eyes darting here and there. It was obvious he had been in this position before.

Miller looked up at Joe with a big smile. "Joe. Nice to see you again. How's the crazy stuff going?"

"Listen, Mr. Miller, dammit, I *am* crazy and you know it. And you're crazy too."

"Yeah, it takes a crazy man to deal with a crazy man, doesn't it, Joe?" Miller said, laughing.

"What do you mean by that?"

"Joe, you might be a little crazy but you've got a long way to go to be really crazy. I just brought you out to let you know you are going to go crazy in the Alcatraz TU and no place else. Put him back in his cell, Mr. Gregory."

Joe started to put up a bit of resistance. He had the muscle to do it. His five-foot, eight-inch frame was all brawn. But I took him by a wristlock and said, "Now, Joe, we don't want to go through this again, do we?"

Joe caught himself and screamed, "I'm crazy, Mr. Miller, and you know it." All the way to TU he kept screaming, "I'm crazy, I'm crazy."

Going up the stairs in TU, Joe tried again in a half-hearted way to cause a little trouble, but I put a real good twist on the wristlock, causing him to howl in pain.

"I'm getting tired of fooling with you, Joe," I said. "Now move it. I'll let you play your game a little bit but don't make me do all the work." He went easy the rest of the way.

I was glad Joe knew when to surrender. My way of doing things was to expend only the energy necessary to get the job done—in this case, to get Joe back into his cell.

To accomplish this, I walked right up in Joe's face and tapped him on the chest just hard enough to throw him off balance. As he threw up his hands to stabilize himself, I grabbed his right wrist with my right hand and at the same time pivoted on my left foot and stepped backward until I was alongside Joe with his right arm laced under my left arm. The execution of a good come-along hold, if done quickly, takes very little effort and causes little discomfort to the convict. Then it is up to the convict. If he tries to break out of the hold, he hurts only himself.

5

A One-Man
Hunger Strike

I was getting fairly well acquainted with a few of the officers, although I had been on Alcatraz less than a week. It's wise to get acquainted rapidly in a situation where your life might depend on knowing the people with whom you work. The officers were friendly, but as in the other institutions where I had worked, they were also respectful of the privacy of others. Down at the Mule Barn, the general rule was "be quiet" because there were officers trying to sleep at all times of day or night.

My first few days on Alcatraz had been far from dull. Even the general routines were clothed in an aura of tension and expectancy. There was never a quiet time in the cell house—at least on the day shift. It would take months at Sandstone, a minimum-custody institution, to experience as much action as I had seen in my first days on Alcatraz. The convicts at Sandstone were not violent people. They were usually serving short terms—in comparison to the Alcatraz population—and chalked up a maximum number of good-time days.

As a new officer at Alcatraz, I received the full treatment from the cons. The general idea was to learn anything about me that might be used against me at some later time. Had I told them where I came from, that information would have been passed around the entire prison to see if there was a convict from my hometown. If there was, he would write a relative or friend to try to dig up something from my past that the convicts could use to their advantage. They wanted to know where I grew up, went to school, and worked, and they wanted to know about my family—who was in it and where they lived. They wanted to know my habits and hobbies. But we officers were taught to tell nothing—to remember

45

that a friendly convict was still a convict. They never forgot that we were officers. We were employees of the Federal Prison Service, which was under the Department of Justice and the Attorney General's Office, and we were charged with the responsibility of keeping them in prison until their time had been served.

I shared friendly conversations with some convicts, but that was after I got to know them. There was a convict from the Minneapolis area with whom I had a number of very pleasant conversations.

One convict who I grew to like better than I had expected was named Kieffer. Bunch called me down from the tier one day and said, "Come on, we've got to go up and help in the hospital."

In the hospital, a convict was strapped in a chair similar to a barber's chair. Shannon, the MTA on duty,* was mixing some sort of liquid in a beaker.

"We have here," Shannon said, "a man who is on a hunger strike. His claim is that he will not eat again until we send him to another institution. He's *not* going to get off Alcatraz that way. Medically speaking, the problem is that, at least to our knowledge, he has not eaten in eight days. So, in order to prevent his developing various side effects of malnutrition, such as brain damage, we are going to force-feed him."

The convict in question was a medium-sized man, fairly well muscled, but very thin-faced, with wide, staring eyes. He looked at Shannon and said, "I don't care what you do. You can tube-feed me if you want to, but as soon as you get it down I'm going to heave it all up."

Shannon held an emesis basin in front of the convict's face. "If you do, we'll just catch it all in this basin and pour it right back down the tube. You want to upchuck again, down the tube again."

The poor convict looked at Shannon and then at the emesis basin. His determined countenance began to dissolve into uncertainty.

"You would do that, too, wouldn't you, Mr. Shannon?" he said, now giving in to complete defeat.

"Yes, I would. It's not going to hurt you. It might sound like cruel and unusual punishment, but it really isn't. We're just trying to keep you alive," Shannon said as he finished blending the mixture. "Ready to go? You can make it easy on yourself, or you can make it hard."

Bunch and I stood on either side of the convict and held his head still as best we could. Shannon expertly ran the tube down into the con's stomach. Holding

*MTA is short for medical technical assistant, an employee of the U.S. Public Health Service assigned to the Federal Prison Service. To be a qualified MTA, one had to have three years of nursing experience and specialize in at least two areas, such as X-ray, lab work, surgical assistance, or psychiatric nursing.

the funnel end of the tube upright, he began to pour the mixture slowly from the beaker. As he did so, he carried on a monologue describing the procedure and the contents of the mixture.

After a few attempts to squirm and claw his way out, the convict resigned himself to the inevitable and sat quietly. When the beaker was empty, Shannon said, "Now I am going to pull out this tube. It won't hurt. Just don't move." Putting the tube aside, Shannon picked up the emesis basin, held it in front of the convict, and waited.

With a sigh of resignation, the con said, "You win, Mr. Shannon. I give up. Take me back to TU."

"Okay, fella, and when you want out of TU just let us know. He's all yours, gentlemen."

Bunch and I unstrapped him and took him downstairs. As we approached TU, Bunch said, "How about it, Kieffer, do you really want to go back to TU or do you want to come out into the population?"

For a moment it looked as if Kieffer was going to cry. "I'll come out if you'll let me," he said in a voice of hopelessness.

"Which cell block would you like?"

"Don't matter, C is okay."

"Kieffer, you're not all that bad. Why don't you just try it the right way for a while? Might be just the thing to lead to a ticket out of here," Bunch said. Kieffer just stared at him. Could there really be hope?

"From now on, I'm going to keep an eye on you. Show me something." To me, Bunch said, "Put him in an outside bottom cell on C Block where we can keep an eye on him." Bunch's twelve years in the Marine Corps had given him a rough, tough personality but he also had a streak of kindness and compassion which I saw on a number of occasions.

Kieffer made the interest in him pay off. A little more than a year later, he was transferred out of Alcatraz. I never heard of him after that.

A few weeks after the Kieffer incident, I took another convict up to the hospital for treatment of facial cuts and a possible fractured bone from a fight in the yard. I took the opportunity to question Shannon. "Would you really have poured that gook back down Kieffer's throat after he vomited it up?"

"Who knows?" grinned Shannon. "I've never had to do it yet."

I got to thinking about a hunger strike in the early days of Alcatraz. An officer who was present at the time told me that the convicts were determined to win better food or die trying. The whole population went on a hunger strike. They didn't create any other disturbance. They went to work every day, climbing up and down the steep stairs to and from the work area. They were exceptionally quiet in the cell house. In those days, there was little sympathy for criminals— quite the opposite. So it never occurred to the administrators to force-feed any of them.

Some of the older cons began to have trouble climbing up the stairs. Finally, just to save them, the leaders of the strike called it off and returned to the dining hall. That was the end of the hunger strike. Give credit to the administration that they let it go at that and did not punish anyone. I laughed to myself and thought, What would it have been like to force-feed a couple of hundred cons?

The first convicts to serve time on The Rock as federal prisoners were military convicts and big crime names drawn from the other institutions in the Federal Prison System. Convicts were transferred as administrators in the various institutions felt it was necessary. Committing murder or attempting to escape often got a convict sent to Alcatraz. Those being transferred to Alcatraz dreaded the limitation of privileges, the individual cells, the thought of the prison's being escape-proof, and the policy of no paroles.

Although no one got paroled directly from Alcatraz, on the recommendation of the Classification Board a convict could be transferred to another institution where he would have the possibility of parole. Being a model prisoner was a start toward a recommendation for transfer. The rule of no paroles from Alcatraz was actually made out of consideration for the convicts. The administration felt that it would be easier on an ex-convict if he could say he was on parole from one of the other institutions in the system. The very name of Alcatraz had a way of striking fear in the minds of the general public. In later years, however, a few convicts were paroled directly from Alcatraz.

On Thursday morning, I idly walked over and looked through the peephole into TU and for a moment was almost paralyzed. The convict orderly had the officer on duty, Lewis, nearly down and was beating the hell out of him.

I yelled to the gun gallery officer to let down the TU key.* Every officer in the vicinity knew immediately that something was wrong and we got the TU door open in record time. I rushed in, followed by other officers, and we soon had the orderly under control. He was completely out of his mind.

---

*The gun galleries at Alcatraz were located at the East and West Ends of the cell house. They were elevated above the passageways and secured with bars and heavy wire. The entries were on the outside of the building. The TU keys were kept in the West Gun Gallery and were let down on lines to officers who needed them.

When we had the convict in restraints and on his way to the hospital, Bunch said, "You all right, Lewis?"

"Yeah, I guess." But he certainly looked quite the worse for wear.

He sat down at the desk and said, "The first orderly I've picked that went wrong. A couple of weeks ago he wanted to know what his chances were of getting out of TU. He'd always been quiet, polite, and no trouble. Since I was losing my orderly, I asked if he would like the job." Lewis paused and then said as though still surprised, "And after two weeks of good work—this."

"Want to take the rest of the day off?"

"No, no. But I would like to have somebody stay in here for a while."

"Greg?"

"Be glad to."

I mused to myself, If I get this kind of action every day, I'm going to stay in pretty good shape even without running up the hill to the cell house every morning. I wondered whether or not I would really like that. Maybe not, but I didn't like boredom either.

With everybody quiet in TU, Lewis and I fell into conversation. I learned he was also a Marine and had entered the Federal Prison Service at Alcatraz prior to World War II.

As I got to know him and work with him, I came to evaluate him as one of the best TU officers we had. He was quiet and had a way of standing square-shouldered and staring at unruly or reluctant convicts. That stare was often all that was needed to convince a convict to honor his demands. He would also fight the front office for anything the convicts were due.

"What did these guys do to get in TU, anyhow?" I asked as we sat at the desk talking.

"Different things. But most of them are in here for their own protection. They are quiet. Don't usually cause a lot of trouble. Several of them were convicted of murder.

"Others are here for only a short term—a day or two—for some infraction of rules. Actually, Greg, this is really a pretty good job. You're busy in here all day. You have two orderlies, one to serve the meals and one to do the janitorial work. But you never let more than one con out of his cell at a time. The lieutenant comes in to supervise the baths. There's a shower at the end of each tier."

"I've heard Mr. Miller sending convicts in here all week," I said.

"Yeah," Lewis laughed. "He knows his convicts. A convict called him a dumb meathead one day and Mr. Miller put him in the Hole, telling him he would never again see the light of day. But that afternoon he came in and told the con, 'Yeah, I might be dumb and you might be smart but you're in the Hole and I'm the associate warden.' Then he broke into a roar of laughter, turned to me, and said, 'Let's get him out of here and back into the population.' He seldom leaves a man in a dark cell very long. It's usually one day or less."

I went down to the officers' mess, ate lunch, and returned to the cell house. Just before the end of the day, an officer whom I had not seen before came into the cell house. A tall, slim man. He said something to Bunch, who motioned for me to come down from my perch on the second tier. The officer looked at me with hard eyes and said, "You Gregory?"

"Yes, sir."

"Don't you ever look at the roster?"

"No, where do you keep it?"

The roster form listed all the posts and shifts. For each day, officers' names were filled in for the various posts. Officers on days off, vacation (identified on the roster as annual leave), or sick leave were also listed. The total number of officers for Alcatraz was around one hundred.

"It's right out there by the side of the captain's desk. You should look at it at the beginning of every shift and especially at the end of your shift to see what you are going to do the next day. Your days off are Friday and Saturday. When you come back on Sunday, do the same thing you are doing now. You will be in the cell house. But you can stand by for further orders because the captain figures you should know enough by now to go to work."

Without further ado, the officer turned and very officiously walked out of the cell house. I watched him as he walked down Broadway and thought, Go to work? What the hell do they call what I've been doing all week if it isn't work?

"Take it easy on him, Greg," said Bunch. "That guy has had some problems. He's Bill Cook, the captain's clerk. In the May riot, he was one of the officers who got shot at point-blank range. Wounded, locked in a cell, played dead to avoid further shooting, he kind of just broke up. You know what it's like. Not much different from combat.

"Some people have lots of courage as long as they can actively and physically come face to face with the enemy. But to have to stay quiet and motionless when somebody is shooting at you . . . "

Memories flashed through my mind. I nodded. Nothing more had to be said.

6

Trouble in the Yard

On Sunday morning after roll call, I returned to the cell house and went about the various assignments Bunch gave me. Mostly I opened and locked cell doors; in between I sat on my perch.

The wall phone at the West End of the cell house rang. Bunch got up from his desk, took the receiver off the hook, listened, put his hand over the mouthpiece, and loudly whispered, "Gregory, it's for you. It's the captain calling."

I went down and took the phone. "Gregory here."

"Gregory, you're going to take the Road Tower on the morning watch starting tonight. Is that all right with you?" The captain's voice was curt, even harsh.

"Yes, sir, captain, anything you say," I said with exaggerated politeness. "Should I take off now?" At Sandstone, when an officer was requested to double back on a shift, he was permitted to go home and rest before his second shift.

"Of course not, finish your shift. You don't come in until midnight, you'll have plenty of time to rest."

"Yes, sir, captain," I said, somewhat subdued. "Whatever you say." Turning from the phone, I happened to catch the look on Bunch's face. A look of disapproval—of warning.

"So?"

"That guy you just talked with . . . ," Bunch started to explain.

"By the way, who is he? I've been here a week and I haven't even met him."

"Just shut up and listen up, man, will you? His name is Lyle Parant."

"That's the guy I've been intending to ask you about."

"He just made lieutenant and he's the acting captain till the new one comes in. But he also wants desperately to be captain. He is strictly for Lyle climbing the promotion ladder—whatever it takes. Get it? Watch him, Greg. He never forgets a grudge. I don't want you to be one of his stepping-stones."

51

"Thanks for the information. I appreciate it. And I'll try to watch my mouth when I'm around him."

I started up the steps to the second tier of cells, which had been my roost during my first week at Alcatraz. I liked this perch because all the convicts coming up or going down the tiers had to face me, at least momentarily. It was a chance to get a good look at their faces, their gait, their posture, their nervous habits, their tics, and their eyes. I looked at how they directed their eyes when approaching me—whether they looked away, stared hard, took a darting glance, or pretended I wasn't there. And just as important to an experienced officer, the convicts had a chance to observe me.

From my place on the second tier, it was also easy to go up to the third tier or down on the flats to let a convict out or back into a cell. Besides the times in the mornings and afternoons when the main work crews went out and returned, there was a lot of movement in the cell house. There were a number of reasons why an individual convict would leave his cell. He might go to see the dentist or doctor, an attorney, the Classification Board, the parole officer, the associate warden for court, or a family member in the visitors' room. Sometimes a painter or mechanic went down to the clothing room for a clean shirt and pants. Or a convict might want to change cells.

I was about halfway up the stairs when the intercom boomed, "Trouble in the yard, Bunch, all officers."

"Come on, Gregory." Bunch was on his way.

I was at Bunch's side just as the gate officer unlocked the heavy steel door that led to the yard and on beyond to the industries. Knowing that Bunch had a tricky knee from a piece of shrapnel he took in World War II, I slipped ahead as I ran down the stairs and saw an officer seemingly paying little attention to what was going on in the yard. Could this fracas be all over? Looking again, I recognized the short, somewhat overweight officer as the one who had tried to push Biff around following the fight in the dining hall. Turning toward the activity, I found myself in the middle of the melee. It was chaos. Convicts were running, screaming obscenities, fighting, and wrestling with each other . . . race rioting had come to Alcatraz. Stopping it quickly was impossible. But we tried to tone it down as much as we could until it played itself out and we could take control.

I saw a white convict running into the center of the fracas, waving a baseball bat. I thought, He's mine, and went after him. I got there just in time to grab him by the cuff of his pant leg, causing him to stumble and fall. Trying to break the fall, he stubbed the bat into the ground, causing the handle to jam into his groin. With a sickly scream, the convict let go of the bat and fell to the ground in what can only be described as exquisite pain. He would cause no more trouble this day.

A black convict grabbed for the bat. I loosened some of his teeth with a stiff elbow and swung the bat, giving him a smart crack on the shins that took his mind off hurting anyone else for a while. Throwing the bat under the stairs, I went after a tall, white, slender convict with a crooked nose who was headed toward the center of the free-swinging, cussing, screeching donnybrook. But when I grabbed him and started applying pressure with a judo hold on his arm, he looked up at me and said, "Jesus Christ, Mac, don't break my goddamn arm. Just get me out of this mess. I'm showboating." All this in a hurried whisper.

Understanding the ever-present need to save face among the prison population, I walked him away from the free-for-all, almost tripping over a con lying on the ground bleeding and apparently unconscious.

All of a sudden, the overweight officer came rushing from the foot of the stairs, grabbed the convict's other arm, and started twisting it unmercifully. With a quick shake of his shoulder, the con sent the officer to the ground in a most undignified sprawl.

Looking down at the prone officer, I wondered, What's with this sorry guy, anyway?

As I walked the convict toward the stairs, he said, "Mac, watch that man. He's day-old shit. Real sneaky."

I thought, He must be one of the guys with no training, trying to ride the coattails of those of us who were trained. Later I learned he was, indeed, an untrained man who had come in during the war and had somehow won the favor of the front office.

At the stairs, I shoved the bent-nosed con hard enough to make him stumble and yelled, "Up the stairs, bub, and fast!" He left the air blue with a lot of phony cussing, playing his part well as he "stumbled" up the stairs to the cell house.

Turning back to the hassle, I noticed a number of officers had come into the yard and were getting most of the convicts under control. I saw a group of convicts surrounding a big black man and went toward it.

Buck Watson, a white convict, had the black convict in a chokehold and was trying to keep him still while his friend, Slick Nichols, hit him with a horseshoe. Slick was having trouble hitting his mark—the black con's head. As often as not he was hitting Buck's arm, which accounted for the stream of obscenities admonishing Slick to "Hit your fucking target!"

I was astonished to see that horseshoes were part of the recreation equipment. Just as Slick drew back for another blow, I grabbed his arm and kept its momentum going back hard and fast, which dumped him on his butt. Grabbing the horseshoe, I glared down at him as he started to get up.

"I won't miss," I said. One look at me with the horseshoe and Slick decided it would be better to stay down.

Just in the nick of time, I ducked under a murderous punch delivered by the black con, whom Buck had released. As I ducked, I went into a field-goal kicking position and followed through with a powerful kick between the legs of the wild-eyed con. Why didn't he go down? He couldn't. Bunch was holding him now in a reverse headlock. He made one attempt to get out of the hold, but the pain caused by his effort reminded him that resistance to a reverse headlock could cause the neck to snap quite easily. Especially if the guy holding you is big and strong like Bunch Tompkins.

"Okay, tiger, it's all over for you," said Bunch. "I've got him, Gregory."

Now the diminishing group of convicts was circled around two more fighting cons, one black and one white. Noting that neither one had a weapon of any kind, I slowed my pace, trying to put on the calm act as I walked into the group.

Watching the fight for a few seconds, I saw the two cons were pretty evenly matched—they were giving each other some punishing blows and both were beginning to wheeze and grunt. I gave them another couple of moments and then stepped between the two, acting much like the referee at a boxing match.

"Break!" I commanded with a hand on a shoulder of each. Both of the convicts stopped. I looked them over and saw they were pretty well banged up.

"You guys all right?" There was a gasping "Yes" from each of them. A couple of officers took over and escorted them up the stairs.

I scanned the yard. So many of these spontaneous riots, whatever their cause, last no more than a few minutes. However, the intensity while in full gear could be alarming. This one seemed to have run out of steam shortly after it began. Now the convicts were just looking for an excuse to get out of the trouble and save face at the same time.

"All right, you guys, spread out. Go on back to whatever you were doing," I said. They were glad to get the order.

Walking over to the officer who seemed to be in charge of the yard, I said, "Any way I can help here?"

"No, everything has calmed down now. You can go back to the cell house. There won't be any more trouble."

"Are you all right, Greg?" Bunch asked after looking me over.

"Yeah, no problems."

"Maybe you better go up to the hospital and check on the big guy. The one that was in the horseshoe match," said Bunch.

Up in the hospital, the big man was sitting on a treatment table. Shannon, the MTA, was shaving parts of his head as best he could and applying bandages. The prongs of the horseshoe had been used to good advantage. He was still plenty hostile.

"Are you okay?" I asked.

"You that real bad Marine just come here." It was a statement, not a question. "Better play it cool, man. Don't give me no hard time." There was menace in his voice.

I sincerely hoped that I would never have to give him any kind of a hard time.

Having fixed a bandage to the last cut, Shannon said, "Well, Mr. Gregory, this is all I can do for this gentleman. He doesn't need hospitalization, so you can take him back downstairs."

I looked at the huge, superbly muscled man. His eyes were still angry and wild.

"By the way, his name is Jones," said Shannon.

"Well, Jones, you heard the man. Let's go."

The big con hesitated for a moment, then slid off the table and looked at me with generations of hatred in his eyes. He turned slowly and walked toward the door.

"I know I'm going to the Hole," he said in a bitter and hopeless voice.

I took my charge through the gate, down the steep stairs, through the door into the dining room, and through the gate into the cell house. I was finding out how difficult it was to go from one place to another on The Rock. In fact, I was beginning to see Alcatraz as a place of ups and downs—up stairs, down stairs, up hills, down hills, and, everywhere, gates or doors requiring an officer with a key.

As I came into the cell house with Jones on the way to TU, I noticed Mr. Miller sitting at a table in the West End. In my first week at Alcatraz, I had seen Miller start off calmly reading the charges to a convict and then work himself into a yelling, arm-swinging, finger-pointing frenzy. He was a big, bombastic man and his face would become florid. Needless to say, he was intimidating to both officers and convicts. He was an enigma. He caught an officer goofing off one day and launched a vicious verbal attack, really shaking up the man, then he turned to me with a big smile and said, "How's it going, Greg?" I could only stare at him and say, "Okay, Mr. Miller."

Bunch and several officers were standing at ease around the table where Miller sat. These officers were veterans of the service, well-trained professionals with lots of experience, officers of the "old school." There was an air of confidence about them. They were all over six feet tall and dressed in full, neat uniforms. These men would get top ratings in any kind of system used to determine superiority among prison officers. They would always win the blue ribbon, so to speak.

On seeing Jones and me, Miller called out, "Bring him over here." Jones made no objection as I steered him to a position in front of Miller.

"All right, Jones, what have you got to say for yourself? You started this fuss. Didn't you? Don't tell me you didn't."

"Why you big motherfucker,* old Meathead, no-good . . . ," and he started over the table at Miller. He never should have done that. Blackjacks popped out of the pockets of the officers and they began tapping, firmly but not too hard, on poor Jones's head.

It was almost comical. All the little pieces of tape that Shannon had so carefully put on Jones's head began to fly up in the air like popcorn a-popping. Slowly, Jones sank down with his elbows on the table, holding his head in his hands.

"Take him to the Hole!" shouted Miller. "He knows where he's going." Two of the veteran officers marched him off to TU.

Wow! This guy is tough, I thought, looking at Miller. He is the boss.

Then I became aware that Miller was looking at me and smiling. He was almost handsome when he smiled. A bit flustered, I quickly came to attention out of long habit.

"Mr. Gregory, they tell me you did a good job out there in the yard."

"Thank you, sir."

Miller stared at me approvingly. "Yeah, good job. Go in and check that fellow and see if he's all right. And if he tries to give you any trouble, let him have it good."

I was about to question this when I felt a hard nudge in the back. I got the message. Bunch wouldn't steer me wrong.

"Yes, sir," I said, and went to the Treatment Unit.

"How's it going, Lewis? Any more excitement?" I asked.

"No. But I've got a few more occupants."

"Mr. Miller sent me in to check on one of them. Jones."

"Yeah, he's right down here."

At the end of the cell block, Lewis stopped. "Kind of dark in there, Gregory.

---

*Strange though it may seem, not much profanity was heard in Alcatraz (except when associated with strong emotion) until the late 1940s and 1950s. A different kind of convict, from the large eastern cities, began to arrive at that time. To them, their pornographic profanity was just their way of talking, but the Alcatraz personnel could never quite get used to it.

Better let me check first, just in case." I could guess about the "just in case." Feces, soft and smelly, can be thrown out of a cell.

But Jones was now quiet and peaceful. I checked him over as best I could. "You all right, Jones?"

Jones stuck his hand through the bars, pointing to a small scratch. "I got this scratch." I looked at him, surprised, to say the least. All that pounding on him with fists, a horseshoe, and saps and he's complaining about a little scratch?

"No problem, Jones. When the MTA comes in, we'll have him look at it," Lewis told him.

Walking back to his desk, Lewis grinned at me. "That's the way they are sometimes. You think they're almost dead and then they complain about a little scratch."

"Hmm," I said. "By the way, Lewis, one of the first guys I sent in here from the yard, a tall, slim man with a crooked nose, don't know his name . . . "

"Panella. He's right down here on the flats in number three."

"Could I talk with him? Is it all right?"

"Sure, go ahead. No problem."

I looked into cell number three. "That was a pretty good act you put on out there in the yard."

Panella looked out and smiled wryly. Getting up off his bunk, he said, "Yeah. Thanks for your help."

"You know you can never fool these guys."

"I know, but I have to pretend to save my neck."

"I'm curious. What's with the 'Mac' routine?"

"I was hoping it might get you to wonder about me. You see, I'm still in the Marines. At least, kind of."

He then told me in much detail about how he had been sent to China after a time in the occupation forces in Japan. While there, he got involved with a Japanese who pulled a knife on him. Panella let him have it with his K-Bar (Marine Corps knife) and killed him. The war with Japan had just ended. There were no friendly witnesses and now killing had suddenly become murder. So Panella ended up with a sentence of life at hard labor.

I turned to leave.

"Wait. Please. There's more. So there won't be any misunderstanding, that act in the yard wasn't because I am all that fond of prison screws but because I have a plan. I'm trying to keep a clean record here and maybe they will ship me back to a navy brig, and just maybe I'll get out someday. But I've gotta get out of Alcatraz first."

"But why Alcatraz instead of in a navy brig from the start?"

"I was in the brig, but some big, so-called tough gob got himself celled with me and then tried to punk me. While I was wrestling with him, I kind of accidentally broke his neck. Putting that on top of knocking off that other guy, I guess they figured I was a real killer, so here I am."

Panella displayed none of the sly and cunning behavior of many convicts who were guilty of murder. He maintained direct eye contact and spoke in a straightforward manner.

I stood for a while thinking about Panella's plight. Governments can get a war started and decide that beginning on such and such a day murder is legal and moral. Then they stop the war, just like that. After a certain date, if you happen to kill one of your former enemies defending yourself in a street fight, it is murder . . .

"Panella," I said shaking my head, "now you know why they call it 'rocks and shoals.'"*

Panella was not the only military prisoner serving time at Alcatraz who was not all that bad. By now he had been in Alcatraz almost two years. Bunch and I watched him over a period of time and decided to write a memo to the warden strongly suggesting he put in a good word on Panella's behalf to the military. The prisoners from the armed forces were supervised by military officers who came to the island to check on them. Eventually the military took back all the armed forces personnel we were holding. Therefore, Panella was finally able to take the first step in his plan. I have often wondered whether he got to take the second step.

Back up on my perch on the second tier, I reflected on the events of the last half hour or so. I thought how different Alcatraz was from the other prisons where I had worked. Officers were not allowed to carry blackjacks at Leavenworth. They could get fired if they were caught with one. I couldn't remember even seeing a blackjack the whole time I worked at Sandstone.

Down on the floor below me, Bunch was talking with Mr. Miller. Other officers were returning to their normal business of the day. Starting off down Broadway, Miller looked up, smiled, and waved briefly. As I nodded back, I thought, I'm going to like working with that man. Sure glad I kept my mouth shut during my first meeting with him.

---

*"Rocks and shoals" refers to the naval rules and regulations concerning punishments for crimes.

7

Road Tower
Morning Watch

Following the midnight roll call of the morning-watch shift, I went to the Control Center and checked out the weapons required on my post—an M1a rifle and a holstered Colt .45 automatic pistol, which I strapped to my waist. In the company of the evening watch lieutenant and the West Gun Gallery officer, I was on my way to my first real assignment at Alcatraz.

The last duty of the evening-watch lieutenant's shift was to escort the morning-watch gun gallery and Road Tower officers to their respective posts. To guard against ambush by escaping convicts, the lieutenant used the military-type tactic of going around a corner and then waving us on man by man.

Outside the cell house, we followed the catwalk around the building and along the side of the library and D Block. As the gun gallery officer ascended to his post, the lieutenant continued on and I followed. The catwalk made a left turn and led us along the recreation yard's south wall to the southwest corner and on beyond a few yards to the Road Tower.

Having finally arrived at my post, I took a look around. I was now on the west side of the island—the opposite side from the dock. The octagon-shaped tower room sat on a platform extending some three or four feet all the way around. Steel barrier rails were mounted at the edge. Underneath, holding up the tower, was a metal framework of crossbars connected to steel posts firmly anchored in concrete. The only illumination of the tower came from the reflection of floodlights mounted on the cell house roof. The tower itself was not lighted—the guard needed to be able to see out and certainly didn't want to be a well-lighted target in case a convict got hold of a weapon.

Inside the tower, I placed the rifle in the horizontal rack beside the door. I put

59

my overcoat on a hanger that was attached to a rope on a pulley and hauled it up into the attic where it would not obstruct the view from the windows. The only piece of furniture was a rather graceful tall chair made of steel—thank goodness it had a cushion. Windows with wide sills went all around the small room. There was nothing to block the view of the outside—not even while using the toilet. A telephone, an open microphone, a flashlight, binoculars, a button to release the security gate on the road below, and an electric heater completed the furnishings. A few feet from the door, an emergency searchlight was mounted on the catwalk.

Above the windows, I found a variety of items on shelves. I was surprised to find gas grenades. Odds and ends of articles of clothing, copies of the post orders, and old administrative notices seemed to make up the rest of the shelf contents. This place could use a good housecleaning, I thought.

Skylights I had seen before—groundlights I had never seen. The floor had a bulletproof window. I looked down to see why: Directly underneath the tower was the gate that secured the road that went around the island.

With my tour completed, I used my flashlight to scan the post orders. The main reason that I was perched in that little wood-and-glass room on the edge of The Rock was to look and keep on looking at everything within my view. I was also there to push the button releasing the gate below for the officer on island patrol. One order said I was to telephone the Control Center every half-hour and report, but this order had been written before the public-address system was installed. The microphone was to be open at all times. Its transmissions were received in the Control Center and other towers. The Dock Tower was also manned twenty-four hours a day.

Tower duty was new to me. Although there were several towers at Leavenworth, I had not spent much time in them. At Sandstone, we had a couple of portable towers we used with the outside work crews. I had supervised crews of fifty to sixty men outside the prison compound. We built roads and fences and cleared land for farming. We used a portable guard tower on such jobs, but truth was, the forests in Minnesota were as much a deterrent to escape attempts as the water around Alcatraz. Most of the convicts were from New York, Chicago, or other big cities and they had heard exaggerated tales of the dangerous animals lurking in the woods surrounding the institution. I did nothing to discourage this belief.

Now on the catwalk of an Alcatraz tower, I gave in to the spell of the magically lighted surroundings. Could I really be here, at the toughest prison of all—filled with the most vicious, murderous, desperate dregs of humanity? I looked at the floodlights shining on the grim, gray walls of the prison. Turning, I saw the beautiful city of San Francisco decorated for Christmas. The yacht harbor was a blaze of colored lights. The handsomely lighted Golden Gate Bridge stood silently while the headlights of cars moved across it. The moon refused to be outdone by the man-made lights, and its reflection across the calm bay joined those of a myriad of lights from all directions, including the water traffic.

Alcatraz. San Francisco, the city by the Golden Gate. A jarring contrast, indeed. As I looked out over the exquisite panorama that surrounded me, everything was peaceful and serene.

My "lunch" was brought out by the main gate officer, who toured the perimeter of the cell house every fifteen minutes. The meal consisted of two sandwiches, a piece of cake, and a thermos of coffee, all packed in a cumbersome wooden box. I looked at one sandwich—fried egg. Then the other—cheese. I opened the thermos, expecting to find the coffee good and hot. I was disappointed again.

Well, I thought, breakfast is only four hours away, and I ate some of my sandwiches, which were tasteless, and the cake, which was good. I certainly had a million-dollar view to go with my meal. The view from the Top of the Mark couldn't compete with the one I enjoyed.

Later, as the water traffic increased, ships passed by, and little tugs pushed huge barges across the bay. Fishing boats also appeared. With the stationary lights of the city and the bridge and the moving lights of land and water traffic to claim my attention, it was difficult to focus on my work.

But I couldn't just look at the entrancing scenery indefinitely—after a few nights I was bored. Tower restrictions at night were severe—no radio and no light for reading. And you had to remain on post for the entire shift. There weren't even any seagulls to feed. Day-shift tower guards had made pets of some of the seagulls, who came regularly for handouts.

What do you do in the Road Tower at night? Nothing but sit and watch, walk around your limited space and watch, contact the Control Center every half hour, and push the road-gate button twice a night. Sometimes the morning lieutenant came out to visit. It was a dull, monotonous, but peaceful post.

A few weeks into my first tour of duty in the Road Tower, the lieutenant who had escorted me out said, "I don't think you are going to be bored tonight. If we get one of our real storms, as has been predicted, you'll be well entertained."

It rained. It rained, and how it rained!

The wind-driven rain smashed against the windows of the tower. I had to tug against the storm to close the door. I got wet and had to use the heater to dry my uniform.

I watched the erratic wind blowing the rain through the floodlights, making it look like a series of moving walls. The Road Tower was the first thing the storm hit as it came through the Golden Gate. I suddenly realized there was no traffic on the bay.

Almost in panic, I hollered into the microphone, "Hey, I don't see any boats or tugs on the bay!" I thought they might have been swamped by the storm.

"Oh, they knew not to come out tonight," the Control Center officer laughed. "This storm was predicted several hours ago, so the boats are all snug in harbor and the operators have pulled the covers over their heads."

At the break of dawn, the wind died down and the torrents of rain diminished. With the coming of daylight, I became fascinated with the flotsam and jetsam stirred up by the storm. The bay was full of parts of buildings, trees, and a lot of other junk I couldn't identify.

I saw a wide stream of muddy water that was easily distinguished from the gray of the bay water. As I watched, a huge timber came into view. It was being carried like a toothpick by the turbulent waters through the bay toward the open sea. Suddenly it went up on end to an almost vertical position, then down into the water out of sight. I called the Control Center and reported the location of the monster timber, which could be a hazard to navigation. The Control Center called the Coast Guard and within a few minutes the protectors of navigation were out there lassoing the timber. As it was towed away, I shuddered at the havoc it could have created for a small boat.

What a show I had witnessed! The lieutenant sure got it right—I had not been bored. As I left the Road Tower that morning, I reflected on what I had seen, heard, and felt. I was deeply impressed with the raw, brutal force of nature—first with the wind-driven water from the clouds as seen in the prison lights, and then by the floodwater rushing down from the rivers to the ocean.

During a lull in the storm, our two boats had been sent to a safer port on the mainland. When the bay waters were too treacherous for the boats, officers who lived on the island or who had finished a shift had to fill in for those who couldn't get to work.

As I had not been notified that I was needed, I had breakfast in the officers' mess and started for the Mule Barn. By this time, the wind had picked up again and when I opened the door to step outside, it smashed into me like ten thousand football linemen. My hat blew off. I tried to catch it but a hard blast of wind was faster than I was, and I lost sight of it. Some days later it was found alongside the powerhouse. It had traveled almost the entire length of the island.

Time had a way of moving along, carrying me with it. At first I found it hard to sleep in the daytime. Although most of the occupants of the Mule Barn made an effort to keep quiet, there was a lot of noise in connection with the everyday activities of the island. The Rock did not afford much space for the three hundred or so people who might be moving about on it at any given time. Not to mention the foghorns' warnings to ships and the ships signaling the tugs for escort into port. The *Warden Johnston,* blowing its whistle ten minutes before departure, came and went on schedule, and barges loaded with supplies put in at our dock regularly.

Aside from the interesting activities on the bay, the morning watch in the Road Tower continued to be boring. I could stand just so much peace and quiet. I began to yearn for action. Correctional officers were rotated from one job post to another every three months and in certain jobs an officer could be reassigned to the same post. The captain made the assignments and his clerk posted the roster. Understanding the rotation of job assignments, I did not squawk when put on a job I didn't like. It was advantageous to the smooth running of the institution for all officers to know the responsibilities of the various posts.

Still, I preferred assignments that involved working with the convicts. At Sandstone I had enjoyed watching some of the convicts assigned to my work crews learn to accomplish goals—simple goals like digging a drainage ditch, hoeing a row of corn, or milking a cow. Some of those kids had never been taught a job and been able to take pride in their achievement. I doubt they had ever been complimented for doing a good job on anything.

Sooner or later I would be back on the day watch in some job that involved working with convicts—the cell house, the kitchen, the hospital, or the clothing room were all good possibilities.

As he made his rounds one night, Crane, the main-gate man, stopped in at the Road Tower and said, "Well, 'Mr. Miller's One-Man Goon Squad,' I've got news for you."

I looked at him crossly and asked, "What do you mean, 'Mr. Miller's One-Man Goon Squad'?"

"That's what everybody has been calling you. Your first week here, you had a lot of action with Mr. Miller looking over your shoulder. He's been talking around about what a good man you are. So somebody gave you a new name."

"Yeah, well I'm not amused by that kind of a title. That makes it sound like I go around beating up on people all the time just for the fun of it."

"Hey, okay. I didn't mean anything by bringing it up. But I didn't make it up, either. What I came out to tell you is, tomorrow night you will be the island patrol."

"I kind of know what that is. I see him every night going around."

"That's what he does. He patrols the island. Why don't you get in touch with him after work? He's a good guy and would be glad to take a little time to tell you the routine of it, so you'll know what to do."

"Sounds interesting. I'll get to see some of this island that I haven't seen yet."

"Let me give you one warning. There are some dangerous spots along that trail around the island. So be real careful."

I watched for the island patrol, Burroughs, to come by. He always came to the gate under the Road Tower to get out of the work area. I called down and asked, "Could I talk with you after the shift is over? I hear I'm going to get your job."

"Yes, I heard that, too. Be glad to talk to you. Tell you what, meet me down at the dock when you get off duty."

Burroughs was waiting for me. He looked to be a man in his mid-forties, good condition, just the beginning of a tummy.

"How would you like to have a decent breakfast for a change?" Burroughs asked. Before I could say no, he said, "Come on up to the apartment. I've already called my wife."

It was a delicious breakfast of ham, eggs, grits, and baking-powder biscuits—the whole works! Mrs. Burroughs was a pleasant lady who laughed easily, and when she found out that I had worked at Leavenworth she said, "That's where we came from. I grew up there and married this guy."

After the meal, Burroughs said, "I'll tell you about the job of island patrol and you write it down. Ask all the questions you want. It is a very responsible and important job. You are pretty much on your own."

During the next hour, I took notes as Burroughs described the island patrol job thoroughly. I never forgot the willingness of this man to help a newcomer.

8

Island Patrol
Morning Watch

That night, as island patrol officer, I went down to the dock after roll call for the last round-trip of the night on the *Warden Johnston.* The boat operator and I waited in the dock office for the "all clear" from the Control Center. The midnight convict count had to be okayed before we could depart. It was, and we made an uneventful trip. There were several officers going home from the evening shift, and on the return trip we had several people returning to their island homes after a night on the town.

Back on the island, I met the lieutenant on duty at the dock office and we talked about what I was to do during the shift. It was Lieutenant Kent, who I had saved from a toilet-dunking on my first day at Alcatraz. He went with me on the first round of the island. It was kind of weird—the fog was coming in—and it was cold.

After checking the social hall for burning cigarettes in wastebaskets and ashtrays, we went along the northeast shore where we spoke to the powerhouse man, made one of the required half-hourly phone calls to the Control Center, and moved on.

Kent unlocked the door to a building that sat right at the edge of the water. He listened, shone his flashlight around, and said, "We call this the old work area. The industrial shops are now farther along the island and this building is used only for storage." He shone his light on the wall phone and directed the beam down the wall.

"Can you see those marks?"

"Yes."

"Those are the bloody marks of Mr. Cline's hands. He passed out trying to reach the telephone to sound the alarm on what became one of the bloodiest escape attempts on Alcatraz. He died later as a result of his wounds.

"Three convicts almost succeeded in making an escape after they bludgeoned Mr. Cline with a hammer. They went out through a window and up the side of the building to the roof. Mr. Stites had just come on duty in the Model Tower, which was near the place the convicts came up on the roof. He grabbed his .45 and shot one of them in the forehead, killing him instantly. Stites hit the next one in the shoulder while he was trying to get through the barbed wire and back down the building. A second bullet got him in the other shoulder, so he gave up. Seeing the trouble they were in, the third convict dived under the tower. He was soon in the Hole."

An MTA later added an interesting note to this story. The convict whom Stites had shot twice recovered from his wounds, went to trial, and continued to serve his time. Sometime later, he complained of chest pains. As the MTA was examining him, he coughed and spat out a .45 slug. Presumably, it was from Stites's gun.

When we left the old work area, I felt somber and greatly moved by Cline's story. Prison officers do get killed in the line of duty. We walked along in silence for a bit when suddenly there was a wild, horrible-sounding noise that was between a scream and a holler, followed by the splash of a heavy body falling into the bay. Tense as I already was, I jumped back, clawing at the holster on my side that held a .45 automatic.

The lieutenant chuckled kindly as he put his hand on my shoulder. "That old sea lion has been scaring island patrol officers for ten years. I think he gets a kick out of it."

We came to another large building, and again Kent unlocked the door, listened, and flashed his light around. "There are several different shops in here," he said. "When you come back on your second round, shake down the glove shop. Turn on all the lights and do a thorough job. It will take you an hour or more to search a shop. There are a lot of places to hide things. When you leave, turn out all the lights and lock the doors. And lock the gates on the second round, too."

We continued around the island, going under the Road Tower, south to the officers' housing, and on around to the Mule Barn and dock. Lieutenant Kent left me there and went up to the cell house.

By this time, I had been at work for three or four hours and decided to have my lunch. I ate in the dock office and chatted through the open mike with the Control Center officer, with whom I had become friends.

On my second round of the island, I searched the glove shop as planned. The only contraband I found was a couple of packs of cigarettes. Using my flashlight sparingly, I continued on around the island, watching for the hazardous places where the trail narrowed to fit between a cliff and the water.

Back on the dock, I searched the dressing room and toilet area used by the convicts who worked on the dock. I also searched the garage and storage areas before checking the boat. By this time, the boat operator had arrived. The Control Center gave me a list of visitors who were expected to make the first return trip from the mainland.

As the boat operator and I walked out of the office toward the dock, I noticed that a number of people had gathered on the balcony of 64 Building: officers' wives on their way to work and children on their way to school. (Although it had been condemned, this building was still home for many officers and their families.) They were waiting for the Dock Tower officer to unlock the gate, which he always did ten minutes before the *Warden Johnston* departed on its 7:00 a.m. trip to the mainland. Many of the island people, especially the children, liked to assemble early to chat with each other.

When we returned to the island, I became a bus driver. The last duty of my new post was to drive the day-shift officers up top. I stopped along the way to pick up island-dwelling officers who didn't want to walk up the steep hill, to drop off officers who had missed the midnight boat and stayed overnight in the city, and to drop off civilian visitors who had come over to spend the day with people who lived on the island.

I parked the bus up top and went in for my breakfast of Danish, dry cereal with blue john, and coffee. It was a good time to review my new assignment. In general, my duties were to patrol the outer perimeter of the island, search the industries buildings for contraband, and serve as the boat officer on the *Warden Johnston* during the first and last trips of the day. As opposed to the Road Tower post, I would be on the go for the entire shift.

I felt good about being the island patrol officer. I would enjoy seeing the children every morning and it was a good way to get acquainted with more officers—those living on the mainland and working the day shift, who came over on the first boat of the morning, and those living on the island who had been out for an evening and caught the last boat of the night.

One night, the lieutenant scheduled the print shop for a complete shakedown. The shop had been created by putting up partitions in a corner of the laundry. During my search, I stood on a chair and looked on top of the lintel over the door. There was a homemade knife, or shiv, which had been there long enough to collect a heavy coating of dust.

Without moving the knife, I called the lieutenant and asked him to come down to the print shop. He was dumbfounded that the knife had been there for an extended period of time. He took it to the armory, where it was added to the collection.

As far as I know, the officers who had searched the print shop in the past were not reprimanded. But there was a curious kind of attitude that it was my fault the knife was there. I guess I should have just thrown it into the bay and forgotten about it.

I heard the phone ringing in the laundry one night as I made the rounds down in the work area. I went in to answer, wondering why anybody would be calling in the wee hours of the morning. It was the Control Center officer, telling me the acting lieutenant wanted me up top immediately. I didn't ask any questions but ran up top on the double, all uphill. When I reached the main building, I was somewhat out of breath. Lieutenant Kent was waiting for me.

"We have work to do," he said.

I followed him into the cell house and then into TU.

"We have to put a convict in the Hole for making too much noise."

Marr was the TU officer on duty. He was the officer who had been in the yard during the riot, acting as if nothing was going on, but had then grabbed Panella the same way he had grabbed Biff in the dining hall. Seeing him again, I couldn't help but feel uneasy. The three of us walked down to the convict's cell.

The lieutenant signaled the gun gallery officer to open the electronically controlled cell door. Just as the lieutenant started in, the convict came bursting out and knocked him flat on his back. And who was this convict? None other than ol' Joe Monde. Joe took off like a striped-ass ape, hitting Marr with his shoulder and knocking him to the floor, where he slid on his backside about fifteen feet on the highly polished surface. Joe ran on down to the other end of TU. I followed casually. After all, Joe couldn't go anyplace, and the more he ran the more tired he would get. Apparently Joe realized that, too. As he started back down the cell block, he made a feint toward me but kept going and ran into his cell, pulling the barred door closed behind him.

"Now if you try to come in again to get me, I'm really going to hurt you," Joe warned.

The lieutenant got up, trying to hide the fact that he had been hurt. Without looking at me, he started back down the cell block.

"Wait a minute, where are you going?" I asked.

"I'm getting the hell out of here."

"Look, you said this guy was supposed to be put in a dark cell. By God, you are not going to let him get away with this—coming out here, knocking down two officers and running back into his cell. Let's get him in the Hole. Marr, you get up here and help."

With the lieutenant and Marr present, I opened the cell again. "All right, Joe," I said, "you pull that stuff again and I'm going to break your neck."

"Mr. Gregory," Joe said with a giggle and extreme politeness, "I'll be glad to go with you. You know that." And he did. He went down to the Hole cell giggling but without resistance.

Back in the work area, I continued the routine inspection of the various shops: print shop, glove shop, tailor shop, brush shop, laundry, and furniture shop. But I was concerned. I did not like the title of "Mr. Miller's One-Man Goon Squad." Neither did I like, in any way, what had just happened in TU. Why couldn't the lieutenant have waited until the day watch to put that guy in the Hole? There would have been plenty of help without calling someone from another job.

Some nights later, there was another call to assist the lieutenant with a convict in TU. I noticed that Marr was again the TU officer. The lieutenant ignored Marr, walked over to a cell, and waved to the man in the gun gallery to open it. The convict was hollering and yelling, making a lot of noise.

"We have to get him out of here and put him in the Hole," the lieutenant said as he opened the door and went in.

The convict had the lieutenant tied up in a second. I rushed in and got my usual headlock on the convict, pulled him out and steered him into the Hole cell, where he was locked in. All this time, Marr was sitting at the desk. When we got back in the cell house where we could not be overheard by the convicts, I decided it was time to talk. It looked more and more like the lieutenant was using me to enhance his own reputation.

"Lieutenant, I don't quite understand this and I don't appreciate it. The TU officer should be able to handle a little convict like that. He's no problem. Why was I called all the way up here?"

"You are to do just what you are told to do," blustered the lieutenant.

"Just cut out the bullshit. I don't appreciate this and I think you should mention in your report that I was called in to move that convict. Maybe I'll write a complaint about it. Just want to let you know that I'm thinking about it."

"You can't write a complaint. You have to wait until I write a complaint on you and then you can answer it."

"I can do any damned thing I want to do. How it will be handled after I do it, I don't know. We'll wait and see."

I continued to think about this situation as the shift wore on. Deviating from the military-type chain of command used in the prison system could get me in trouble. I thought, I need some advice from an experienced officer on just where I stand at Alcatraz. On my way to breakfast at the end of the shift, I checked the roster. Burger was not due to report until four in the afternoon.

Down in the Mule Barn, I knocked on Burger's door.

"Who's there?" came a growl from inside the room.

"Gregory. May I talk to you?"

I translated Burger's second growl as an invitation and went in.

"Sit down, shut up, and be still until I get some coffee made," mumbled Burger.

I did as I was told, and when Burger had got the coffee going he unlocked his footlocker and brought out a bottle of very good whiskey. Pouring me a generous amount, he said, "Keep this to yourself. I don't want everybody knocking on this door to get a drink."

It sure was what I needed.

"Ready?" Burger said after a few sips of coffee. "I am."

"I think I need some help." I went on to tell about Crane calling me "Mr. Miller's One-Man Goon Squad."

"Yeah, go on."

I described the incidents in TU.

After some thought, Burger said, "You're going to have to accept that nickname. You're already a personality on The Rock. As to the other, let me start by giving you some sound advice. Put everything on paper and see to it that a copy goes to the proper authority. In this case, Mr. Miller." Burger got up and put a portable typewriter on the table, opened it, and said, "I'll write your first letter." Whereupon he had me describe again the TU incidents.

"Okay, I'm going to write this up in a formal way." When he finished, he removed the letter from the typewriter and handed it to me. I signed it, and Burger said, "Now, you keep the carbon forever. You never know." He put the original in an envelope. "I'm going to take this letter and get it to Mr. Miller. It's just as well you are not seen giving Mr. Miller a letter this early in the game."

I was still a bit puzzled, wondering at the underlying politics.

"Look. There are things that I do for people I like. When Mr. Miller gets this letter, he'll know your side and your problems. You can be sure that Lieutenant Kent is going to write up these incidents in his way. He certainly won't tell it like it was."

I stood stretching and yawning and said with a smile, "You know, Burger, you're ugly as hell, but I love you much."

"Get out of here!"

Two days went by without my hearing from anyone about the letter, which was on my mind constantly. Much as I wanted to speak with Mr. Miller about the situation, I was damned if I would go to him directly. It would appear that I was just whining and complaining. So I waited.

I was down on the dock getting the boat ready for the first morning trip when I saw Miller coming along in my direction. At the same time, Miller saw me.

"Son, I got a letter about a problem of yours. When can I see you?"

"Whenever it is convenient for you, Mr. Miller."

"When you get off, do some fast sleeping and be in my office at 4:30 this afternoon." I didn't sleep much, but I was in Miller's office at 4:30.

Before anything was said, Miller pointed to the gap at the top of the partition that separated his office from the office next door. It was obvious that conferences held here were not private.

"Let's take a walk," he said.

As we walked through the outer offices, I could feel the stares from the officers working there: the captain's clerk, mail officer, record clerk, and others in the office for various reasons. I had not wanted a lot of attention paid to the fact that I was having a conference with Mr. Miller.

"What those rabbit ears in there don't hear won't hurt them. Mr. Gregory, I have Lieutenant Kent's memos on what happened in TU. I didn't pay much attention to them because I thought the lieutenant and Mr. Marr had handled the convicts in a simple, routine way. I realize now that the lieutenant brought you into TU for the sole purpose of having you handle the con . . . inmates.* His memos sound as if he and Marr took care of things. Mr. Gregory, be assured I am going to talk with Lieutenant Kent about these incidents. Anything else?"

"No, sir. And I appreciate your giving attention to this because it did bother me."

"Anytime you have a problem, feel free to come in to see me." It was the end of my being used as a "one-man goon squad."

The first boat trip of the day got to be my favorite part of the island patrol job. While the women chatted with each other, I enjoyed getting acquainted with the children. I talked sports with the older ones and teased the younger ones. It was a good group of kids, always laughing, teasing, socializing with each other. As long as they sat down, put on their life jackets, and weren't too noisy, I didn't hassle them. I liked them and they liked me. We got along just fine. The one or two who challenged me soon joined the others in being cooperative—which accounts for my consternation when the acting captain called me in after the shift one morning.

Parant didn't even look up when I walked into his office. Talking down to the top of his desk, he said, "Can't you keep those kids in line? We are getting com-

*By this time, bulletins coming from the Bureau of Prisons referred to "inmates" instead of "convicts" and we had been instructed to change the way we referred to the prison population.

plaints that they are making too much noise on the boat. The women say they can't carry on a conversation."

"Captain, I haven't heard any complaints at all. I don't think they are making too much noise. They're just being normal kids," I said in total disbelief at the accusation.

"I said they were making noise and you have to quiet them down. The least I expect of you is to be able to keep those children under control."

I was about to take umbrage at this and really unload, but then thought, What the hell, I guess this is my day to be walked on by another "acting" something or other.

I said, "Yes, sir," and walked out.

The next morning on the boat, I went to the front of the cabin and asked for quiet.

"Now, hear this," I said in a deep, stentorian voice. There were a few nervous giggles from the kids as they quieted down.

"I want to talk to you people, especially you women. The acting captain called me in yesterday morning, and said the kids were making too much noise, that you women couldn't hear yourselves think. Now, if the kids are making too much noise I can quiet them down in a minute. But I want to know which of you women, if any, have made a complaint about the kids."

"Mr. Gregory, we think you are handling these kids real well. If anybody has a complaint, you tell them to come see us," one woman said.

Putting on a real stern face, I said, "Now, kids, do you hear that?" The kids burst out laughing and we continued on our way to San Francisco.

When I was through with the shift that morning, I went back to the acting captain. This time I didn't wait to be acknowledged.

"Captain," I said, "I just talked to the people on the boat. To all of the passengers, and not a one of them voiced any complaint at all about the children. They don't think they're too noisy. In fact, they think they are real good kids and so do I." As I turned and started walking out, the captain took off his cap and slammed it on his desk. I kept walking.

This incident, as ridiculous as it was, illustrates the kind of behavior we had to put up with from some of the "acting" officers. At least two of these became my nemeses. But they were only a couple in a large group of well-trained men with integrity and leadership ability who served as acting lieutenants, captains, associate wardens, and wardens during my tenure at Alcatraz. It was a pleasure to work with these men.

As boat officer, I checked the water inside the slip to make sure there were no obstructions. One time, I found a sea lion that had found what he thought was a safe place at the stern of the boat. It took several of us to push him out of the way so we could get the boat out of the slip. On another occasion, there was a striped bass, the biggest I had ever seen, swimming around the stern. A large bite had been taken out of his stomach and his insides trailed behind him as he swam around. Sometimes logs or timbers lodged in the slip.

One morning as I finished my inspection, Captain Emil Rychner escorted an overnight visitor down to catch the early boat.

"Greg," Captain Rychner said, "would you take a picture of us by the *Warden Johnston*?"

"Sure," I said as I took the camera.

"Did you say 'Greg'? Is this Gregory?" the visitor asked with a chuckle.

"Yes," the captain said. "Greg, meet Warden Culver from Florida. He worked here at Alcatraz before your time."

Extending his hand to me, the warden said, "I've heard about you, Mr. Gregory."

"How do you do, Warden Culver. How 'bout my coming to work for you?" I asked.

"Come on. Get on this boat right now. From what I've heard about you, you can work for me anytime," the warden said with another chuckle.

When we docked at Fort Mason, I said good-bye to Warden Culver and wondered which stories he had heard. I must be doing something right, I thought.

It was a cold, cold, foggy night. Although I had on an overcoat, I could barely keep warm, but for a guy with sinus trouble it felt good. I made my first stop at the laundry. Opening the door, I was almost bowled over by a strong, sweet-sour smell. Pruno! I'd know that distinctive odor anywhere. Pruno, or moonshine, was easily made with a little dough or yeast and fruit—anything that would ferment. It always smelled the same regardless of the ingredients. Making it seemed to be the favorite pastime of prisoners everywhere.

I circled around the laundry several times trying to locate the source of the smell. I would get close to it and then lose it.

I was reminded of a time in Sandstone when the convicts were making pruno in the bakery but, search as we would, we could not find that booze. One night an officer happened to look up in what was called the rising room, which had a rather high ceiling. In one corner was a pipe that came out from one wall and went into the adjoining wall at a right angle, forming a convenient perch. Sitting right on it was a five-gallon can of fruit, just a-bubbling away.

When I finally gave up and reported to the Control Center, the lieutenant came down, walked over to a big hamper of sheets, and pulled some off the top.

The jug was sitting inside the warm sheets and fermenting very nicely. We emptied it out into a sink.

A few nights went by before I smelled pruno again. This time I started with the clothes hamper. Sure enough, there it was. After I poured out the pruno, I got to thinking that finding it was too easy. The convicts would know I was still on island patrol. Going back, I emptied the hamper. Below the sheets there was a false bottom hiding more pruno. Those clever rascals—a jug for me to find and one for them to drink.

I got to leaving notes for the moonshiners after pouring out their latest poison. When a convict reached for his container of booze, he would find a note attached that said, "Due to the fact that you have not paid your federal alcohol tax, we have confiscated the contents of this jug. Sorry." One time I got an answer saying, "You better stay out of Kentucky!"

One night, Frank Zubke was the acting lieutenant. I hadn't been around him very much, but what little I had seen of him I liked. He had a direct way of talking and an infectious chuckle, plus a lot of experience. Before coming into the Federal Prison System, he had worked at a real hard-line state prison.

After my boat-officer duty on the last trip of the night, we were sitting in the dock office getting better acquainted and discussing what I was to do during my shift. Frank pointed to the intercom and then motioned for me to follow him outside the office.

"That guy in the Control Center has rabbit ears and he listens to everything and reports everything. It's all right with me, but let's take a walk. I'll go with you on your first round."

"Good."

Frank went back into the office and hollered, "Control Center!"

"Yes, lieutenant."

"I'm going to walk around with Mr. Gregory. I haven't been down in the work area for a while. So if you want me, ring any phone down there. We'll hear it."

"Check."

As we walked along, Frank said, "How are you doing so far?"

"All right, I guess. I haven't had too many complaints. I'm learning a lot. There are things I don't understand, but I guess every prison has its own philosophy and you just have to learn it."

"I'm sure you know that Parant doesn't exactly like you."

"Yeah, I've noticed, but I don't know why."

"I don't think he needs a reason. Don't worry about it, as long as you have one good friend. And you have. That's Mr. Miller. He is a damned good friend of yours. I know him pretty well. He and I are old, square-headed Dutchmen. He hasn't had much formal education, but he sure is one good prison man. As they say about him, he may not always be right, but he is never wrong.

"Mr. Miller runs his ship and takes responsibility for everything that goes on. Doesn't try to lay it on anyone else, doesn't try to lie about things. If you are wrong, he bawls you out. But that's usually it. Unless it's real serious, of course, and then he will probably fire you. He fires an officer every now and then and nobody complains. I've known some guys that he fired. You can believe they deserved it."

"Well, Frank, except for the first week, I've been on the morning watch. So I haven't been around him much, but from what I've seen of him, I'm impressed."

As we went from shop to shop, Frank pointed out things of interest here and there and told me stories that I had not heard. He told about two escape attempts from the industrial shops—both of which were thwarted by extra officers who happened to enter the shops as the regular officers were being tied up by the convicts. One of these officers was Paul Madigan, who later became warden. One of the convicts wanted to kill Madigan for disrupting their plans. But a convict known as Big Red talked him out of it.

Years later when a problem came up about Big Red, I talked with Madigan about it. His comment was, "Well, I owe that man, he saved my life once. That's why I'm kind of soft on him."

I was called up early one morning on one of my days off and told to fill in as the culinary officer. Although it was not my favorite post, I had served some tours of duty in the kitchen at Sandstone.

So on this morning I went up for the early shift in the Alcatraz kitchen. The regular officer had called in sick. As I walked back through the dining hall and into the kitchen, I noticed the floor was about an inch deep in soapsuds. Cleanliness is one thing, but all this soapy water on the floor?

Just as I walked into the kitchen, two guys went at each other with French butcher knives, which, to say the least, caught me by surprise. I moved toward the convict closest to me, hoping I could control him. But just as I reached him, someone hit me in the back, knocked me down, and sent me skidding across the soapy floor. I didn't stop until I hit the wall on the other side of the kitchen. When I tried to get up, I was too hasty, and of course fell down again.

While I was sliding around on the floor trying to get control of myself, the two convicts, for reasons of their own, dropped their knives and chased each other around the dining hall. I finally got up and thought, To hell with 'em—I'm not about to run after them.

I picked up the knives and locked them in the cupboard. Then I called over the intercom to report the ongoing fight and request help. By that time, the convicts were out of breath and were just sort of playing tippy-toe with each other. Finally, a couple of officers got there and escorted the fighters off to the Hole.

I looked around for the person who had prevented me from wading in between those two knives. He had saved my life or at the very least kept me from getting a few more scars. It was Big Red. He was a balding, red-headed man with blue eyes. He was not physically big as his nickname implied. He was about five feet ten inches tall, with a medium frame, but he kept himself in good physical condition. The reference to size came from the respect the convicts thought was due him for his quiet, stable personality and the no-nonsense way he went about his work. Walking over to Big Red, I started to thank him.

"Make no mistake about it, Mr. Gregory, if I ever get a chance to blow this joint and you are in my way, you had better move," Big Red firmly said.

I knew just what he meant. "Well, I thank you anyway."

Wondering about the knives, I checked with the steward and found they had been issued to the convicts for necessary chores.

Frank Zubke wasn't very keen about being an acting lieutenant. He had been around tough prisons long enough to know that everything can go fine and you can look good and start thinking, Maybe one of these days they will get kindhearted and make me a full lieutenant. On the other hand, all of a sudden something can happen out of the blue over which you have no control but which makes you look bad. A black mark on a record can follow a man for years, keeping him from being promoted. One of these potentially troublesome situations came up one night when Frank had the watch. It just added to my puzzlement about Alcatraz.

Frank called me from my job as island patrol and said, "Look, I've got a problem and I'm going to ask you to help me, but I know it is above and beyond, as it were."

"Well, let's have it."

"The hospital staff has got into the habit of leaving instructions instead of coming up here themselves in the early morning to take care of things. They have somehow finagled around so that they lay it on the officer of the morning watch to dish out prescription pills and even hypodermic shots. That's what I've got tonight. I'm supposed to give a shot to a convict, and if I don't do it, he's going to start one hell of a mess. He's up there in the hospital now in A ward."

This, I realized, was another part of the drug situation that I couldn't figure out. I looked at Frank. "Well, so?"

"The simple fact is, I've never given anybody an injection of any kind. I don't know how to do it. I know that you do know how."

Now I had to make a very ticklish decision. Of course, the smart, common-sense choice would be to protect myself and say absolutely not, I wouldn't have anything to do with such a thing. I was not legally qualified to give an injection. I could be held responsible if anything went wrong, such as an embolism or the convict dying as a result of a reaction to the drug. There was no way to get drugs or equipment that might help reverse a reaction. On the other hand, I really liked Frank and I knew he would stand by me if something did happen.

Looking at him, I said, "You know, I don't understand this drug situation. It baffles me. In fact, the whole mystique of Alcatraz baffles me."

"It's a personality problem, Greg," Frank said with a wry grin. "This institution is run by personalities. They pretty much make their own rules, but they stand up for them. So here we are, stuck with carrying out the orders."

His pleading eyes got to me. "Come on, I'll do it," I said. The chart in the hospital indicated the injection was of a painkiller. Not unusual if a convict is in pain, but this convict didn't have the miserable expression of a person in pain. This made me hesitate, but I knew if I didn't give him the shot, he would cause a big problem for everyone for the rest of the shift. Besides, instructions had been issued that it was to be done.

I shoved the needle into a shoulder muscle and wiggled it to make the convict thoroughly aware that he had been stabbed with the needle. Then I pulled it out. As Frank and I walked down the aisle, I emptied the syringe. Nobody saw me do it. The con could not have a bad reaction because none of the medication had gotten into his system.

I wondered if I could get Shannon into conversation, maybe away from the institution, and find out what was going on with the drugs being dispensed. One thing about Shannon, he was a wise man. When it came to prison medicine, he had been around long enough to have seen it all.

One night as I made my first round through the industries, unlocking doors, listening, and using my flashlight sparingly, I distinctly heard footsteps somewhere above me. I thought it might be coming from the second floor of the building. That didn't seem quite right, but I knew it was from up above somewhere. As I listened, the steps stopped, went on, and then stopped again.

Staying low so my silhouette would not be seen through a window, I got to a phone and dialed 333, the Control Center. Frank had the Control Center on that watch. I spoke softly, telling what I had heard.

"Yeah, Greg, if you go out and look on top of the Model Building, you'll see Lieutenant Kent trying to get you for something," Frank said.

Seldom had I been so enraged—such a stupid thing to do, trying to slip up on an armed person!

I shouted into the phone, "Frank, you had better tell that S.O.B. if he wants to live he had better come down here making plenty of noise."

I watched the lieutenant retrace his steps up over the catwalk. When he got back to the Control Center, Frank told him, "You better not be playing tricks on that guy. You know he spent time in combat and he's liable to shoot first and ask questions later."

This scared the hell out of the lieutenant. Then he went out to the Road Tower to look down in the industries area—still checking on my activities.

The Road Tower officer had seen the lieutenant out on the catwalk and also had a few words to say. He told him, "You should never go over that catwalk at night. It just isn't done. That Gregory is liable to take a shot at you."

Following these two lectures, when the lieutenant came down to the industries during my shift he would whistle, sing, and flash his light all around. However, this did not stop him from dogging me, looking for some infraction of the rules.

The acting lieutenant apparently never recovered from his embarrassment concerning the awkward position he was in when I first met him—with a hopped-up convict trying to stick his head in the toilet. Maybe I should have just let the convict go ahead and do it.

A year or so later, I was again on island patrol and my nemesis was again the supervisor of the watch. I had stopped in the powerhouse and was having a cup of coffee and a chat with the operator, O'Connel. Suddenly O'Connel tensed, looking startled and scared. I looked around to find the acting lieutenant giving me a hard stare and shifting his weight from one foot to the other.

"You know, Mr. Gregory, you're supposed to be patrolling, not drinking coffee in the powerhouse," he said with a half-smile.

I got up and left.

The lieutenant had gone down to the powerhouse to get a cup of coffee for himself. Everybody used to stop in for a cup of O'Connel's coffee—he made it for us. It helped him cope with the boredom of the long nights when his only human contact came from his half-hour calls to the Control Center.

I went on about my work, thinking little of it until the following morning when the city-dwelling officers started boarding the boat and giving me knowing looks. I didn't know what was going on until one said, "That was a dirty trick."

"What do you mean?" I asked.

"The lieutenant bawling you out for having a cup of coffee in the powerhouse.

He makes regular rounds all shift long from one coffee urn to another." It was such a petty thing that it aroused the ire of the entire staff of the institution.

The outcome of that third-of-a-cup of coffee I drank with O'Connel was several letters concerning it in my file and the sudden closure of all the coffee urns in the institution to the acting lieutenant. With his coffee-drinking habit, I'm sure he hurt more than I did. It was actually good for my ego to know I had that kind of support from my fellow officers.

By the time the lieutenant realized the uproar he had caused, it was too late for him to alibi out of it. He tried to say he was just trying to warn me, but the coffeepots stayed closed to him for some time.

Being on the morning watch, I was well aware of the fact that I was missing quite a bit of action in the institution, but I was not unhappy about it. It was the same kind of activity I had experienced during my first week—drug and racial problems. Although I liked to work with the convicts, I still didn't feel I had a handle on just what was going on at Alcatraz. Many of the incidents I heard about served only to increase my confusion about the drug situation.

9

A Change of Command

One night at roll call, we were greeted with, "Warden Johnston is going to retire." Johnston didn't want to retire but he was overage. He had already been given one extension and his request for a second extension had been refused. He had to go.

I knew little about Warden Johnston. I had had only two meetings with the man.

Shortly after my arrival, I had been called into his office. It was a long office, and way down at one end was the warden sitting at his desk. I walked up to the desk and stood looking around. There wasn't a chair for me to sit in. This was one of Johnston's little eccentricities. You didn't sit down in his office. You came in, stood, had your interview, and walked out. No sitting around for idle chatter.

The warden called me in because I had written a piece for a prison magazine while working at Sandstone. Larry Carpenter, the personnel training officer, had asked me to write an article about a study program he had instituted at Sandstone. By the time the article was published, I had been transferred to Alcatraz. Warden Johnston was profuse in his praise. I thanked him, turned, and walked out.

A few days later when I was relieving the main-gate officer for a while, here came the warden going into the cell house. He always traveled with an entourage. He was a short man, roly-poly, and almost always presented a stern face.

"Aha," he said as he looked up at me and broke into a big smile, "the big Swede from Minnesota."

With a hard stare and no smile, I shot right back, "Don't you dare call me a Swede." That wasn't the way junior officers spoke to wardens. The entourage was shocked. Even the warden showed surprise. Then he broke out laughing.

Therein originated another nickname that stuck for a long time—"The Big Swede." Actually, I was proud to be called a Swede. A number of Swedish men immigrated to this country and came to work in the steel mills of Duluth, where I grew up. I went to school with and socialized with their children. They taught me many things about their culture and invited me to their celebrations. My reserved English background was in sharp contrast with the exuberance of the Swedish people.

Warden Johnston was one of the last of the political appointees in the Federal Prison System. He had been the warden in a state prison and had done some very good work. When Alcatraz was opened as a federal prison, he got his appointment. Warden Johnston also had an office in the main post office building in San Francisco, where he spent a great deal of time. He was very much involved in state and national politics.

When Johnston was on the island, no one ever spoke to him without his having spoken first. There was a story that a new officer said, "Good morning, Warden," and the warden curtly said, "When I want to talk to you, I will let you know." That scared everyone, and as a result no one ever talked to the warden without his special invitation.

On Sundays at the evening meal, the warden stood at the gate that separated the dining hall from the cell house. As he stood in the center of the gate, the convicts had to file past him on either side as they left the dining hall. This disturbed the officers; they were afraid a convict with a grudge might let the warden have it. In the past, a convict had knocked the warden down. The belief among the officers who knew the warden's methods was that he did this just to let the convicts know he had no fear of them.

Before I had time to get accustomed to the idea of Warden Johnston's impending retirement, I heard that Mr. Miller was being transferred to another institution. This was a bigger shock to the officers than the retirement of the warden. Although it might be considered the warden's program at Alcatraz, it was Mr. Miller who carried it out in his own way. Miller was truly "a good man with bad men," as Warden Johnston described him at his going-away party. Whoever the replacement might be, Mr. Miller would be sorely missed.

Meanwhile, it was business as usual on the morning watch. Toward the end of the shift one morning, I had just come down to get the boat ready for the first trip to the mainland when I heard an urgent call over the intercom to come up top immediately. I got in a truck and drove up.

Frank Zubke was in the visitors' room, where convicts were searched and dressed before being taken outside the prison. His problem was a guy named

Snuffy Dolin. Snuffy was the most unsightly and repulsive convict who ever came to Alcatraz. His nickname was given to him because of all the cocaine he had sniffed. He had been a drug addict all of his adult life, and his nasal septum was completely eaten away. He was harmless but exasperating because of his constant sniffling and snuffling. His table manners were so atrocious that the other convicts refused to eat with him. He was given a private table in the dining hall. Even so, the other cons could not keep from staring at him in disgusted fascination. Perhaps he was sent to Alcatraz because he was such an impossible pest.

As I approached the gate to the visitors' room, Frank walked out and briefed me. Snuffy's time was up and he was due to be picked up by the next agency with a hold on him. He had just submitted to a complete search, including body cavities. But Snuffy was adamant—he was not going to get dressed until he got the shot of dope he claimed the hospital staff had promised him. It was possible someone had told him he could have a shot just to get rid of him.

"Open the gate and let me come in," I said.

Snuffy stood there clothed only in his resolve to get a shot. I walked up to him and stepped on his foot, just hard enough to make him feel it. Snuffy screamed loudly in exaggerated pain and began hopping around. As he did, I grabbed his undershirt and pulled it down over his head. Then we put him on a chair and held him down while pulling on his shorts. A rap on the shins gave him something else to yell about while we got a shirt on him. Item by item, Frank and I got the allotted clothing on Snuffy, including a tie and handcuffs.

I escorted him down to the dock. By this time, Snuffy had given up on getting a shot and was talking about the great job he was going to get when he got out. The truth was that if he lived long enough to leave prison, his first job would be to get a shot of heroin.

Frank and I had to laugh about Snuffy, the first convict we ever knew who didn't want to leave Alcatraz.

I was assigned for another quarter on the island patrol morning watch. The policy of rotating job assignments every three months had been ignored, but I didn't really mind. I was learning quite a bit about the geography of The Rock. There were tunnels and caves down along the beaches. I explored an old building that had served as a storage place for gunpowder during the army's days on the island. Now it held fuel oil. The guns had been located near the dock. The turn circles for the big guns had been bricked in and the area was used as an office and storeroom by the boat operators.

Nothing ever remained the same for very long in the prison service. Something was always happening to cause a ripple or wrinkle in our activities from one day to the next or, in my case, from one night to the next.

I lost my wristwatch on patrol one night. I backtracked and searched the areas I had just left but didn't find it. I called the officer in charge, Lieutenant Johnson. He came down and we went all over the industries again—we searched through the clean laundry, we ran our hands down into bags of dirty laundry, we looked under sewing-machine tables and workbenches. By the time we got off duty it was daylight, so we searched all the paths I had walked on patrol. We searched the foliage beside the paths. We did not find my watch.

Some weeks later I was called in to see our new warden, Edwin B. Swope. An odd sort of fellow. He came from the Southwest and displayed his fondness for that part of the country by dressing in the style of that area. His sombrero, cowboy boots, turquoise belt buckle, and rings looked out of place on the island. But I don't think anybody ever told him. He was about five feet nine inches tall with a slender build. He and his wife were both big fans of horse racing, especially the betting aspect of it.

Swope's strong ties to a powerful U.S. senator and other Washington figures of the day no doubt accounted for his appointment to his new position. He was the last political appointee to serve as warden of Alcatraz.

"Recognize this?" Warden Swope asked as he held up my watch.

"Yes. It's my watch," I said. As it had my initials on the back, I could hardly deny it, nor did I have any reason to.

"How come an inmate had it?"

"I don't know. I lost it on patrol duty."

"Why didn't you report it?"

"I reported it to my supervisor, Lieutenant Johnson."

Johnson was called in. The story was that these two had worked together at another institution and had no use for each other.

I stood there listening to the warden chewing out Johnson and watching the lieutenant turn red and then pale.

"Warden," I said, "Lieutenant Johnson and I searched for that watch every chance we got all night long, and then, in the daylight, after our shift was over, we went back and searched along all the paths to see if I had dropped it outside somewhere."

The warden glared at me for a long moment and then finally, with seeming reluctance, gave back my watch. As I walked out of his office I thought, By gosh, that sucker was hoping he could catch me in an illegal deal with a convict.

That got me to wondering how my watch had gotten to the warden. Eventually, I got the complete story. An officer had found my watch on a convict during a routine shakedown. Instead of assuming my innocence, he assumed my guilt and turned it over to the warden. It always seemed to me that the officers who were hell-bent on a promotion thought a sure way to go up the ladder was to make everybody else look bad.

Some of the officers at Alcatraz had worked with Warden Swope in other institutions. It wasn't long before the grapevine started carrying stories about his being soft on inmates—as he called convicts—and hard on officers. Well-trained and conscientious officers had been fired by him, according to the stories. Perhaps the most disturbing of the grapevine tales was that he seldom supported an officer. An officer who put a convict on report became the one on trial instead of the convict. When an officer was called in for a disciplinary hearing, the warden pulled out a notebook of possible infractions and read a few aloud, implicitly accusing the officer. The officer would walk out of the meeting mumbling that he didn't remember doing whatever the warden had accused him of doing.

While on island patrol, I had lots of time to think and little opportunity to talk with others. I found I couldn't shake an uneasy feeling concerning Alcatraz. What was Alcatraz? Where did it stand with the bureau? Did the bureau know how it was operated? For that matter, did anyone? There were so many special privileges for convicts and so many drugs being administered.

Alcatraz was the first institution in the Federal Prison System with maximum security and minimum privileges. The population transferred from other institutions was considered to be incorrigible. Many of them were violent, homicidal, drug users, or had tried to escape from other prisons. In other words, a man didn't get to occupy one of our cells for talking out of turn in Sunday school. Most of them came from federal prisons but the states also sent incorrigibles to Alcatraz.

From what I had been able to observe during my brief time at Alcatraz before the change of command and from what I learned by talking to other officers, two very strong men—Warden Johnston and Associate Warden Miller—had run Alcatraz for fourteen years in their own unique way. Rewards were given to individual convicts, such as the two I had seen in the kitchen cooking steaks for themselves. Some convicts were allowed to keep items in their cells that would have been considered contraband in another cell. With a new warden and associate warden (Paul Madigan), it seemed unlikely that the same system of special privileges could continue working as it apparently had in the past. Perhaps the convicts had been kept in line by the fearless attitude of Johnston and Miller.

I began to hear reports that the drug problem was escalating and that convicts were failing to comply with institution rules more and more often. Taking advantage of the change in administration, the cons had wasted no time in demanding more drugs. The users forced many nonusers to collect drugs for them in order to pay off debts, and some convicts collected drugs to sell. The asking price was usually sexual favors or protection from other convicts.

Speaking of the drug habits of convicts reminds me of a problem I had with drugs one night during a stint on the island patrol morning watch.

When I came out of World War II, my headaches became a nuisance. The diagnosis was migraine headaches and I was put on a mixture of aspirin, phenacetin, and codeine—referred to as APCs. I kept some of these pills in my pocket and when I felt a headache coming on I took one.

One night on my way to work as island patrol, I developed a headache. At the time, I had an apartment in the city and had boarded the *Warden Johnston* when the headache hit. When I felt in my pockets for an APC, I didn't find any. There was no turning back—I had to go on to work.

Along with the headache I often had nausea. So there I was leaning over the port rail of the *Warden Johnston* getting rid of my dinner and feeling very ill when Askew, a new MTA, came up to me, thinking I was probably drunk. I told him about the headaches.

"Well, here, take these. They should help you."

On the island I got some water and washed down one of the pills. It made my stomach feel a bit queasy. But by the time we were through roll call and I was out walking my beat around the island, I was feeling pretty good. Then I remembered I had another pill. According to my philosophy, if a little is good, more is better. I took the second pill.

The time was coming to make one of my half-hourly calls to the Control Center. I went into the dry-cleaning shop and noticed I still had six minutes before it was time to call. I began to feel dizzy and sat down.

They found me a couple of hours later. Everyone had screwed up. The Control Center officer who was supposed to take my calls had not followed up on my failure to call. I could have been deathly ill down in the work area and no one would have known the difference. In fact, I was practically dead.

It was the Control Center relief who came in and noticed on the call-in chart that I had not been checked off. He alerted all officers on duty. Finally, the lieutenant found me sound asleep with a Colt .45 on my belt. He had an awful time waking me. As he was ranting and raving at me for falling asleep, he was already thinking that he had to write up this incident for the captain. Although he liked me, he had a job to do.

After I washed my face, I carried on the rest of the night. But I knew I was in a lot of trouble.

In the meantime, I began to put two and two together. I had never fallen asleep on the job before, was seldom even drowsy. Then it dawned on me. It had to be those pills. I went to see Askew.

"What in the devil was that you gave me?" I asked him.

"I gave you a couple of sleeping pills. So you could go home and go to bed. I thought you were living on the island and you were coming home to go to bed," Askew said. Now it was his turn to do a little sweating. If I told what had actually happened, he would be in trouble. Even though he was an MTA, he wasn't authorized to be running around with that kind of drug in his pocket.

"Tell you what, Askew," I said, "if I only get a suspension then I won't say anything about the pills and you can go free. But if they're going to fire me, then I'm going to have to tell the whole story."

"That's okay with me," Askew said.

I was called in front of the disciplinary board, which was made up of all the brass—the warden, associate warden, captain, and two lieutenants. I was well aware of the possible outcome of this meeting. At the same time, I was near the completion of my studies at the San Francisco College of Chiropractic and felt that I'd have something to fall back on if I got fired.

Warden Swope read the charges concerning my being asleep on the job and then went through my history—you did this and you did that. I never did figure out how much of it came out of his little book. He reminded me that at one time I had owed the institution at Sandstone one dollar for some reason and that I habitually went around with my coat unbuttoned—which was true, but didn't seem to me to be worthy of action on the part of this austere group.

The warden ended his presentation with, "How do you plead to this charge?"

"I guess you mean sleeping on the job," I said. "Yes, I was sleeping on the job."

There was a long silence during which I got more hard stares from the warden, while the others looked at the tabletop and at the warden. The first requirement of the associate, the captain, and the lieutenants was to keep the warden happy—that was the way to get a good rating and look forward to a promotion. In this situation, they were trying to figure out what Warden Swope wanted to do with me so they could vote with him.

Finally, the warden almost snarled at me, "You can leave now."

I got up and walked out, feeling I might as well make plans for my farewell to the Federal Prison Service. Knowing I would have thirty days to respond to any action of the committee, I waited to see what would happen.

A day or two later, my good friend Lieutenant Stucker came to me and said, "You goofed."

"How did I goof?"

"Swope wanted you to cry, plead, and beg for mercy. And you wouldn't. If you had made a defense and done some pleading, he would feel free to just suspend you for a while. Now he feels he has to fire you."

"Well, I thought the only manly thing for me to do was to plead guilty and let the chips fall where they may."

Stucker shook his head. "None of my business, but why don't you go in and talk to the warden? It might help and I'm sure it won't make your case any worse. It can't get any worse."

So I went out front to make an appointment to plead with Warden Swope. Bertrand, the warden's new secretary, went in to see whether he would see me. I was immediately invited into his office and directed to sit down. There had been a change in the warden's office—chairs were now provided for visitors.

I told the warden I was sorry about sleeping on the job and that I didn't make any plea to save my job because I just wasn't built to beg for mercy.

Warden Swope stared at me for what seemed ages. He finally said, "So what do you think we ought to do with you?"

"I think a suspension would be in order," I said.

"Fine. How much of a suspension would you say?"

"Oh, thirty days ought to do it."

"Thirty days?" The warden looked astonished. "Thirty days—we can't do that. That's too much, my boy."

Following another long pause, he said, "I don't know what we are going to do with you. I can't let you go free. You have a way about you, my boy—it would look like we let you talk yourself out of trouble. And if we should have to try another officer and gave him a suspension after not punishing you, he would think it was because he didn't have the ability to talk himself out of his predicament. Go on back to work and we'll let you know what we're going to do."

I got up, said my thanks, and was walking out of the office when Warden Swope said, "My boy, there is one thing I have intended to mention. I notice that several of you people still say 'convict' instead of 'inmate.' The bureau would like us to say 'inmate'."

Standing in the sally port waiting to get back into the cell house, I found myself smiling about being in the warden's "my boy" camp.

"What's all the smiling about? I thought you just came out of the warden's office," the main-gate officer said.

"That's what I'm smiling about, my boy," I said, and strolled on down to the West End.

With Square Deal Eddie's reputation (the warden had acquired this nickname shortly after his arrival on Alcatraz), I certainly didn't expect any leniency from him. However, his final decision to suspend me for three weeks was more than a square deal and much appreciated by me. I used the time to concentrate on my courses at the chiropractic college.

Lieutenant Johnson, who was on the disciplinary board, told me later, "When the warden asked whether or not you should be fired, everybody on the committee voted yes, including me and your very good friend, Mr. Madigan. We all thought that was what Swope wanted."

That hurt me pretty good. On the other hand, Swope was a powerful man and these guys had families and had to work for a living. They had to get along.

"We can't fire that man with the wonderful war record he has," Johnson quoted the warden as saying.

There is an odd little sequel to this episode. During my suspension, I moved back to the island. One day, I was down on the dock to catch the boat to the city. I was standing somewhat apart from the rest of the people—mostly wives and children, along with a few off-duty officers.

Warden Swope walked over, put his arm around me, and said, "Well, my boy, how are you getting along?"

"Just fine, Warden, just fine," I said. He always put his arm around you if he liked you. If he didn't like you, he held you at such a distance that you felt small indeed. He could also be very sarcastic.

As we chatted, I couldn't help but notice the stares from the officers and wives on the dock—surprise, envy, and jealousy. With my suspension, they couldn't believe Warden Swope and I could be on such friendly terms.

On one occasion when he put his arm around me, I reached back, caught his arm, pulled it around, and looked at his hand.

Startled, the warden asked, "What are you doing?" People just did not get that familiar with him.

"I just wanted to see if there was a knife in your hand, Warden," I said.

For a moment he stared at me with cold, wide eyes. Then he broke into a dry little chuckle as he walked away. There are times when even the "great" like to be teased. The trick is to know just when those times are.

Incidentally, even though Askew's job was secure because I didn't tell why I had gone to sleep in the dry-cleaning shop, he decided he didn't like being an MTA and abruptly quit. I thought about going in and telling the whole story, just to clean the slate. But I knew it just wouldn't sound right. So to this day, many of my colleagues have not heard the truth about why I fell asleep on the job.

I remember another headache, one that Robert Stroud—the Birdman of Alcatraz—helped me get through. Again, I was assigned to island patrol morning watch and I didn't have any APCs. The lieutenant on duty, seeing that I was in pretty ragged shape, said, "Why don't we just give you the hospital for tonight? You can handle that, can't you?"

"Sure, I can make it."

And thus was I subjected to an eight-hour exposé of Stroud by Stroud. I kept walking up and down the hall, trying to take my mind off my headache. Stroud came to the bars of his roomy ward cell. Due to the administration's difficulty in finding a place to house Stroud in permanent segregation, he was finally assigned to one of the small wards in the hospital. His being the only one on the ward meant he was given the most space—in fact, it was the biggest "cell" on Alcatraz.

He asked me what was wrong. I told him I had a little headache. So he started a long lecture on headaches. At first I was kind of glad to have somebody to talk with, just to kill time. I had not paid much attention to Stroud before that night. He went on and on about all kinds of exercises that would help the head. None of it was exactly new, neither was it very profound. It all sounded like something I had heard before, but he was talking as if all the information came from his own experiences or original research.

He changed to other topics, but maintained the same involved tone. As I paced up and down in front of his cell, I would nod or say something occasionally. Every time I got within range, he would start discoursing again. It was all about himself. I began to understand how a man could live his entire life, or most of it, as Stroud did—with his kind of ego, it could be done.

This made me wonder just who this Stroud was. He was the first con of national notoriety that I saw during my training at Leavenworth. Officers I respected told me in some detail about his activities. His involvement with birds was a ruse to get alcohol. He claimed he needed the alcohol to make slides of bird tissues. Officers who had the opportunity to know said he drank the alcohol and that they never saw a sick bird become healthy as a result of Stroud's treatments.

There were a lot of stories floating around about Stroud and for some reason I never understood, the administration seemed to believe most of them. The more I talked with him about his treatment of birds, the more I realized what a phony he was.

Once I noticed that he had a book on pathology, and he gave me the name of the author. I wasn't familiar with the name, but it was a human pathology textbook. This began to open up something for me. After that I would check his books when I went up to the hospital. He had all the books he wanted, even though the rule was that an inmate could have only four books at a time in his cell. I suspected that Stroud was simply putting together information from all these books to write his articles on birds.

There was a rumor that Stroud had learned how to speak French in six weeks, or maybe it was six months, but even so, it made people think he had a fantastic brain. It so happened that one day a French priest came over to the island for a visit. He had been invited by Father Scannell, who was the island's priest at the time. When the French priest, who also spoke excellent English, came up to the hospital, I happened to be there and, of course, I had a devilish thought.

"Father, would you like to do a favor for me, just for fun?" I asked him.

The priest stared at me with questioning eyes. He was obviously surprised to be approached in this manner. When he saw my smile, he said, "What would you like me to do, sir?"

"Would you go over there and talk to Stroud in French? At least enough to see how much French he knows. Just carry on a conversation with him. Let's see what happens," I said.

Stroud was very flattered to have the priest stop to talk with him. But when the priest started speaking French, Stroud started saying, "What? What?"

"Do you speak French?" the priest asked.

"Oh, yes, yes," was Stroud's reply. But it was clear he was not able to understand or speak more than a few words in French.

He made every effort to get people to believe he was some sort of a genius. But in all honesty, in my contacts with Stroud I saw nothing close to genius. In fact, I saw the guy as a poor damn fool. He was his own worst enemy and people on the outside took him for whatever money he had made on his writings.

He displayed no concern for the past or future. Stroud's world was Stroud right now—he was the one and only one in that world. His rather odd and severe type of imprisonment didn't seem to bother him at all. I never heard of his being depressed. On the other hand, he would often make real threats to correctional officers and he was constantly raving against Mr. Miller. Stroud's idea for improving discipline was to let every inmate carry a knife. According to him, we would be surprised at how well behaved everyone would be.

During my stints as mail censor, many a letter came in from women begging to be granted custody of Stroud. They offered marriage and a good home. With his record as a cold-blooded killer, I could imagine what might happen if he were released to one of these women.

There was a story on the grapevine that Stroud had been approached concerning a possible parole. As the tale goes, Stroud brusquely and bluntly said, "No parole. I want an absolute presidential pardon before I go out."

Stroud died of natural causes in the federal prison hospital in Springfield, Missouri, at the age of seventy-three. He had spent fifty-four years in prison.

10

Acting Lieutenant

One night when I reported for duty on the morning watch as island patrol, the evening-watch lieutenant said, "You are the lieutenant tonight, Gregory."

"What?" I said in disbelief. I was a junior officer and there were any number of senior officers who would have liked to show they could be a lieutenant.

"That's what the roster says."

"I don't know the lieutenant's job, not the first thing about his responsibilities." I wondered why the acting captain wanted me in this position. I wasn't exactly his favorite officer.

"I'll hang around for a while," said the evening lieutenant, "but there's really nothing to it. The first thing is . . . ," and he went on to tell about making the first round of the cell house and how to make the count. "And the rest is just go along and hope nothing happens. When in doubt about something, call the captain. Or call me. I'd be glad to come up and help you out. I live here on the island."

Roll call on the morning watch was informal. There were usually only seven officers, but the number of officers changed as posts were activated or discontinued. The main thing was to see that every post was filled and that the officers were ready and able to do their jobs. Observation and informal chats determined whether they had consumed alcohol and were unable to perform their duties. You also listened to the grapevine on such topics. Secrets were hard to keep on Alcatraz; besides, it was to the advantage of all for everyone to be fit.

I went into the cell house along with the cell house officer, the TU officer, and the hospital officer. While the cell house officer made a count of the cell house, the hospital officer and I made a count of the hospital.

We went into the open ward and used flashlights to check each convict, looking to see whether they seemed to be okay. The rules demanded that no less than two officers go into the ward, for safety reasons. We often had very dangerous convicts in the hospital.

I left the hospital officer to his book. This was the only post where reading on the evening and morning shifts was allowed. He could sit in the office and read. But there was a catch to this privilege—the hospital officer had to call the Control Center every fifteen minutes.

I went down the stairs and back into the quiet cell house. Walking silently along the aisle, I could hear the grinding of teeth but not much else. Such a difference from the daytime, when there was noise from every direction and almost continuous movement of people from one place to another. Even when no one else was moving about during the day, the convicts with janitorial duties could be found mopping and polishing the aisles. Being a cell house floor janitor was considered a good job. A broom pusher could get around and collect all the gossip.

The cell house lights were subdued. As I moved down the aisles, the few lights that were on cast long shadows and, along with the overpowering hush, concocted a ghostly atmosphere. During the late 1950s, the tailor shop made slippers from old wool blankets that we were supposed to wear over our shoes when walking in the cell house at night. I never wore them. A number of convicts can attest to the fact that I didn't need them—they never heard me coming. However, that didn't keep them from good-naturedly reminding me that the rules said I was to wear the awkward shoe covers.

My next responsibility was to make the count in the brightly lighted TU—no reduction of lighting for the night here. I went in and found the convicts had covered the fronts of their cells by hanging blankets and towels on the bars.

"What's this all about?" I asked the TU officer.

"They started this a few weeks ago. Said the light bothered them."

"Has it been reported?"

"I reported it, but the captain didn't do anything about it."

I went along the aisle making the count and tearing down the covers, dropping them inside the cells. There were no complaints from the convicts. During the following nights when I was the acting lieutenant, the makeshift curtains did not reappear. However, I was told that when I went back on island patrol the curtains reappeared. When the regular lieutenant tore them down the convicts made so much noise that he gave in, knowing he would get no support from the front office. The convicts knew I didn't care what the front office thought.

Technically, the TU officer was not allowed to read on duty but since there was plenty of light the rule was ignored. That is, until an officer brought a whole course of study to work one night. That was a bit too much. It seems as though there is always someone who has to spoil a good thing.

Back at the West End of the cell house, I checked the counts against the current listing of convicts by location—cell house, hospital, and TU. The counts being correct, I called the Control Center officer to give the word and he called the boat operator to say it was okay to depart on the last round-trip of the night to the mainland.

I walked down the hill to the dock and waited for the return of the *Warden Johnston* so I could observe the people as they disembarked. Getting off the boat was sometimes tricky, especially when the winds were high and the water was rough.

With the boat secure, the island patrol officer and I went into the dock office where I gave him pertinent information and we decided which shop he should search. On the following nights, I sometimes went with him on part of his rounds or made a tour of 64 Building before going back to the cell house.

Then came the dullest part of the lieutenant's job on the morning watch. I was to sit at the captain's desk out in front. I tried shooting the bull with the Control Center and main-gate officers, but they were a bit reluctant to talk with me. They were both senior officers and were probably wondering why I, instead of one of them, had been put in the lieutenant's position. I understood their attitude, and spent most of my inactive time in the captain's office or wandering around outside the front door in the fresh air.

The lieutenant was not allowed to read on the job, but I figured it was legal to read the convict résumés. In the warden's office there was a file on every convict who had been issued an Alcatraz number. I took a few at a time, sat at the captain's desk, and read them.

Each file told me about a convict's educational background, employment record, family, and childhood. There was also information on his criminal activities. I spent a lot of time learning about the convicts—which gave me a better basis for dealing with them.

At 3:00 a.m., I went back into the cell house to see Macky, the cell house officer. After World War II he had stayed in the Naval Reserve for a while. He liked to bet on horse races. He was very careful about his bets, making only one or two a month and usually winning. According to Macky, he made as much money on the horses as he got in salary from the prison service.

Macky used the morning watch to study the racing forms, bringing them to work in the back of his shirt. I told him one night that he should be careful about taking off his coat. He gave me a noncommittal grin. I was just warning him that others might squeal on him. I wouldn't report him because he was doing his job.

Macky's grin, even in the dim light of the cell house, could be seen from some distance down Broadway. He whispered, "The guy in the last cell has been talking in his dreams to some detective inspector. He told the detective to go shit in his hat. Just listen to the way he's grinding his teeth."

During the quiet of the night, a convict would lightly tap his tin cup on the bars if he needed to get the attention of an officer. If it was a legitimate request, the lieutenant would be called to take care of it. An ill convict would be taken to the hospital and the doctor or MTA would be consulted.

Taking a convict up to the hospital took a lot of time. If two officers were required, the island patrol had to be called to come up and help. The cell house officer could not leave his post. The keys to the lock boxes that controlled the cell doors had to be picked up from the Control Center. After getting the keys and opening the lock box and then the cell, the keys were put on a line and the West Gun Gallery officer pulled them up into the safety of the gallery.

When the sick convict, accompanied by the lieutenant, was ready to leave the cell house, the line was dropped from the gallery with the keys to the dining hall and the door at the bottom of the stairs leading up to the hospital. The hospital officer would unlock the gate at the top of the stairs—mission accomplished. As many as six of the seven officers on duty could be involved in the various aspects of transferring a sick convict to the hospital.

If a convict was being cantankerous and made a lot of noise with his cup on the bars, there might be some yelling and screaming at him from other convicts, but if the noise was being made by a convict who really had a problem, the others seemed to accept it without complaint. Convicts were jealous of their time to sleep. It was a chance to escape the reality of where they were.

I went into the kitchen and dining hall to make a routine inspection, looking for contraband, safety hazards, anything unusual or out of place. By then it was time for another count. I made my rounds and, again, went back to the West End to total the counts and call the Control Center.

The first steward and the kitchen officer came on duty between 4:00 and 4:30 a.m. For convenience, the convicts on the kitchen crew were celled in the same block, referred to as "kitchen row." The kitchen officer and the cell house officer opened the cells on kitchen row, synchronizing the pulling of the levers so as to minimize the noise. After the officers hand-searched the convicts, I counted them and admitted them to the dining hall, which led to the kitchen, where they went about their various chores of setting up for breakfast. At the West End, I changed the count to show the number of convicts in the kitchen.

Then I went into the kitchen, for two reasons: one, the steward would have the coffee made by now and, two, I wanted to talk with Blackie Audette, a convict who worked there. I got a tin cup of the black, hot brew and found Blackie. It always helps to know the right people—and in this case, Blackie was the right person.

"Blackie," I said, "you know everything there is to know about this kitchen. So, tonight and every night that I'm the lieutenant, make me a good sandwich and hide it someplace. Can you do that?"

"Sure can. I'll put it up on the top shelf behind the cooking pots."

"Good." I was sick of the wooden-box specials.

Blackie, an American Indian, was a good-natured bank robber. He had a medium build and a fringe of very black hair. He liked to work in the kitchen—he would rather be in the kitchen than go to a movie or out to the recreation yard.

Blackie found a variety of sandwich makings for me: roast beef, steak, chicken, or cold cuts if he couldn't find anything else. Of course, this was illegal but the sandwiches were certainly welcome—they sure beat fried eggs and rat cheese.

I went back to sit at the captain's desk and take calls from officers who were sick and would need a replacement on the day shift.

The day's activities really got going between 6:30 and 7:00 with several things happening simultaneously or in quick succession. A bell sounded at 6:30 to wake the convicts and the lights were turned on, bringing the cell house back to life. A stand-up count was made, the boat left for the first run, a few officers reported for early duty, and breakfast was served to the main line.

I went into the dining hall and served as the lieutenant in charge of breakfast. The kitchen officer and four others took the stations around the dining hall.

The day-watch lieutenant called his roll and the day-shift officers came into the cell house. By this time, some of the convicts had finished eating and we were letting them out of the dining hall. They were allowed twenty minutes to eat, but we never pushed if someone needed more time. I went to the West End and stayed with the day-watch lieutenant until the last convict left the dining hall. My first watch as an acting lieutenant was over. It had been an easy shift.

It puzzled me somewhat that my nemesis, Acting Captain Parant, had made me the acting lieutenant. I couldn't figure it out, but orders were orders and I took them. I continued as the lieutenant of the morning watch for several weeks. Everybody cooperated with me, and I tried not to exercise any more authority than necessary.

Nothing dramatic happened during my stint as acting lieutenant. I didn't find much contraband in my searches of the kitchen or officers' mess. However, one night I saw a stainless steel can in the back of a lower cupboard in the officers' mess. Not having seen it before, I investigated. It held seven or eight nicely cooked pork chops.

I thought, I know some guys who will appreciate these, and headed for the stack of box lunches. One pork chop per box and the can was empty. I put it back in the cupboard. The next night it was gone.

I got knowing looks from the recipients of the pork chops that morning as we went off shift and more the next night at roll call—but not a word was said about the addition to the lunches. Several weeks went by and I was back on island patrol when an officer named George Black shyly thanked me for the good lunch, saying he hadn't said anything because he didn't know where it came from or whether all the officers on duty had received a pork chop.

I had been looking for booze when I found the pork chops. I knew that one of the kitchen workers, a con who was doing time for bank robbery, was getting alcohol from somewhere. I never did find his stash. He was a good guy, didn't cause trouble with convicts or officers. I really didn't care that he had his booze— I just hated to admit I couldn't find it.

This con told me stories about banks and bank robberies. He would go into a bank with a vial of water, show it to the teller and say it was nitroglycerin, and demand money. The teller, not being willing to call his bluff, would cooperate. Later, while holed up in a motel drinking Jack Daniel's, his favorite whiskey, he would read the newspaper account of the robbery. The bank president would be quoted as saying $30,000 had been taken. As he was the robber, he knew only $15,000 had been taken. He didn't like being used to cover up what was stolen by the bank employees.

He also told me about getting messages by way of the grapevine, asking him to rob a certain bank on a certain day at a certain time. This meant the bank management was trying to cover an inside theft before the bank auditors came to audit the books. He didn't mind helping them out until robbing a bank became a federal offense and punishable by a twenty-year sentence.

One night I came to work expecting to continue in the role of lieutenant, but I was told I was back on island patrol. This suited me fine, but I wondered why I had been assigned to be the lieutenant only to be abruptly put back on island patrol. I said to myself, Alcatraz gets odder and odder.

It was years later that I learned a number of the senior officers had signed a letter to the captain, complaining about my functioning as a lieutenant while still classified as a junior officer.

One night after I was back on island patrol and Carter Selig was the lieutenant, he called down to the industries saying I was needed up top. When I got there, he told me a convict was hanging himself, and began running toward TU.

"You can't go rushing in there like that, lieutenant," I told Selig. "If he's already hanging, he's gone by now. Rushing in there, you're going to get the whole prison upset." He did slow down some, but hurried along as much as he could.

In TU we found Smitty, a black professional jailbird with a sense of humor, tied under his bunk as if hanging himself. Perhaps he was feeling wakeful and decided to play a joke on the officer making the count. We went in and untied him without a problem.

"Let's put him in hand restraints so he can't hurt himself," Selig said.

"Well, we can put him in restraints, but I don't think he'll be in them very long."

Smitty smiled.

"Frankly," I said, "we should put him in the Hole."

Smitty stopped smiling.

At Selig's insistence, Smitty allowed himself to be tied into the long gloves that restricted hand movement. We locked him in a cell in the hospital and, sure enough, Smitty removed the restraints.

Smitty could get into or out of most anything. He worked for me in the clothing room one time. I made the mistake of locking my keys in a cabinet. No point in getting excited about it as long as Smitty worked for me. I called him over and asked him to unlock the cabinet door. He wouldn't let me watch, but he opened the cabinet.

Another night, I was in the tailor shop marveling at a big cutting machine. Fabric was laid out for army suntans, as the khaki pants were called, and with this machine hundreds of pants could be cut at one time. The phone rang and I was told to hurry up top.

I was needed in TU to help take a man up to the hospital. Entering the cell, I pulled off the blanket—what a mess! The convict had picked at the veins in his wrists until he was well on the way to bleeding to death.

It was only by accident that the officer in charge of TU discovered there was something amiss. He was standing across from the cells with his butt up against the radiator to keep warm. Idly looking around, his attention was drawn by something dripping from under a con's bunk. Although the officer immediately called the Control Center for help and we got the convict to the hospital as quickly as we could, it was too late. He had lost too much blood and his veins had collapsed. According to the other convicts in the hospital that night, just a minute or so before the end he sat up in bed and said, "I feel good," then laid back and died.

There weren't many suicides at Alcatraz. Only a fraction of the attempts were really serious. Most of them were fake attempts by convicts hoping to be transferred off The Rock to another institution.

One suicide attempt might have succeeded had it not been interrupted by an officer who happened to be walking down the aisle. An inmate had removed the lightbulb from the ceiling fixture in his cell. He then put one foot in the toilet and was trying to reach the active light socket when the officer stopped him. The inmate was doing life for kidnapping. He had been sentenced just days before the Lindbergh Law went into effect. Had he committed the crime after the law took effect, the courts could have solved his problem for him by giving him the death penalty.

Word came that a new captain was coming in. It was Ralph Tahash, of all people! He had been the captain at Sandstone when I worked there. He's not going to like it here, I thought, he's too easygoing for this place. Tahash could be a tough officer but it seemed that to be captain at Alcatraz you had to grow into it— spend time working with the population before moving to a front-office position. Everything at Sandstone—convicts, celling, discipline, and work programs—was so much easier than it was here at Alcatraz. Just getting accustomed to the rules and the reasons for them would be a big transition for Captain Tahash.

I was told that when Parant found out he was not going to be made captain— that someone was coming in from another prison—he said, "Well, I guess I might as well get that Gregory off the morning watch. That will be the first thing the new captain will do if I don't." I was serving about my third consecutive tour of duty on the morning watch; I don't remember why Parant wanted to punish me.

When I heard this, I thought how glad I was that Parant was not going to be captain. He was mean and didn't believe in fair play. One thing I knew about Captain Tahash is that he was a firm taskmaster but fair. People in other prisons had liked working on his shifts. Even though they had to work harder and pay more attention to the rules, it was easier than working under some of the other officers.

11

Cell House Day Watch

I went back on days, with time off on the weekends. That was a pleasant change from having time off in the middle of the week. I was assigned to the cell house, where the activities of the day started and ended. For this quarter I had a job called Cell House Two. Most of my time was spent in the East End of the cell house but I worked anywhere I was needed. Bunch Tompkins was now the acting lieutenant on the day watch, so I didn't get to see him as often as when he was in charge of the cell house.

As the Cell House Two officer, I was up and down the tiers letting inmates in and out of their cells for various reasons, shaking down cells, escorting inmates to wherever they had to go, observing meals in the dining hall, delivering mail, and keeping an eye on the orderlies cleaning the aisles. Every day, and sometimes twice a day, the aisles in the cell house were cleaned. On Saturday the mop was used generously and on Sunday the floors were waxed with a special waxing machine. It sure made the floors look nice.

"B-1," Lieutenant Tompkins called out.

"Forty-four," came the response from the officer who had just counted all the inmates in B-1. Bunch, who was down at the West End, checked the number against the official inmate count.

When Bunch called out, "C-2," he said to me, "You might as well get ready to go up there and make the count. This guy can't count a tier of cons."

"Twenty-seven," called the officer in C-2.

"Count it again," Bunch said, and we waited.

When a count did not tally it was usually because the record on an inmate had not been changed at the West End when he was taken to the hospital or to the Hole. This was easily corrected by checking with those units. Otherwise it was because an officer couldn't keep his count straight or an inmate decided to trick the officer who was counting his tier. A new officer or one who was not liked by the inmates was sometimes forced to open a cell to find an inmate. Of course, the only place an inmate could hide was under the bunk.

There were a few officers who were more or less excused from making the count because they could never come up with the right number. Some tried counting a few cells, writing down the number, and then counting some more, but mistakes in addition often nullified this effort. Some tried using mechanical counters, but even that didn't work.

"Twenty-seven," again came the call from C-2.

"Call out the numbers of the empty cells," Bunch said.

"Twenty-one and twenty-five."

"Well, what do you know? He got it right this time. Twenty-one went to the hospital and twenty-five is unoccupied. Okay, C-2." And the count continued.

When Bunch had checked off the count from each tier and found that it tallied with the cell house count, he called the Control Center and reported the total. Other locations where there were inmates did the same.

The inmates were filing out to work one morning when I happened to think of something. Seeing Met Mullin in the line, I called out to him, "Met, step out of line."

I said quietly to Bunch, "Watch this little trick I learned from an officer down at Leavenworth. He couldn't stand boredom."

"Now look, Met," I said to the inmate, "you better straighten that out and you better do it pretty fast; otherwise, I won't have any choice but to put you on report." My tone was very serious.

Met's eyes registered puzzlement, confusion, and then fear. "What you talking about, man?"

"Get on to work now, but if you don't get it straightened out, you can't say I didn't warn you." Met, of course, began to worry. He wasn't worried about any particular thing he had done, but which one of several things I had discovered.

"Now you've got poor Met all shook up," Bunch said, his voice showing no sympathy. "He's a good one to pull that on because he's always into one thing or another."

"It's really surprising how that little ruse can bring a lot of nasty stuff to the surface."

Some days later as the inmates were filing out to work, Met gave me a big wink and kept on walking. I wondered what he had corrected.

• • •

By now I had collected quite a lot of information on many of the inmates. I felt I knew some of them quite well, but I was still learning. While shaking down their cells, I continued to add to my store of information: their likes, dislikes, talents, hobbies, needs, and the extent to which they corresponded with their family and friends. The contents of a cell told a lot about the occupant. The inmates were a varied lot, as any group of a like number would be.

An illiterate inmate might treasure a fancy, expensive fountain pen. Some cells showed their occupants to be serious students who took extension courses from the University of California in Berkeley. Several took courses in creative writing. Others were avid readers, checking out books from the reasonably well-stocked prison library.

Many of the old-timers played bridge and studied improvised problem hands. Others played chess after being locked in their cells at night. In the interest of not disturbing their neighbors, a third man was sometimes required in a chess game. When the players' cells were far apart, the third man, who also had a chessboard, received the plays and quietly relayed them to the participants. This stopped a lot of verbal fights with the inmates who wanted a quiet time after supper.

The majority of the inmates were considerate and respected the need for reasonable quiet. Those who did not study, read, paint, or play quiet games were the ones who made the most noise after supper. Their entertainment was talking, joking, and teasing, which often led to arguments. In fact, when the cells were opened for breakfast, we had to be on our toes—there just might be somebody who remembered a squabble from the night before and wanted to make it physical. The inmates had had time to build up steam for a fight. I learned it was just as well to let them exchange some blows. A few direct hits would usually help them to forget about it.

The athletic Big Red took an interest in music. While taking an extension course in the subject, he became so captivated that he ordered a saxophone. From seven to eight each evening, Big Red's practice sessions could be heard by all. Several inmates complained quietly that it was a painful assault on their ears and dispositions. But their respect for and fear of Big Red was such that they didn't dare make a big issue of it.

Big Red recruited other "musicians" and eventually formed a band of five or six members. They were allowed to play in the dining hall on holidays. They were only a cut above a fourth- or fifth-grade band, but it did wonders for their self-esteem. Again, there were complaints from some inmates, tongue-in-cheek this time, that it was cruel and inhuman to subject them to the band during a special holiday meal.

John Paul Chase's cell was interesting because of the paintings in it. John had a decent education and a talent for painting. He took extension courses in art. After a few failures and some pretty successful paintings, he started his masterpiece.

It began as a sketch on a canvas approximately two-and-a-half by four feet. The seven hills of San Francisco encircled the portrait of an orchestra conductor. Woven in between the hills were a cable car, a musical staff, and some musical notes. Slowly and painstakingly, the scenery and the portrait came to life on the canvas. It was recognized by the officers as a very special work.

Comments or questions to John concerning the painting were met with a smile but no concrete information. However, he did seem to be especially pleased with it.

Then one day the masterpiece was gone. Its sudden removal caused much speculation concerning its whereabouts. John still answered questions with only a smile. He wouldn't talk.

The mystery was solved a few weeks later by Herb Caen, a *San Francisco Chronicle* columnist. Caen reported on the retirement party for Pierre Monteux, the conductor of the San Francisco Symphony. Monteux received many beautiful and expensive gifts at the party but the gift he cherished most, Caen wrote, was a painting of himself conducting the symphony with the panorama of San Francisco in the background. The column went on to report that the portrait had been painted by an inmate on Alcatraz. It is doubtful that Caen knew that the talented artist was doing time because he and his partner, Baby Face Nelson, had killed a treasury agent during a mail train robbery.

Knowing the inmates gave me clues as to why certain items might be in a cell and when to be watchful of specific inmates. If an inmate with a penchant for creating firebombs started a collection of incendiary materials, you paid attention. A Molotov cocktail could be made by stuffing the heads of matches in a small glass bottle and inserting a piece of cotton for a fuse. The flying glass could cause a lot of damage to anyone who happened to be nearby when the bottle exploded. Many inmates were quite ingenious at using whatever was at hand to make tools or weapons. Stout string coated with resin or pieces of sandpaper could be used to cut bars. Anything that was rigid enough to penetrate human skin and tissue could be made into a shiv. A piece of metal could be sharpened on the concrete floor and a handle could be formed by inserting the metal into the heated plastic of a toothbrush handle.

Some seemingly harmless things from the kitchen, such as ginger, could be used as an intoxicant. Other substances were so poisonous that by the time the inmate became intoxicated, death would not be far away. A couple of inmates wanted to reach euphoria so badly that they strained paint thinner through loaves of bread, hoping this would remove the lethal substances. One of them died and the other suffered permanent damage to his vocal cords.

One time when I was assigned to the cell house I kept after an inmate named Conlin to clean up his cell. Finally I said to him, "I've asked you several times to clear out and clean up your cell. And I told you I was going to clear it out if you didn't. So today I'm coming in here with a big box and load up all this junk and get rid of it."

"You better not do that," Conlin said.

"What do you mean, I'd better not?"

"You just better not," he smiled.

"Now you've put me up against the wall, haven't you? I've told you what will happen if you don't clean up your cell, and you've suggested that something is going to happen to me if I do." Conlin grinned and said nothing.

"Suitcase Sally" was the nickname given Conlin by his fellow inmates. It was almost a respectful name. During World War II he had worked in the research lab of a defense plant, where each day he went to work with an empty suitcase, filled it with various metals, and slid it, by way of an old drain, under the fence. On leaving work he would retrieve the suitcase. Most of the metals were marked with identifying numbers, but Conlin had a way of shaving off the numbers before selling the metals on the local black market. His downfall was a new type of X-ray that showed the imprint of the numbers inches deep in the metal. He was given the "Sally" part of his nickname because he was much sought-after for homosexual favors.

Conlin was one of the few inmates who came directly from sentencing to Alcatraz. During the body-cavity search that was required on entrance into the institution, two rolled-up bills were found in his rectum—a twenty and a one-dollar bill.

Judging from the math books Conlin ordered, he must have been a mathematical whiz. You would have to be to understand those books. However, he did not show very good social judgment. He was prone to make disparaging remarks about blacks in their presence. But other than that and his bad housekeeping habits, he was a nice guy, pleasant and easygoing.

As the work crews filed out, I told a cell house orderly to get a box and bring it to Conlin's cell. I loaded up all the contraband, mostly junk. One odd thing I found under the bunk was a pillowcase stuffed with socks. Why would anyone want all those socks? Each inmate was issued six pairs a week and could get more with a note from an MTA or the doctor. So why hoard a pillowcase full of socks? As I put them into the box, I reached into the pillowcase one more time, checking to make sure there wasn't anything else in there. I came up with something pink. The prison-issued socks were white. Pulling out the pink item for examination, I found myself holding a pair of ladies' panties.

So this is who has been stealing the warden's wife's laundry, I thought.

Just then I looked around and found Conlin standing in the cell door watching me. He had started out to work but had doubled back to see what I was doing. I got him inside and said, "Okay, drop your strides."

"Why, Mr. Gregory?"

"Never mind why, just do it."

Conlin ducked his head and coyly smiled up at me with inviting eyes. I stared hard at him and he decided I meant it. Slowly he began to open his jeans and again broke into a smile.

"Where did you get those puce panties, Suitcase Sally?"

"Mr. Gregory, these are pink, they're not puce."

"All right, out with you, off to work."

As I slammed shut the door of the cell, I wondered what in the hell I was going to do about this situation. I knew the warden's wife had been complaining about losing laundry but I didn't know it was her panties. My main thought was that this delicate situation would require careful handling.

Later in the afternoon, Bunch came to me and said, "The warden wants to see you, Mr. Gregory."

"Yeah? What about?"

"Look, I'm the lieutenant now, on the other side of the fence. So just go on in and see him."

Warden Swope was standing by a big window that looked out on the bay.

"Sit down, Mr. Gregory," the warden said. "I understand that you searched an inmate's cell and took away some of his personal property. Plus the fact you tore up the cell. Mussed up his bed. My boy, did you really do that to this inmate's cell? He's a pretty good inmate."

"Well, I know he's okay as an inmate, but I also know that his cell was crammed with a lot of useless junk. And as far as any personal things, I left his personal items in his cell. I took away only the excess prison-issued items. There was quite a bit of that kind of stuff in his cell, including a pillowcase full of socks. As to his bed, I took it apart in order to give it a thorough search."

With a look of irritation and a sweep of his hand as if brushing all that away, the warden said, "Mr. Gregory, you must realize that a man's cell is his home. You wouldn't want anyone to come into your home and tear it apart, would you?"

Looking him straight in the eye, I said, "Warden, if someone had a search warrant to come into my house, there wouldn't be much I could do about it."

The warden returned my stare. Then his eyes softened and he began to chuckle. "Mr. Gregory, you have a reputation around here of being rather hard on these boys."

"Just what do you mean, Warden? I'm only enforcing the rules and regulations as they have been written up by the bureau and by the administration of this institution."

"And you're doing a very good job."

The warden seemed to be leaving a lot unsaid concerning his philosophy on the handling of incarcerated people. I felt he was trying to tell me that he wanted me on his team—or maybe warn me. I had seen officers actually quiver like a puppy in the presence of a warden. I did not feel like quivering—never did. Wardens seemed to like me and respect me for sticking to my principles.

"Warden," I said through a mirthless grin, "I read you loud and clear. And after all, it is your prison to govern."

As I turned to walk out, the warden said, "Anytime, my boy, you feel you need to talk with me, you come right on into this office, you hear?"

I was going through the main gate into the cell house when Paul Madigan, who had become the associate warden, caught up with me. Madigan had worked at several prisons and was now back for his third stint of duty at Alcatraz. He probably knew more about Alcatraz than anyone else in the prison service at that time. He took my arm and steered me over to a corner where we would not be overheard.

"This guy, Conlin, whose cell you just shook down . . . "

"Yeah, I was just called in to see the warden about that. And there is a wrinkle here, Mr. Madigan." And I told him about the panties.

Madigan grinned a bit and then his face became grave again. In a very quiet voice he said, "Conlin found a fully loaded .38 caliber pistol and turned it in."

He said no more, nor did he need to. Here was an inmate who had risked his own life by turning in a weapon. Somebody had gone to a lot of trouble to get that .38 into the institution. They must have been very unhappy when it disappeared.

"Thank you, Mr. Madigan." As I walked away I thought, Okay, Suitcase Sally, if you are the kind of inmate who turns in a loaded gun, you can have *two* pillowcases stuffed with socks and panties as far as I'm concerned. Back in the cell house, I felt sick to my stomach. A fully loaded .38 could have made widows of six officers' wives and left their children without fathers. Socks and the warden's wife's panties seemed a small price to pay.

I've often speculated about how the gun could have been delivered to the island. I do not believe it was brought in by an officer. My theory is that it came in through the laundry. Alcatraz did the laundry for the island occupants and for all the military bases in the area.

I wondered whether the warden knew about the loaded gun. Although the grapevine—and the plumbing line*—at Alcatraz worked extremely well, there were things I told no one other than Mr. Madigan, and he in turn told me things that I never heard from any other source. The loaded gun was one of those things.

I liked Madigan's reason for letting Conlin keep his collection much better than the warden's "keep 'em happy" reason. I certainly understood the warden. This was more of what I had seen coming while still at Sandstone. The policy seemed to be "Keep the boys behind bars happy and quiet, whatever it takes." Maybe that kept the bureau happy. Warden Swope even had the cell house walls repainted in more cheerful colors, pink and yellow.

The warden understood that I would continue to do the job I was trained to do within the constraints of his policies as head of the institution. He knew that though I did not wilt in the presence of authority, I respected the chain of command. So, I thought, it's going to be a prisoners' prison.

Trying to keep the warden happy by keeping the inmates happy could get to be a problem. I knew very well that if the warden didn't back up correctional officers in their dealings with inmates, there certainly wouldn't be any support from the administrative staff. It was comforting to know that Madigan trusted me.

The inmates learned something from the Suitcase Sally incident. They knew they could do things that they would not have considered during the administration of Warden Johnston and Mr. Miller. It didn't take long before they refused to shave and get standard haircuts. They also began to call the officers disrespectful names.

Officers bucking for a promotion learned not to "shoot"—write a disciplinary report on—an inmate for any infraction of the rules. That left the rest of us to try to keep the inmates in line as best we could.

Actually, my behavior didn't change much because I never wrote a shot unless it was about something really serious, like a knifing, or something that had been seen by others that I couldn't get out of reporting. I preferred to handle minor infractions on the spot without dragging them out for days. Soon, other conscientious officers also stopped writing shots on inmates.

Things had been different under Mr. Miller's reign. He encouraged the writing of shots on inmates who broke the rules. When they came to disciplinary

---

*No one has been able to adequately explain how news can travel so fast in prisons in spite of efforts to keep information private. Prison grapevines seem to be very efficient and always in working order. In Alcatraz, the toilet plumbing line was the conduit used for communication.

court, appropriate action was taken. And he didn't allow inmates to call officers disrespectful names. He left no doubt how he felt about name-calling.

Miller made himself available to the inmates in the cell house after lunch on most weekdays. Anyone who wanted to make a special request got in line and waited his turn in front of the table where Miller sat. One time, a new inmate, wanting to change his cell, asked a seasoned Alcatraz inmate how to go about it. "See that line in front of Meathead? Just get in line and tell Meathead what you want," was the helpful reply.

When the new inmate got up to the table, he very respectfully said, "Mr. Meat-head, I . . . " The feces hit the fan. Miller's face turned red, he jumped up, knocked over the table, waved his arms around dangerously, and screamed something unintelligible at the poor kid. The polite new inmate jumped back several feet and ran as fast as he could to his cell, with Miller's glare following him.

When Miller's yelling subsided, the West End became unusually quiet. A couple of officers set up the table and chair. Before sitting down again, Miller looked around at the officers and burst out in one of his raucous laughs. The tension was broken and the officers joined in the laughter.

One of the inmates waiting his turn ducked his head into his shoulder and said quietly to me, "One of his better performances." Inmates did not join in laughter with officers. For their own well-being among their peers, they had to seem unconcerned by such commotions.

Filling all the various posts to cover days off, vacations, and sick days was not an easy task. We were often asked to vary our schedule or our post of duty to accommodate a temporary vacancy. I was asked to fill in on the late daytime shift. This gave me an opportunity to experience the change from daytime activities to the quiet and more relaxed period after supper.

The only place in Alcatraz an inmate felt reasonably safe was in his single-occupancy cell with the door locked. Inmates are much like animals in the wilderness: alert, fearful, restless. After a full day of being watchful, inmates seemed relieved to be back in their cells.

The inmates had different ways of walking. Within the safety of the cell they were quite casual, might even put their hands in their pockets and saunter around. Outside the cell, no one walked with his hands in his pockets. There was more action in the stride from head to foot. Some walked on tiptoe as if sparring, ready to throw a punch. Some walked with their chin tucked into their shoulder as if protecting themselves from a blow. Some developed specific ways of swinging the hips. In the days when the inmates tailored their own clothing, the swinging-hip inmates wore extremely tight pants. I remember one fellow who had a soft, mushy kind of walk. He took about fifteen steps to the average person's one step. He shuffled along like a ball of mashed potatoes with appendages.

The really disturbed inmates sometimes just sat and did nothing, or they might pace up and down the cell talking to themselves. They were the sad ones—the ones you felt would never be able to live on the outside. About all you could do was protect them from other inmates and try to get them transferred to an institution with better facilities for taking care of them.

Some inmates had had the same habits for so long that they were unaware of the trouble they caused themselves and others. These inmates considered force to be the only solution to any problem, and blaming someone else was standard behavior. They were unaccustomed to having anyone think of them as a worthwhile individual or care what happened to them.

Such was the case with one inmate, a very strong black man. In the recreation yard, the inmates made their own decisions about how to spend their time. Some sports equipment was provided—balls, bats, and a tetherball. Some inmates preferred table games and still others preferred walking, jogging, or just visiting with friends.

On one occasion, a group decided to see who could throw a baseball the hardest. When it came around to the strong black inmate, he threw as hard as he could. The humerus—the bone extending from the shoulder to the elbow—in his throwing arm snapped. He was carefully taken up to the hospital. The jagged end of the broken bone bulged under the skin.

A couple of doctors came over from the Public Health Service Hospital, set the bone, put the inmate's arm in a cast, and asked that he be kept in the hospital for a few days so he wouldn't have to move around much. Why the bone broke was never explained.

This guy had been a pretty blustery character. After this event, I noticed a change in him. He seemed more at ease, had a more pleasant expression, and readily complied with orders.

One day he said to me, "You know, Boss, when I broke my arm? That was the first time in my life anybody ever did anything for me."

"Help! Insulin!" was the cry I heard coming from the second tier.

I rushed up the stairs and found Bates, a young black inmate, going into shock. He was a diabetic and had just returned from the hospital, where he got a shot of insulin. The noon meal was being served but Bates had not felt like eating.

I ran down to the dining hall shouting, "Open the gate!" I filled a bowl with milk and was scooping sugar into it when my nemesis Lieutenant Kent came up beside me.

"Gregory, you can't do that," the lieutenant said.

I looked up just as I finished and started out. The look on the lieutenant's face clearly said, I've finally got you, Gregory, there's no way you can get out of this. What he thought I was doing, I didn't have time to consider.

I ran back up the steps and said, "Here, Bates, let's see if we can get some of this down you." I held his head up and got some of the sweetened milk down and he began to come out of shock.

"Thanks, Mr. Gregory. I was about gone."

"Yeah, I could see that you were. I'm sure glad you shouted soon enough." I stayed with him until I was sure he was okay.

The lieutenant must have found out from someone else what I did with the bowl of milk. He never mentioned it to me.

It was hard to change the habit of saying "convict." I was getting the bureau word "inmate" out about half the time when an inmate asked me, "Why do you call us convicts 'inmates'?"

I was a bit surprised at the question but the inmate, or convict, went on to say, "'Inmates' are in insane asylums. 'Convicts' are in prison."

"To tell you the truth, man, I think you're right. 'Inmate' does sound like some kind of patient," I said.

Everything at Alcatraz revolved around or was governed in some way by the Control Center. Calls to and from the outside went through the Control Center. Everything that happened in the towers or the dock office was heard through the public-address system there. Entry into the cell house was controlled, in part, from the Control Center. The count of the inmates was reported to the Control Center, where a final total was made and checked against the number of inmates assigned to Alcatraz. The boat operator couldn't depart for the mainland until he got the nod from the Control Center. At night, when quiet was the rule, the Control Center still had phones ringing with reports from the various posts.

Most officers underwent a long apprenticeship before being left alone with all the equipment and responsibilities of the Control Center. But this did not always happen. On one occasion the captain grabbed me and said, "Get in there and straighten out that mess." With the warden on vacation, the captain wanted a smooth-running institution.

I went in and was assaulted visually and aurally. Every phone was ringing and every light on the switchboard was flashing. The poor officer who had been assigned to the job was doing the best he could with the limited training he had received. I told him to man the telephones and I would take the switchboard.

I sat down in front of all those flashing lights, put on the headset, and thought, Here goes nothing! In my usual "if a job's gotta be done—do it" fashion, I started pulling lines, a handful at a time, and stuffing them in somewhere else. In the process, I somehow created a conference call between the bureau in Washington, D.C., the vacationing warden in the Midwest, and the captain on Alcatraz. These three gentlemen were very pleased to be able to speak directly to each other without having to relay messages and were highly complimentary of my ability to set it up for them. I never admitted to them or to others, who wanted desperately to know how I had done it, that I didn't know how I had worked the magic. It was a fluke.

A couple of the officers who worked the Control Center often and who were really good with all the equipment tried to find out what I knew that they didn't know. Like John Paul Chase when asked about his painting, I smiled but didn't talk. I guess they thought it was very selfish of me not to tell them how to set up conference calls.

Later, I asked a telephone company engineer about making such a hookup. He said it couldn't be done with the equipment we were using.

Many things happened during any day shift. When we took days off or went on vacation, it was still business as usual on The Rock, and on returning to work, there were stories to hear. One story that everybody was laughing about involved a certain young officer who had been given the responsibility of supervising the yard while it was being used by the occupants of TU. The officer had to be over twenty-one but looked to be about seventeen or eighteen years old. He had blond curly hair, friendly blue eyes, a medium build, and was of average height, and came equipped with a shy smile and a somewhat apologetic expression.

The TU officer had sent a couple of good friends, Canvasback and Kimo, to the yard at the same time. In the free world, Canvasback had tried to be a professional boxer. That's where he got his nickname. Apparently he was the only one who didn't know he was not a fighter. But he kept trying.

On this occasion, Canvasback and Kimo decided to jump the new, innocent-looking officer. An officer in the yard tower saw the attack and shouted frantically into the intercom for help. He continued to shout excitedly even after help was on the way. Suddenly the frenzied shouting stopped. A burst of laughter told the Control Center that the tables had turned.

When the cell house officers got to the yard, they found the young officer standing there holding the wrist of one of the two "brave" cons—giving it a little twist when necessary to keep him flat on the ground. The other con was also on the ground, yelling in pain, and perhaps humiliation. His ankle was under the foot of the officer, receiving enough pressure to keep him in a prone position.

Sick call for the cell house inmates was held by the MTA after lunch each day. Those who wanted medical advice or drugs lined up and went up to the hospital. As in any group, the complaints varied but most were of a minor nature and the MTA could handle them. The MTA listed those who asked to see the doctor and any whom he thought should be seen by the doctor. The list requesting to see the doctor was always long—the inmates had to see the doctor in order to be put on the list to receive drugs.

The MTA also made a daily trip to TU to hold sick call. On his way back to the hospital one day, Shannon reported to Bunch in my presence that for some reason there was a shortage of hot water bottles. A TU inmate had asked for one and got quite huffy when told there weren't any. He had more or less threatened Shannon.

Over the past few weeks, a number of the TU inmates had asked for hot water bottles. No records had been kept of which inmates made the requests, so a general search of TU would have to be made to locate them. I volunteered.

"I think I'll go along with you. Something doesn't seem right here," Bunch said. "Has any one inmate ordered more than one hot water bottle?"

"No, I don't think so. They seem to be spread out pretty good," said Shannon.

"How about Barns, did he ask for one?" Barns was constantly in trouble for one reason or another; as a result, he spent a lot of time in TU.

"No, not that I recall."

"Hmm," said Bunch.

Inside TU, Bunch said to Lewis, "Let's get Barns out of his cell. Put him in a vacant cell."

Lewis raised his eyebrows, but seeing the look in Bunch's eyes, led the way up the stairs to Barns's cell.

"We're going to move you to another cell," Lewis said.

Barns was lying on his bunk. "What in the hell do you mean?"

"Open the door, Lewis," Bunch said.

As the door opened, Bunch stepped quickly in and grabbed Barns by the front of his shirt, pulling him erect and moving him without pause out the door. Lewis and another TU officer, Rich, took over and started him on the way to an empty cell.

"What in the hell do you goddamned screws think you're doing here? You can't move me out of my cell without a reason. I want to see the warden."

"On second thought, put him in the Hole," Bunch said. As the two officers hustled Barns off to the Hole, Bunch said to me, "He may not be there for very long. But at least we'll have him there for a little while."

When Lewis and Rich returned to Barns's cell, they were accompanied by much noise from the new occupant of the Hole. However, the rest of TU was strangely quiet.

"Now," said Bunch with a knowing look at me, "pull those blankets and mattress off that bunk and I'll show you some hot water bottles."

With one swift move, I dumped the mattress and blankets on the floor. Not only were there a number of hot water bottles but also rolls of adhesive tape and several pairs of rubber gloves.

After a moment spent silently staring at the loot, Bunch said, "All they need now is a paddle or an outboard motor and they could be on their way to San Francisco.

"Don't touch a thing. I'm going to make a phone call," he said as he started down the stairs to the phone. Bunch's booming voice could be heard all over the cell block as he all but ordered the warden to come to TU.

In a very short time Warden Swope appeared, looking indignant and bewildered.

"Warden, would you come up here? We have something to show you," Bunch said.

The warden stared in disbelief at the hot water bottles and other materials.

"This is 'a man's home,' Warden, according to you," Bunch said.

When the significance of what he was seeing became clear to the warden, his face went through a number of changes and ended up with a look of fear.

Some days later, an order came down saying that hot water bottles could be used only within the confines of the hospital.

Even this incident was not enough to cause the renewal of systematic and thorough searching of cells. In years to come, Alcatraz was to pay dearly for this laxness. There were escape attempts, some of which led to deaths, and many hours of searching for escapees by Alcatraz officers, the U.S. Coast Guard, and local police units.

Aerial view of Alcatraz Island, 1949. *Photo by Pacific Aerial Surveys,*
a division of HJW GeoSpatial, Inc., Oakland, Calif.

Emblem above main entrance to Alcatraz, 1990. *Private collection of George H. Gregory.*

The four wardens of Alcatraz, clockwise from top left: James A. Johnston, warden from 1934 to 1948; Edwin B. Swope, 1948 to 1955; Paul J. Madigan, 1955 to 1961; and Olin G. Blackwell, 1961 to 1963. *Johnston, Swope, and Blackwell courtesy Federal Bureau of Prisons Archives; Madigan courtesy Golden Gate National Recreation Area, Phil Dollison collection, P 89-055.041pl.*

Two officers on Broadway. *Courtesy Federal Bureau of Prisons Archives.*

Adjoining cells and two unidentified inmates, ca. 1960. *Courtesy Golden Gate National Recreation Area, Phil Dollison collection, P 89-055.005n.*

Inmates on the recreation yard. *Courtesy Federal Bureau of Prisons Archives.*

Mess hall during a meal, ca. 1950. *Courtesy Golden Gate National Recreation Area, Don Denevi collection, P 83-166.050n.*

Inmate band playing in the mess hall at Christmastime, ca. 1960. *Courtesy Golden Gate National Recreation Area, Arnold W. Peters collection, P 85-116-012.*

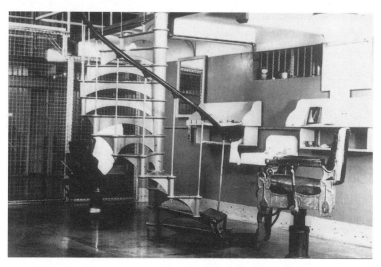

The Alcatraz barbershop, ca. 1950. *Courtesy Golden Gate National Recreation Area, Don Denevi collection, P 83-144.118.*

Inmates returning to the cell house from the industries building, ca. 1955. The Hill Tower, Model Tower, and catwalk to the Model Building are in the upper section of the photograph. *Courtesy Golden Gate National Recreation Area, Phil Dollison collection, P 89-055.009p.*

D Block Treatment Unit with dark cells. *Courtesy Federal Bureau of Prisons Archives.*

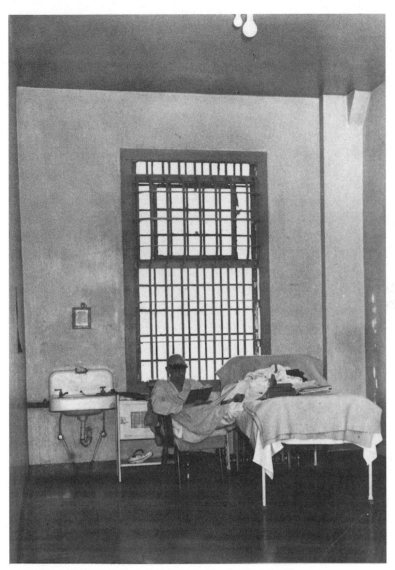

Robert Stroud, the "Birdman," in his segregated cell in the Alcatraz
hospital. *Courtesy Federal Bureau of Prisons Archives.*

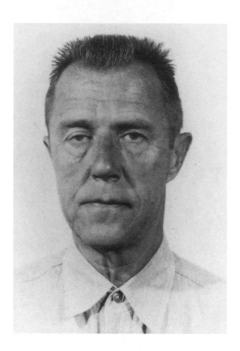 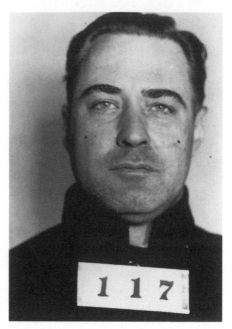

Clockwise from top left: Alvin "Creepy Karpis" Karpavicz, one of the inmate leaders and self-appointed head of the kitchen crew; George "Machine Gun" Kelly, bank robber, kidnapper, and accomplished storyteller; James "Blackie" Audette, the "right person" to know in the kitchen; Joseph Barsock, who was killed by another inmate in the prison barbershop; and Aaron Walter Burgett, who died in a 1958 escape attempt. *Courtesy National Archives and Records Administration—Pacific Region, San Francisco.*

The Control Center, ca. 1950. *Courtesy Golden Gate National Recreation Area, Don Denevi collection, P 83-144.115.*

Correctional officer operating the locking system for opening and closing cell doors, ca. 1960. *Courtesy Golden Gate National Recreation Area, Phil Dollison collection, P 89-055.089.*

Gregory wearing officer's uniform, ca. 1960.
Private collection of George H. Gregory.

An inmate and Gregory in the San Francisco federal court building, ca. 1961.
Courtesy San Francisco Chronicle.

S. P. ALCATRAZ, CALIFORNIA
WEEK DAY ROSTER

POST	8 AM to 5 PM	POST	9 to 5:30	DAYS OFF
Captain	Bergen	W. R. 8:30-5:30	Kirkpatrick	Starbuck
Construction		Captain's Clerk	Walters	Kinahelos
Construction		Cellhouse West	DeVincenzi	Mitchell
Garbage Detail	Collet	Truck Officer	Peterson	Hudson
West Gun #2	Fisher, J	Yard Wall Relief	Royl	Barnett
Tower #3	Meushaw	Yard Week Days	Cropper	Ward
Tower #4	Robbins	Barber Shop	McGoren	Roy
Laundry #1	Bloomquist	Utility #1	Jennings	Fisher, F
Laundry #2	Abend	Library	Henry	Fontenot
Model Shop	Blair	Cell Inspection		Sutfin
Brush Shop	Christopherson	Cell Inspection		O'Branovich
Tailor Shop	Burns	Cell Inspection		Allen
Glove Shop	Barker	Lock Inspection	Holbrook	Ryohner
Cell Inspection	Smith			Prindle

POST	12M to 8 AM	8 AM to 4:30	4 PM to 12M	DAYS OFF (M)
Lieutenant	Severson		Mahan	Moore
Cellhouse	Carew		Willmore	Tennison
Control Center	Baker, G	Black	Orr	Burrows
Dock & Patrol	Dolby	Baucom	Buell	Long, W
Tower #1	Gregory	Bush	Shelton	
Hospital	Davoren	Valentino	Chapman	DAYS OFF (B)
Main Gate	Norris	Schwab	Levinson	Greiner
Tower #2	Mattox	Sendek	Pepper	Griffiths
Treatment Unit	Burlingame	Martin, D	Munyon	Spencer
West Gallery	Winegar	Martin, J	McPherson	
Barge	Hart			

STOREROOM: Keefe
Moffitt
Segelstrom

POST	7:30 to 4 PM	7:15 to 3:15	7:15 to 3:45	ANNUAL LEAVE
Lt. Cellhouse	Siminski			Whitaker
Cellhouse I/C		Butterfield		Baker, R.
Construction		Kidney		Boylas
Locksmith		Dove		Craven
Mail Censor		Reische		Landers
Clothing Room		Greenwood		Duncan
Yard Wall		Richberger		Ordway
Cellhouse #2			Collinge	
Utility #2		Midstokke		
Cell Inspection				
Cell Inspection				
Cell Inspection				

	7:15 to 4:15		
Dock In-Charge	Welch		

	5:45 AM to 2:15	10:15 to 6:45
Tower #5	Bowen	Cox

SICK	SPECIAL
Waller	Rifle Range: Irving
Welwyn	(9 to 5:30)
Pehrson	Work Area: Pahl
Schaefer	(8 to 5)

	6 AM to 2 PM		10:45 to 6:45
Culinary #1	Yates	Cul #2	Glaum

Seward: Clothing Room (9:30 to 4:00P) 7:15 to 3:45
Training: Winthrop: Hospital (8:00A to 2:30P--Cellhouse (2:30P to 4:30P)
LaCentra: Work Area (8:00A to 5:00P)
Herbert, S.: Culinary (8:00A to 4:30P) to 2 PM
Inman: West Gallery (8:00A to 4:30P)   TOTAL 107   *M Bergen*

(11-27-54 → Hamilton)

CAPTAIN P. R. Bergen   DATE MONDAY, NOVEMBER 22, 1954

Copy of a weekday roster of officers' assignments.
Private collection of George H. Gregory.

Personnel F ~m No. 45
Approved r~oruary 1, 1951

UNITED STATES DEPARTMENT OF JUSTICE
FEDERAL PRISON SYSTEM

EMPLOYEE PERFORMANCE RATING REPORT

ALCATRAZ
(Institution)

GEORGE H. GREGORY
(Name of employee)

(Initials
of employee)

4-1-61 - 3-31-62
(Period covered)

CORRECTIONAL OFFICER
(Position title)

CI-22
(Position No.)

☐ Satisfactory
☒ Outstanding
☐ Unsatisfactory

Fred D Malan
(Rating Officer preparing rating)

April 5, 1962
(Date of Preparation)

T D Bradley
(Reviewing Officer)

FP1—LK—11-10-51—3750 sets—8433

4-6-62
(Date of Review)

Gregory's final performance rating, April 6, 1962.
Private collection of George H. Gregory.

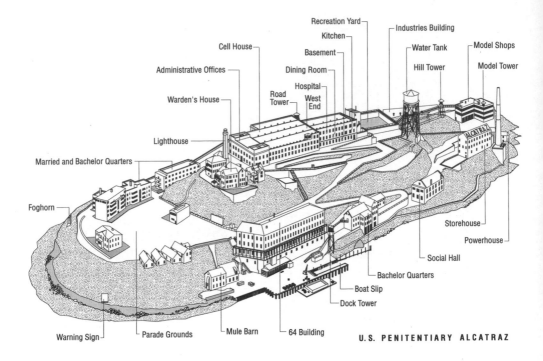

Recreation Yard

Kitchen

Basement

Dining Room

Hospital

West End

Road Tower

Cell House

Administrative Offices

Warden's House

Lighthouse

Married and Bachelor Quarters

Foghorn

Industries Building

Water Tank

Hill Tower

Model Shops

Model Tower

Storehouse

Powerhouse

Social Hall

Bachelor Quarters

Boat Slip

Dock Tower

Mule Barn

64 Building

Parade Grounds

Warning Sign

U.S. PENITENTIARY ALCATRAZ

Clockwise from top left: Diagrams of the U.S. Penitentiary, Alcatraz; the Alcatraz cell house and administrative offices; and the Alcatraz kitchen and dining wing, hospital wing, and clothing and shower room. *Courtesy Federal Bureau of Prisons Archives, edited by Greg Coiner of Art Works.*

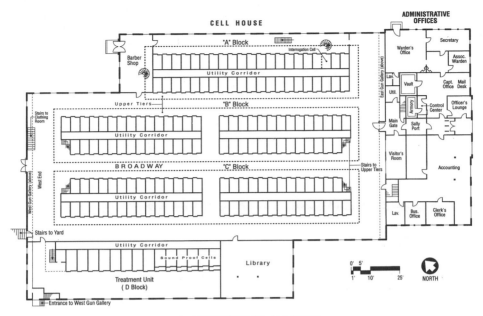

CELL HOUSE

ADMINISTRATIVE OFFICES

U.S. PENITENTIARY ALCATRAZ

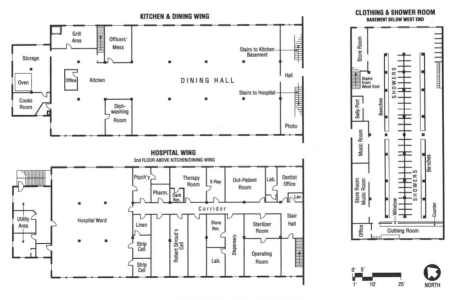

KITCHEN & DINING WING

CLOTHING & SHOWER ROOM
BASEMENT BELOW WEST END

HOSPITAL WING
2nd FLOOR ABOVE KITCHEN/DINING WING

U.S. PENITENTIARY ALCATRAZ

12

Alcatraz and the Courts

Alcatraz hated to go to court. For some reason or other, no matter what the case was or how seemingly clear-cut the facts, it was not the inmate or inmates involved but Alcatraz itself that ended up being put on trial. In my long tenure at Alcatraz, I can think of only one inmate—and one officer—who was found guilty in the federal court of San Francisco.

San Francisco had a great dislike for Alcatraz. The general feeling was that the prison hurt the image of the city. Every time I heard this, I would smile weakly because I couldn't see how Alcatraz could affect the image of such a beautiful city. But perhaps this attitude influenced the decisions made in the courts.

The officer found guilty was a sorry person who had been hired off the street with no investigation and given very little training. He was caught bringing in some innocuous contraband to an inmate. Unimportant as it was, it was still illegal. The inmate immediately informed on the officer. Swope was the warden at the time and made a big issue of it. This fellow was convicted, and deservedly so.

The inmate who was convicted committed a most bizarre murder. It occurred in the barbershop as the result of a lovers' quarrel. The killer was the barber for black inmates, Curly Thomas, and his victim was Joseph Barsock. When Curly was given the job of barber, several of us questioned the assignment. We knew a number of the other black inmates didn't like him and would resent his cutting their hair.

It is still not clear to me why Barsock was let out of his cell and allowed to go to the barbershop. He was not on the schedule for that day.

They were lovers, these two. Curly was older and smaller than Barsock. On this day, Curly took his scissors—a pair of long-bladed shears with sharp points—and, according to the report, shoved them into the carotid artery of his lover, who was sitting in the barber's chair. Barsock jumped out of the chair, ran a few steps, and fell. Curly knelt at the side of this man whose life was spurting away and began sucking up the blood and mumbling in his peculiar speech, "I love you. I love you. I love you."

Meanwhile, I was having lunch in the officers' mess. Selkirk, an inexperienced and naive officer, had just relieved me at the hospital. I had said jokingly as I left, "Well, Selkirk, I hope nothing happens today, but if it does I hope it happens while you're the hospital officer."

When I returned from lunch it was to find a very pale and glassy-eyed Selkirk. Hurriedly opening the gate, he said, "You got your wish. It happened while you were at lunch."

"What happened, for goodness sake?"

"You'll see," a much shaken Selkirk said as he rushed down the hospital stairs.

And I did see. Barsock was laid out in the storeroom with an identity tag on his big toe and a look of childish serenity on his face in spite of the ugly gash in his neck. He looked so young one couldn't help but wonder what might have been in store for him had he grown up in a different environment. Although hundreds of children in the slums became criminals in order to survive, thousands of others seemed to be able to overcome the obstacles and make it in society.

During my testimony at Curly's trial, I was questioned by the defense attorney. "Mr. Gregory, did you search Barsock's clothing?"

"Yes, sir, I did." It was in the line of duty that I searched his clothing.

"Did you find a weapon in his clothing?"

"Yes, I did."

"Could you describe it?"

"It was a metal crochet-type hook, about six inches long, that's used in the making of brushes. The hook had been filed off, making it very sharp."

"Would it have been hard for him to get at the hook?"

"It would have taken a modicum of effort."

"What's that?" said the judge. "Speak up, Mr. Gregory."

I turned toward the judge and repeated my answer. There were stares back and forth among all concerned.

During a recess when we were all standing around jawboning, the judge came up, looked at me somewhat distastefully, and said, "What in the hell did you mean by 'modicum'?"

We all laughed. It was as good a way as any to ease some of the tension of a murder trial.

Curly's defense attorney made good use of my testimony concerning Barsock's weapon and was able to get a sentence of twenty-five years to run consecutively with Curly's current sentences. Otherwise, Curly might have got life—which was what most everybody thought he deserved. Even so, it was a rare case of a conviction of an inmate at Alcatraz.

All the trial and sentence meant to Curly was that he got to be the star of the show for a brief time. He wore a nice brown suit, compliments of Alcatraz. He put on the best act you ever saw of writing copious notes as he listened to the different witnesses. I never saw those notes but I knew from censoring mail that he couldn't possibly have been writing down the complicated testimony that was being given. He was all but illiterate.

It was difficult to understand Curly when he spoke. He had a jargon of his own. He never initiated conversation with officers but responded politely and respectfully when spoken to. And he ignored the other inmates—except when they crossed his path. He was forever being sent to TU for various acts of aggression directed toward other black inmates—never toward white inmates. In TU, Curly often served as the orderly because he was efficient, dependable, and didn't give favors.

Curly's mind was strictly on the most brutal and cruel aspects of life. He could make deadly weapons from almost anything. He even sharpened the bone from a T-bone steak and carried it in his pocket. It was well suited to Curly's preferred kind of attack, which was to sever the carotid artery, and it went through the snitch boxes* without being detected. After Curly's T-bone weapon was found, we began to remove the bones from steaks before serving them.

Curly certainly was an odd individual. He was a slight fellow, and terribly ticklish—it was difficult to shake him down. If you touched him anywhere, he would jump and quiver. When you asked him to raise his bare feet so you could see the soles, he would shake all over for fear you would touch him there. He could not tolerate that.

Curly received letters occasionally from his family, wishing him good luck and so on. Judging by the letters, they were proud, hard-working people. Once, they sent a picture of their new house. They were very poor, and being able to buy a house was quite a thing. Curly was really impressed. This was one time he approached other people. He couldn't help but show the picture to everybody.

Curly had several behaviors that were peculiar to him. One example that comes to mind occurred when I was in charge of TU and Curly was my orderly.

*A "snitch box" was a metal detector constructed in the shape of a door frame that the inmates walked through when returning from the industries. Metal detectors were also used on the dock and at the main gate to the cell house.

He was out of his cell taking care of the janitorial duties when there was a stabbing in the yard.

Somehow, Curly knew something had happened. He jumped up on the sink and looked out the TU window into the yard below. Of course, I also looked. Mann, an inmate, was lying there on the concrete, bleeding bright red blood from his head to his feet. Officers were steering another inmate, Laiten, toward the stairs—he had used a knife on Mann.

Curly started giggling, laughing, and keening in a weird, high-pitched voice. It was a sound I had never heard before and hoped never to hear again. There he was up on the sink, shivering, shaking, and dancing on tiptoe. It was as though he was in some kind of orgiastic ecstasy. He was completely out of this world.

Knowing the officers would be bringing Laiten into TU, I had to get Curly locked in his cell. I told him to get down, but he paid no attention to me. It was all I could do to pull him off the sink. He continued wailing as I guided him to his cell and locked the door.

By the time I got to the TU entrance, the officers were there with my new charge. The lieutenant stayed to help me with Laiten. As we stripped him, he kept repeating over and over again in a hysterical yet joyful kind of voice, "He had the knife. He had the knife." Laiten gave no indication that he was aware of us or his surroundings. It was unreal.

The crazy talk from Laiten was bad enough, but I kept hearing Curly in his cell, which was right around the corner. He kept up his inhuman, hellish giggling and mumbling in a bizarre, terrifying garble.

Then the lieutenant's voice joined the din as he stood there staring into Laiten's face, repeating, "He's not going to make it. He's not going to make it." Although his voice was more normal than the other two, it was no less disturbing. The color was draining from the lieutenant's face and his arms hung loose at his sides. He was no longer helping me with Laiten. He was about to go into shock.

I grabbed Laiten by the arm and said, "Let's go." His eyes flashed me a look of hatred but he went along without resistance as I paraded him down to the Hole. I'd had enough of this psychodrama.

Except for the insane babbling from Laiten and Curly, TU was absolutely quiet.

On another occasion, I heard that strange voice from Curly again. This time, I was the TU officer on the evening watch. In the evening after supper had been served, the TU inmates liked to stand at the bars in their cells and watch the lights come on in the city. They also told stories of their lives. Some of them were good storytellers, very interesting, and I used to enjoy those times.

In addition to watching the lights and telling stories, they did a lot of studying, especially on their Spanish courses. Several of them were taking Spanish: The word was out that Bolivia would accept escaped inmates if they had plenty of money and if they married a native woman. In the event of a successful escape, these inmates wanted to be prepared.

On this evening, strangely enough, Curly Thomas decided to take the floor. This surprised everybody because he was never one to talk very much. But this time he got up to the bars in his cell and began to talk and laugh. Everybody stopped their activities and listened to him. He was putting on quite a show. He spoke in the same weird, high-pitched, screechy voice he used when Laiten stabbed Mann, and he continued for twenty minutes. It was difficult to understand him, but after a few sentences you sort of calibrated your mind to comprehend his jargon.

He was telling about his life on the outside, specifically about how he used young girls who had just reached puberty. He got them started on drugs by stabbing them with a knife and then giving them a little taste to get them high and ease the pain. He bought them candy and soft drinks. And, of course, he used them sexually. He enjoyed them most when they were thoroughly hooked and dependent on him for drugs.

While dancing around in his cell, Curly described in detail what he did to those girls when they began to suffer from withdrawal symptoms. He teased, tortured, and forced them into inhuman sexual acts. He reported their cries and screams for mercy in ugly detail.

Tough as the other inmates were and as much as they were used to the raw side of life, they listened with looks of disgust, horror, anger, and even hatred on their faces. I think everybody in TU believed every word of what Curly said. I certainly did. He was not the type who would have made up something like that, nor did he think there was anything wrong with what he did. It was just a way of life. A way for him to enjoy himself.

Several black inmates from Washington, D.C., had known Curly, or had known about him, on the outside. They wanted nothing to do with him. They told me how he would cheat at dice or cards. If challenged, he would pull a knife. He had a reputation, even when he was a teenage kid, of being a killer. He wasn't very old when he came to Alcatraz. I doubt if he was any older than his late twenties.

It seemed no black inmate was safe from Curly's cutting weapons. One day in the dining hall, he seriously stabbed a fellow inmate from D.C. When the victim recovered enough to leave the hospital, he sorrowfully told me that he couldn't understand Curly's attacking him because their families were very close.

It is a wonder Curly lived as long as he did. When Alcatraz closed, he was transferred to Leavenworth. As it was told to me, you couldn't count the number of holes in Curly when the other inmates got him where they wanted him and stuck their knives in him.

Following my testimony at Curly's trial, I watched the attitude toward me change subtly. The prosecuting attorney didn't appreciate my testimony because he wanted a life sentence and didn't get it. Many of my colleagues didn't like it because they also felt Curly should get the maximum penalty. I didn't *want* to help the defense, but my testimony had that effect.

I wondered what my colleagues would have done. Would those who were making snide remarks about my testimony have handled the discovery of the weapon differently? It caused me some introspection and I came to the conclusion that I couldn't have handled it any other way.

As an officer of the law, I was to turn in any weapon I found. I found the weapon in Barsock's clothing. I turned it in to my supervisor. I had fulfilled my responsibility as I saw it. As to my testimony at Curly's trial, I swore to tell the truth and did just that.

Although Curly never said anything about my testimony, I got the feeling he thought I had testified for him. He didn't understand that I had testified to the truth—not for or against anyone. He did not understand "honesty" and "truth" as I do.

Apparently as a result of my testimony, I came to be known among the black inmate population as an officer who could be counted on when they were in trouble. It was not my intention to build a following among the black inmates, but something like that developed over the years. Although no one ever directly spoke of it, I could tell when a black inmate changed his attitude toward me.

I was called on many times to represent black inmates at good-time disciplinary trials.* I'm not sure why, because I never won a case. However, the inmates seemed to feel they got good representation.

Before a case came to disciplinary court, it had been thoroughly investigated by an officer other than the accusing officer. Guilt was involved. I didn't like being in the position of trying to defend a guilty inmate, but it was part of my job. I did the best I could.

My defense was more or less tongue-in-cheek. I would say something like this: "We have to consider that Joe here is doing hard time. He is having difficulty adjusting to our strict rules and regulations here at Alcatraz. Then he also has trouble at home."

*A "good-time trial" was one in which an inmate's misdeed was serious enough to cause the loss of all or a portion of his accumulated good time.

The usual response from the court was, "We will take that into consideration."

From accusing officers, my colleagues, the attitude was, Thanks a lot, you bastard. Again, I don't know why, since I never won a case.

With the exception of a few inmates like Curly, there was a code of truth and honesty in the black population that I can best explain by relating an incident. This occurred when I was serving as the kitchen officer, with a mostly black crew. A meal requiring knives had been served. After the meal, I counted the knives carefully in the dining hall. The number tallied. Then another officer picked up the knives and put them in a stainless steel tray for the washing process. The knives were under the supervision of an officer the entire time.

When all the inmates were back in their cells except the kitchen crew, I counted the knives into the security cabinet. One knife was missing.

I looked at Irwin, one of the kitchen crew. He sensed by the way I looked at him that something was wrong. He also knew that he was the last inmate to legally handle the knives. Suddenly his face became a mask of fear, puzzlement, and anger. That told me Irwin had not taken the knife. I looked around at the other inmates—all of them stood silently with eyes averted.

I called the crew together.

"The last one of you to have had a chance at the knives was Irwin. He will be the one blamed. You have put him in a bad spot. And you know what will happen to him. Irwin will miss his chance to get out of Alcatraz and then to be paroled."

I stared at the tops of their heads. Their eyes were on the floor.

"Now," I continued as I pointed to a place on the counter, "I am going to walk from here to the dining hall door. I will not look back. When I get to the door, I am going to turn around and come back. I want to see that knife right here when I get back."

I walked to the door, turned, walked back, picked up the knife from the spot I had pointed to, and locked it in the security cabinet. The inmates were busy with their assigned duties. Nothing more was said about the incident.

One case that shows how difficult it was to convict an inmate is the sickening trial of Laiten for the merciless killing of Karney, a very popular inmate. Laiten was a powerfully built, good-looking man—blue eyes, baby face. One's first impression would be that he was a really nice fellow. Laiten came from a broken home, went from reform school into the army during the Korean police action, immediately got into trouble, and was finally shipped to Alcatraz. His vicious antisocial behavior was such that a simple fistfight was never good enough to settle a problem. He had to hurt badly, even kill.

When Laiten got to Alcatraz, he was soon in trouble again. In fact, he seemed to be a chronic troublemaker. He was in and out of TU. It was when he was not confined to TU and therefore had yard privileges that he attacked Mann with a knife, stabbing him repeatedly, nearly cutting out his tongue. Miraculously, Mann lived. The population was not offended by this mutilation because they didn't like Mann and wouldn't have been disturbed had he died. Laiten was tried for that and acquitted. Then he had a fight with Karney, who was an on-and-off buddy. As opposed to Laiten, Karney had grown up in a good home. When they became adversaries, they were very bitter adversaries.

Laiten had been in TU a long time for trying to attack Karney. The attempt was made in the yard and Karney had run fast enough to stay out of reach. They were both put in TU as a result of the fracas. Karney did his time and was released with an assignment to work in the clothing room.

Some time later, after many promises that everything would be okay, Laiten was brought out of TU and put back into the population. After a few days, he complained about his shoes not fitting and was let out of his cell to go to the clothing room to get another pair. At the top of the stairs, according to the rules, an officer hand-searched him.

At this time, officers were timid about touching inmates near the genitals. There had been many cases of inmates falsely claiming to have been hurt during searches. The limited extent of the search made it possible for Laiten to carry a knife into the clothing room. He had secured it alongside his penis.

On seeing Karney, Laiten wasted no time in wielding his knife. His first slash was down the left arm, which he laid wide open. The second was into Karney's heart, which was cut practically in two. Karney staggered a few steps and fell dead.

Laiten was taken to court in what would seem to be a tight case against him. He had definitely killed Karney. The case lasted a couple of weeks. I was one of those who took a turn escorting Laiten to court.

The defense, thinking they might help their cause, found some pretext to ask Laiten to remove his shirt and undershirt, showing his bare torso. He was all muscle, a fine specimen of a powerful physique. It was a smart move. There was no question about the favorable impression made by Laiten's body, blond hair, and baby-blue eyes. Surely such a lovely lad could not commit so brutal a murder.

One woman reporter was especially impressed. She couldn't keep her hands off Laiten. She got as close as she could to him and "oohed" and "aahed" while asking questions. It was enough to nauseate anybody, not to mention me. I had seen what those beautiful muscles had done to other human beings.

Laiten was acquitted on self-defense. He claimed to have been unarmed until he took the knife from Karney.

Although Laiten was acquitted by the federal court, the inmate population did not acquit him. They hated Laiten for the cold-blooded murder of Karney, whom they had liked.

Laiten spent the rest of his Alcatraz days in TU. To have put him into the population would have been tantamount to setting him up to be murdered.

13

Mail Censor

Many officers coveted the job of mail censor because it required little direct contact with the inmates—but not me. I wanted to be where the action was.

Needless to say, I was bored stiff with this assignment. Reading every inmate letter, going out or coming in, was part of the job. A typical incoming letter might read: "Dear Son, The White Sox won today. Hope you are O.K. Love, Dad." Pulling the inmate's correspondence file, I recorded receipt of the letter. Then, leaning back in my chair, I pushed my cap off my forehead and read another letter.

As the mail censor, you could choose to ignore what you learned about the inmates or you could become depressed. The life some of them had before finding themselves in prison had been very grim. The life they would go back to after serving their time didn't look any better. However, in some cases I learned that an inmate had a family that cared about him and looked forward to having him return home. These relatives would write regularly to keep the inmate informed of family and community news.

When the inmates talked about their families, they usually bragged about how much money their fathers made and how well educated various members of their family were. Walking down an aisle in the cell house one day, I overheard one of these sessions. As I walked in front of the cell of the inmate who was talking, he stopped and gave me a murderous stare. I had interrupted his illusion, his fantasy—his escape into a dream world. To him, I represented the reality that he was in prison and the truth about his family—his alcoholic father worked part-time as a day laborer. In that instant, the inmate hated me for knowing that what he was saying was not true. The fact that he knew I would never divulge the information to other inmates didn't matter.

Inmates could write any number of letters to members of Congress, the bureau, or the courts. A locked box was provided in the cell house for letters going to the bureau. Each day, two officers opened the box and put all the letters into a pouch for direct shipment to the bureau.

The inmates' correspondence to family and friends was supervised in the hope that they would lose contact with people who might be a negative influence on them. They were allowed to write a total of seven letters per month to people on an approved list. Similarly, inmates could receive letters only from these people. The parole board investigated and approved the correspondents in advance. The investigations were performed by whatever law enforcement or social service agency in the local area could handle the job.

If a letter came in from a person who was not approved, it was to be returned. However, when I read such a letter I considered the inmate, whether or not he was getting any mail, and the letter itself. Did this sound like a stable person with whom the inmate might be interested in corresponding? If so, I told the inmate about the letter and asked if he would like to have the person approved.

In one case the inmate said, "No, I don't want anything to do with that guy. He's a do-gooder that just drives everybody crazy." The letter was from a minister in his hometown.

If the inmate wanted the person added to his list, I went to the parole officer and asked him to start the proceedings for approval.

You could almost tell how long an inmate had been imprisoned by looking at his correspondence file. They often started out getting mail from wives, parents, siblings, friends, teachers, and ministers—everybody on their approved list. After a few years, the number of letters began to dwindle. As almost all of our charges had been in prison a number of years before they got to us, we had a minimum of mail coming and going. A great many of the inmates had lost all contact with family and friends—no entry had been made in their correspondence file for years.

Some inmates corresponded with members of their family who were also in prison. One guy wrote to his mother and wife at a federal women's prison.

One man who wrote to several people in his small hometown did not want to put a return address on his letters. I put his letters through without the return. When another officer refused to accept his letters without the return, the inmate sent a kite* out to the associate warden requesting permission not to use the return. The associate warden put the letter on my desk. I put it in the mailbag. The inmate enjoyed corresponding with the people on his list and he didn't want the

*"Kite" was the prison term for a written message from an inmate to the administration.

postman and whoever else might see his letters to know they came from Alcatraz. An unreal kind of fear had built up in people's minds about Alcatraz and its occupants.

The inmates were allowed to write on both sides of one sheet of paper. One day, I read a letter written on both sides from edge to edge and top to bottom in writing that was so small and jumbled it was almost impossible to read. After struggling with it for several minutes, I sent it back to the inmate with instructions to rewrite it so I could read it if he wanted it mailed. Although I could decipher the worst handwriting in the world, I couldn't see any reason why this guy should not write so it could be read easily—he had the skills to do it.

A day or so later, Warden Madigan walked by and dropped the same letter on my desk without saying a word. I put it in an envelope and sent it back to the inmate. The next time a letter came from that guy, I could read it.

A number of officers were unable to handle the demands of the mail censor's job; they especially lacked the particular skill of being able to read between the lines. This ability came from knowing something about the inmate involved and having some understanding of his problems in the institution as well as on the outside. The inmates had many clever ways of trying to sneak out messages.

Quotes, or perhaps misquotes, from the Bible were used in letters to convey covert messages. The name of a friend, partner, or enemy might be sent out in this way. The location of stolen money could be hidden in a story or poem. Some quotations were innocent—you had to know the inmate to determine which letters to send out and which to send back. There wasn't much you could do about messages such as, "Say hello to Annie and tell her it wasn't that way." I didn't know what this message meant, but I knew there had never been an "Annie" mentioned in the inmate's file. I sent the letter on its way to the addressee.

Many letters were requests for money—attorney fees was usually the reason given. Seldom did an inmate admit to his own guilt—it was his attorney's fault that he was sent to prison. This accounted for a large number of the writs that ended up on the mail censor's desk. Making pruno and writing writs went neck and neck as a favorite pastime. Not that the same inmates engaged in both activities. Some of those who wrote writs made a full-time job of it. They might send out several a week. The serious writs were sent on to the intended recipient. As a favor to the busy court system, the unfounded, ridiculous writs were put in the wastebasket.

In one case, a physically slight inmate had mouthed off to a very tough con. Officers broke up the fight before the little con got hurt and put both inmates in the Hole. The little con sent out a writ claiming the officers had brutally beaten him, burned his forehead with cigarette butts, and tried to make him sterile by injuring his genitals. None of this had happened, so the writ went into the wastebasket. The little con was trying to get a transfer to another institution in order to avoid facing the tough con when they were released from the Hole.

The mail censor shared an office with the captain and his clerk. The office was located in the administrative wing to the right of the front entrance to the main building. Next door on the right was the associate warden's office and the warden's secretary; a sharp turn to the left took you into the warden's office. The business and accounting offices were in the left wing of the administrative offices. One thing about being out front—when it was time to go home, you just left. There was no waiting around for gates to be opened.

The mail censor also escorted inmates to court appearances. On one of these occasions when there was a recess and the inmate was locked up, I was invited into the judge's chambers by the clerk. As the clerk was discoursing on the behind-the-scenes workings of the office staff, he mentioned that they read every writ that came to them, regardless of how foolish it might seem.

I smiled at the clerk and said, "Well, I guess we mail censors on The Rock are doing you a big favor."

"Oh? How could that be?"

"We read all the mail sent out by the inmates and if a writ is foolish or plainly untruthful, we simply file them in the 'round file.'"

"What?" shouted the judge. He had been sitting at his desk reading some material. Even sitting down, he was a very impressive, powerful-looking man, with a thick mane of white hair, white moustache, steely blue eyes, red cheeks, and a stern demeanor. "What do you do with those writs?" he said in a hard voice.

I was taken aback by the judge's reaction. Before I could get my wits together to repeat what I had said, the judge said, "I don't want to hear what you said and I don't want you or your colleagues ever in the future to destroy a writ. Mister, uh . . ."

"Gregory."

"Mr. Gregory, any writ will be judged by the courts and only by the courts as to its merit. Even a writ written on toilet paper is a legal document and must be handled as such. It must be given serious consideration. It is up to a judge to decide whether or not the courts will hear it."

"Yes, sir," I meekly said. But the judge was already back to his reading.

After being bawled out by the judge, I sent all the writs through. It must have been at least a year or so later that I again escorted an inmate to the same court. On a lunch break, I happened to see the clerk going down the hall with a big stack of legal documents.

"See these?" he said to me. "These are all writs from prisoners and every one of them has to be read."

"That doesn't surprise me. I probably dropped most of them in the mailbag myself."

"Don't get me wrong, we don't want you to start throwing them away again."

One inmate sent out at least one writ a day. His writs all made the same plea—that he was not guilty of the charges, and if he had had a good attorney, he would not be in prison. Eventually I opened a letter from the judge in which he returned the inmate's writ, stating that it was being "denied with prejudice." I found myself smiling—so the judge had heard all he wanted to hear from our writ-writing inmate.

Although he didn't write any more writs, this inmate didn't stop writing. He wrote a simple but pleasant letter to his "wife." I couldn't find anything in his file about his having a wife. But by this time, society had become less strict about who might be called a spouse. Not seeing any harm in the letter, I put it through.

The response from the woman seemed like double-talk, but it also sounded as if she knew the inmate and had some feeling for him. The following day, a letter crossed my desk addressed to the woman. The con was boldly telling her to become a prostitute and send him the money she earned. He told her he wanted to hire an attorney so he could get out of prison.

I sent the letter back with the explanation that the woman would have to be approved by the parole board before he could continue his correspondence.

I had a lot of overtime built up and was more or less shanghaied by the captain and sent on vacation. Inmates knew which officer was assigned to what post, what his days off were, when he went on vacation, and when he would return.

When I returned after a week off, the warden—who at that time was Olin Blackwell—came out to the mail desk, handed me a letter, and walked away. This indicated he was giving me full authority to handle it.

I took out the letter and read a blistering attack on the warden for allowing "the enclosed letter to be mailed." It was from the inmate's "wife" and the enclosed letter was the one I had refused to send.

I checked the inmate's correspondence file and noted that the letter had gone out to the woman while I was away. The inmate had simply kept it until I went on vacation and then sent it out again. Frankly, I was glad the woman was so infuriated about being told to prostitute herself for the writ-writing inmate. But I was also sorry that such a letter had been allowed to go out.

I went in and told Warden Blackwell what I had done—or, in this case, not done, since I had refused to send the letter. By way of response, the warden gave me an ingratiating smile and just looked at me with his big blue eyes.

After assuring myself that that was his total answer, I left, taking the two letters with me. I thought maybe I should write to the woman explaining how the letter had been sent out. Then I thought that might lead her to further action. I round-filed the letters and never heard any more about them.

As I have said, I also dealt with letters involving the infamous Birdman. Women kept writing to Robert Stroud or to the warden on his behalf, begging that he be released in their custody. Warden Madigan had answered such letters, trying to discourage the women's interest in Stroud—saying he was not the fellow they thought he was. We often got requests from women who asked to be allowed to visit Stroud or some other inmate who was unknown to them except by name and reputation.

One day I was sitting in the mail office, swearing under my breath at an inmate's letter, when Mr. Wages stopped in front of my desk. He put an official-looking document under my nose and said, "Here, sign this." Wages was one of that ever-increasing group of officers who, because of their closeness to the higher-ups and ability to use a typewriter, were getting jobs far removed from inmates. It was an aspect of the growing bureaucracy of the Federal Bureau of Prisons.

Wages was short, fat, and rather insipid. He tried to act like a real stalwart prison officer. I sort of pitied him, but I also felt some contempt for him.

"So what kind of crap do you want me to sign now?" I asked sarcastically.

"It's your promotion," Wages said loudly and curtly. Then he looked around, leaned over, and said to me in a whisper, "You could have got this a long time ago if you had shown respect for people you have no respect for."

"Never end a sentence with a preposition," I said. Wages gave me a blank look. Obviously he didn't get it.

I smiled as I signed at the X. I was now a senior officer, no longer a junior officer. The Alcatraz plumbing line had already spread the news, so this was no surprise. I handed the paper back to Wages and said, "Say 'thank you' to the warden for me, will you?"

Wages said over his shoulder as he left, "This came from the bureau, not the warden."

I remember that promotion with some irony because it was at the same desk as mail censor sometime later that I almost lost my job, along with an impressive amount of money.

Inmates sometimes received money in small amounts from family members or friends. These amounts were credited to their accounts and deposit slips were sent to the inmates.

In this case, a large check was made out to an inmate who was a state prisoner. The check was drawn on the treasury of his home state. Wondering why this should be, I went to the cashier to ask whether this could be a mistake and the check was actually intended for Alcatraz. (When a state prisoner was transferred to Alcatraz, the state paid the cost of keeping that prisoner.)

"Don't bring your problems to me. I've got enough of my own," was the answer I got from the new cashier.

I went to the associate warden, who said, "Well, you can never tell about these cons."

Reluctantly, I finally made out a deposit slip and sent a copy to the inmate. About a week later, Mel Kidney, a wise prison officer, told me to come see him after work.

"Greg, one of my informers gave me some information that is not very good for you," Kidney gravely said. "I don't know what it's all about, but this guy, Logan, a Massachusetts con, apparently got a lot of money and is buying savings bonds as fast as he can. My informer told me he didn't want to see a good officer like you hurt by a bum like him. He knew there had to be something fishy about the money, but didn't know what."

I headed for the front office, thinking, So much for going through channels and the chain of command. I'm going straight to the warden.

I waved to Bertrand and bolted into the warden's office. "Warden Madigan, I've got problems. Have you got a minute?" It was the end of the day and the warden was on his way home.

"Sure. What's the problem, Gregory?"

I told him about the check I had credited to the inmate's account.

"That would be the money for keeping this character here. Apparently he was quite a problem back in his home state," the warden said as he picked up the phone and dialed. "I'm calling Sherman."

Sherman was an F.B.I. man working in the San Francisco office. He was a special agent assigned to Alcatraz. I had worked with him on a number of cases and knew him fairly well. I was confident he could get me out of this mess if anybody could.

While waiting for the call to go through, the warden said, "Do you realize that if the money is not returned you could become liable and have to pay it back?"

I felt a tingle go down my spine and my eyes narrowed as I estimated the number of paychecks it would take. Here I was doing the administration a favor by staying on the mail desk because it was hard to find a replacement, and now they were going to try to make me pay back the money? Somehow it didn't seem fair.

"Greg," the warden said as he looked at the clock, "you'll have time to catch the boat. Go over to town, have a couple of stiff ones and a good dinner. Try not to worry about this. I'm sure we can work it out."

I went to town all right, had some stiff ones and a good dinner, but I can't say I didn't worry. For one thing, it would be a long time before I would have another evening out if I had to pay back the money, and I would hate being taken by a con.

But Warden Madigan was as good as his word. He did work it out and retrieved all but about twenty dollars of the money.

As for me, I got a written reprimand handed to me by the warden.

"Warden," I said bitterly, "all the time I have spent on this damn mail desk I never even got a 'thank you' or commendation for a job that most of your officers can't even handle. I make one mistake and I get a written reprimand put in my file."

The warden turned and walked away.

It was at a going-away party for a retiring officer that the warden asked permission to make a little speech.

"Actually, all I want to do is take this opportunity to make a presentation to Gregory. You won't object to sharing the limelight, will you, Harvey?"

"I don't know, Warden. I can't figure out how a no-good bastard like Gregory could ever get an award," laughed Harvey.

I looked at the warden in surprise and thought, Now what is he up to?

"Come up here, Greg. I'd like to read it to you." Attempting to sound stern but with blue eyes twinkling in merriment, the warden read, "This certificate is presented to Officer Gregory as a commendation for the excellent work he does when assigned to the mail desk."

Practically everybody in the room knew about my reprimand and felt the same as I did about it. Reprimands were plentiful but commendations were all too few.

For a second, there was absolute quiet. Then the group rose to their feet, clapping and laughing because an officer was actually being recognized for work well done.

14

The Hospital

One area of the Alcatraz penitentiary that always interested me was the hospital. The personnel working in the hospital were U.S. Public Health Service employees assigned to the Federal Prison Service. Most of them were highly trained professionals with years of experience in the prison environment. The Public Health Service was usually able to attract good doctors and medical technical assistants. For the most part, they were very cooperative. The prison staff held the medical staff, especially the MTAs, in high regard. They were respected for their knowledge, their efficiency in handling medical matters, and their courage in dealing with difficult and dangerous inmates.

From the beginning of Alcatraz as a federal penitentiary to the 1950s, there had been a physician in residence on the island. When the civil service started cutting expenses, the prison administration decided the Alcatraz physician had to go. Private physicians from the area contracted with the Public Health Service to hold sick call for the inmates.

At first the MTAs tried to coach the contract doctors concerning the drug situation, but they soon gave it up when they found too many of the doctors just wanted to get through the list, prescribe the drugs, and get off the island as quickly as possible. It didn't take long for the doctors to realize that the drug situation was a sticky problem, and they wanted no part of it. Some doctors lasted a couple of days, some a couple of months; a few of them made a feeble effort to cut out the drugs, but they could see the problem was too big for them. Not to mention the fact that when a doctor told an inmate he could no longer have drugs, the inmate would threaten him in such a way as to scare him half to death.

One day, Dr. Cummings arrived. He was a Public Health Service doctor who had previously done service as a prison doctor. His present assignment was to the

Federal Bureau of Prisons as a supervisor of medical personnel. I knew him from other prisons and from his previous trips to Alcatraz. This time he was on a very serious mission. He represented the Surgeon General, who had announced to the Federal Bureau of Prisons that the doling out of drugs to inmates had to be stopped. Cummings said that a special doctor would be sent out from head-quarters to direct the program at Alcatraz.

According to the grapevine, Belcher was the name of the doctor being sent to Alcatraz. I asked Shannon if he knew anything about him.

"No. He couldn't have been around the prison service or I would have heard of him."

"So what do you think?"

"I don't know," Shannon said with a puzzled look. "All we can do is 'stand by for a ram.'"*

An officer came up to the hospital, where I had been helping to supervise the sick call, and said, "Gregory, I'm relieving you. The warden wants to see you right away."

"My boy," Warden Swope said as he motioned me to a chair, "I think you know as much about our medical problem here as anybody."

I wondered why he didn't just say "drug problem."

"So," the warden went on, "I want you to spend as much time as you can up in the hospital. I'm aware there are certain times of the day that you will have to be in the cell house. I don't know what in the world is going to happen when this new doctor arrives, but I want you to be on top of it as much as you can. And I want you to report to me anything you think I should know. Even minor inci-dents—feel free to let me know what is happening." Getting up from his chair, he wandered over to the window and stood looking out. Mumbling more to him-self than to me, he said, "After all, I didn't start this stuff. I don't know why I should be stuck with it."

"I'll do my best, Warden," I said, getting up and shrugging my shoulders. My head was full of questions. I mainly wondered why the warden seemed afraid.

Drugs were not brought in from the outside. There was no hint or suspicion that officers were trafficking. But Alcatraz had become home to many of the more incorrigible military prisoners. These inmates were prison-wise and knew all the angles and tricks to use on the contract doctors to get drugs. As doctors came and went from Alcatraz, drug dispensing continued and became worse. If inmates were not given drugs, or even if they just wanted more in the middle of the night,

*"Stand by for a ram" is a nautical expression used to alert those on board a ship to prepare for a collision.

they would bang their tin cups on the bars, making sleep impossible for others. The MTA would finally give them another pill. It got to the point that anything was done just to keep them quiet. In short, it was way out of hand.

Back in the hospital, I said to Shannon, "Sorry, mate, but it looks like I am permanently assigned to the hospital. That is, except during troop movements. I'll have to be down in the cell house then. I don't know what in the hell I'm supposed to be doing here, but if I can be of any help to you at all, just let me know."

I was sitting in the examining room drinking a cup of coffee when I said to Shannon, "I see the new doctor came in today. What's he like?"

"Come on, I'll introduce you. He's turning up his nose right now at his little office." As Shannon and I appeared in the doorway, Shannon said, "Dr. Belcher, this is Senior Officer George Gregory."

The doctor, whose training was in psychiatry, was a young, smooth-faced, slightly chubby, innocent-looking man with big, brown eyes and an adolescent handsomeness.

Shannon said, "Doctor, Mr. Gregory will be assigned to the hospital on a permanent basis to be of whatever service he can."

Dr. Belcher stared at me for a long moment and finally said, "It certainly looks like I am going to need a whole lot of help. I don't even know what this is all about." He was very soft-spoken. "Come in, sit down and let's have a powwow. Don't you have powwows out here in Indian country?" he said with a silly laugh.

Shannon and I exchanged glances that said, Do we really have to put up with this every day?

Dr. Belcher pushed an ashtray toward me, saying, "Go ahead and smoke. I don't use them. Now, can you tell me about the sick call?"

"Well," said Shannon, "in theory it's the opportunity for inmates to come up here and tell their problems to the MTA. If they have something wrong that merits the doctor's attention or if they ask to see the doctor, the MTA puts them on a list."

"I understand there is always a lengthy list to see the doctor. Surely they're not all so sick they need a doctor's help."

Shannon looked at him and bluntly said, "No, doctor, the only thing they want from you is drugs. They want sleeping pills, tranquilizers, or whatever."

For several moments Dr. Belcher thought this over, tapping the desk idly with a pencil.

"And if we don't give them the drugs?" Dr. Belcher asked quietly.

I said in a very even voice, "Doctor, it's going to take some effort to stop this. We could have riots, and it could be quite taxing on the medical staff as well as the correctional staff."

"I see. I don't know just what to do yet. But there is one thing you two could do for me to help me learn more about these inmates who are getting drugs. Make me two lists. List number one, the nonviolent or weak ones, the ones with loud talk but not much to back it up. The second list should be of the really dangerous inmates—the violent ones."

"Right," said Shannon, "two lists on the way."

"Now another thing. It sounds as if we would have this hospital full of people all during sick call. Is there any way we can schedule these inmates so that we only have four or five at a time up here in the hospital?"

"I can talk to the warden about it," I said with a bit of trepidation. The doctor and the warden represented two autonomous government bureaus—the Public Health Service and the Federal Prison Service. Although the doctor was small of stature, that said nothing about his ego or how much he wanted to be boss. I already knew the warden thought of himself as the boss of all Alcatraz.

"Is he the man to see?"

"Yes, eventually he is the one to make the decision."

"I think I will talk with him about this myself."

The phone rang. I answered on the extension in the doctor's office.

"Gregory here."

"Greg, we got what looks like a nasty cutting down here, self-inflicted. He's in his cell," reported Lieutenant Tompkins.

"Got it," I said. "Shannon, cutting in the cell house. Could be bad."

Shannon grabbed his kit and raced down the hall. I got to the door before him and unlocked it. The door at the bottom of the stairs was unlocked by an officer in the cell house. I remained there to let Shannon back in with the injured inmate.

Dr. Belcher came to the top of the stairs and asked, "What is this all about?"

"We probably will have an inmate coming up here who's trying to get an extra dose of drugs. He's cut himself, thinking this will sway you to give him whatever he wants."

"I guess we had better get ready for a little sewing."

When Shannon and an officer from the cell house escorted the self-mutilated inmate to the door, I saw that it was Lindo. Not a really bad inmate. He had been sent to Alcatraz because of an escape he made from another federal penitentiary. It cost the Department of Justice a pretty penny before they caught up with him, and of course his warden's feelings were very much hurt, so Lindo ended up at Alcatraz. Now he was another inmate who was getting into serious trouble because of the drug situation that was sweeping all the institutions.

Once Lindo was on the table, the doctor loosened the tourniquet that Shannon had applied and examined Lindo's arm.

"Um," said the doctor. "Looks like we got to you just in time. This is a pretty big artery you've cut."

"Artery?" squeaked Lindo in a frightened voice.

"Let's give him a unit of blood."

"I'll take care of it, doctor," Shannon said as he left the examining room.

It was only minutes before the inmate nurse had all the equipment. As soon as the blood was flowing properly, the nurse opened a surgical kit and helped the doctor with his rubber gloves. Lindo raised his head and said, "Oh, come on Doc, you are going to give me a shot before you do that, aren't you?" The tone of his voice revealed that he knew it was useless. Within seconds, Dr. Belcher had Lindo's wound neatly sewed together.

"What the hell is this?" said Lindo. "You can't get away with this. This is cruel and inhuman treatment."

Then the doctor did an unusual thing. Putting his hand on Lindo's chest, he looked for a long moment at close range into his eyes. "Tell me, friend," he said in a gentle voice, "it didn't hurt, did it?"

Lindo looked up at the group staring down at him and who, indeed, were as astonished as he was. "This guy is a creep," the inmate muttered in wonder. Not having put this together myself, I was about ready to agree with Lindo.

"When the I.V. has run out," said Dr. Belcher, "put a light cast on his arm to protect it from overstretching and he can go back to his cell. We'll see him again tomorrow at sick call."

As the doctor walked out the door, Lindo yelled at him, "You're not going to get away with this!"

A large portion of the hospital was taken up by a sixteen-bed open ward. This was a constant headache for the correctional officers because the inmates would often get into fights. At the back of the ward was a small room with a toilet and shower for the use of the hospital occupants. Although this room was not equipped with a door, about half of it could not be seen without going into the ward.

The ward was usually full of inmates, most of whom were there to get drugs by complaining of various and mysterious illnesses. Headaches and imitations of near nervous breakdowns were among the favorite ailments.

Inmates habitually checked into the ward on weekdays for the treatment of their alleged ills and to avoid work. Strangely enough, on Friday morning they would begin to have remissions of their various illnesses. We cynical officers thought it was because they wanted to get out into the exercise yard on the weekend. (Only work-assigned inmates, if their job permitted, could use the yard on weekdays. Inmates in the regular population had yard privileges on the weekend.)

However, there was no rest for the ward because another group would check in for the weekend. These inmates weren't interested in exercising in the yard but they were very interested in the privacy that the ward bathroom afforded for sex. Although the hospital personnel knew perfectly well what was going on, they had no visual proof. Most of the illicit activity took place at night when there was limited lighting and limited staff.

An inmate named Lonnie was kept permanently in the ward because his medical file contained a diagnosis of insanity. He liked to go around saying, "I'm crazy, and I have the papers to prove it." In fact, he was a pretty smart cookie. He served as the hospital orderly for several years. Through a number of sessions with Lonnie, I got the whole story of the weekend homosexual orgies in the bathroom, including names and numbers.

The more I was around Dr. Belcher, the more I appreciated the man and his working style. He carried in his coat pocket the lists of violent and nonviolent drug users that Shannon and I had compiled for him. As he made notes on his contacts with the inmates, I often saw him pull out the lists and study them and his notes side by side.

Dr. Belcher called me into his office one day and said, "Greg, look at the names I have marked on this list. This is step number one in our new drug program."

He handed me the nonviolent drug users list with checks by about fifteen names.

Dr. Belcher continued, "I think the ones I've marked can take it if I just tell them to go to hell, they are not going to get any more drugs. I've studied them and, of course, they are going to holler and yell and threaten. I can take all that. Are you still of the opinion that they will not cause too much trouble? And if we have misjudged someone, do we have the personnel to handle him without his getting into a completely murderous state? Hurting one of us or himself?"

Looking at the names Dr. Belcher had marked, I couldn't help but admire him for being able to correctly profile these inmates in such a short time.

"No," I said, "these guys won't be any problem. But if they do try anything, we can handle them, doctor. We'll take them into the examining room one at a time, close the door, and let them blow it all out. There is one here that, if you will allow me, I'd like to handle for you."

Dr. Belcher raised a questioning eyebrow but said nothing.

"He's been here a long time but is still comparatively young. The parole board is seriously thinking about transferring him so that eventually he can be paroled. He's been using the drugs to go to sleep at night and to escape for a little while from 'doing time.' I think when I tell him about his very good chance of transferring and parole, you'll never again see him on sick call just to get a sleeping pill."

"That will be just fine."

"And may I suggest the order in which you see the inmates?"

"Yes."

I took the list and organized the names for the interviews. "The first one is just a goofy guy, playing this game because it's the game of the day. When you tell him he won't be getting any more drugs, he'll just laugh and walk out. He does have a peculiar habit that might respond to psychiatric treatment, though."

"Oh, what's that?"

"He likes to snip off the testicles of mice with his big buck teeth."

The doctor winced slightly and said dryly, "Kind of hard on the mice, isn't it?"

"The second one," I continued, "is not likely to get too excited. He'll make some noise but not until he is safely out the door. The next several guys are not at all violent. They'll plead their case eloquently for a few moments. When they see they're not influencing you, they'll save it to try on other people."

"Other people?"

"Oh yes, the warden, the associate warden, the priest, the minister. The minister dearly loves to hear the inmates' complaints. And we have an army psychiatrist who's been hired by the bureau to visit inmates and determine their psychiatric state. I hesitate to say this, but I've noticed he is quite sympathetic to these drug addicts. Quite a number of the inmates are getting drugs because he has ordered them."

"Hmm."

"Just thought you would want to know."

It took a few days before the doctor decided the time was right to begin his antidrug program. All the inmates on the list behaved as expected. You can believe the news spread rapidly throughout the institution. At first the inmates were amazed, actually nonplussed. How could this young, boyish-looking doctor dare to be so tough? It was unbelievable to the inmate population in general.

There was a lot of hollering and dissatisfaction from the inmates who had been cut off drugs. The ones who were still being given drugs were very quiet. They thought they were being favored for something they were doing, and stayed quiet for fear they might lose their drug issues.

Drugs prescribed for the inmates were routinely put in pharmacy-type pack-

ages and sent down to the West End desk for the evening-watch cell house officer to deliver on his rounds. Every day or so for about a month, the doctor elim-
inated one or two inmates from the drug dole. Although you could sense the tension developing in the inmate population, there were no overt remonstrances
other than the usual blaspheming of the doctor. Once in a while, there'd be a
mild tussle.

During roll call one day, the lieutenant told me that the warden wanted to see
me. When we broke ranks, he sidled up to me and said, "What the hell is going
on up in that hospital?"

I shrugged my shoulders and proceeded to the warden's office.

"Greg, what in the world is going on?" asked Warden Swope in a pleading
voice.

"Warden, when you first assigned me to this special hospital duty, I didn't
know what I was getting into. I'm not even sure yet. But let me tell you what Dr.
Belcher is trying to do here."

I explained the doctor's program at some length and then said, "Warden, I
think you should have a conference with Dr. Belcher." I didn't say it, but I was
trying to make sure I didn't become a middleman between the doctor and the
warden—between the Public Health Service and the Federal Prison Service.

Although the warden still looked puzzled, I turned and left his office.

Up in the hospital, I said, "Shannon, I've just come from the warden's office.
You know the warden and the doctor have simply got to get together."

Dr. Belcher was working like a man with a mission. Although he took care of
all his duties as doctor, his main interest seemed to be in reducing the number of
inmates on drugs. He had already studied the inmates and systematically removed a large number of them from the drug list. We thought that some of their
friends might still be collecting drugs for them, but we couldn't be sure.

The warden, on the other hand, could not limit his interest in the institution
to a certain department. In addition to keeping the bureau happy, he had to consider the safety of the staff, the safekeeping of the inmates, and public relations
in the area. Information from the plumbing line could be invaluable to the warden and his staff. Sometimes there was a price for such intelligence, perhaps an
exchange of favors. Drugs could be involved.

Shannon nodded speculatively. "Greg, Dr. Belcher and I are getting pretty
close. I think we can work something out. Let's go talk to the good doctor."

The doctor looked up from his paperwork and said, "The both of you? What
have I done wrong now?"

I cleared my throat, feeling very awkward. This was just about as difficult as a kid telling his parents what to do. "Doctor, I've just been in to see the warden. Well, just to put it bluntly, we think you should talk with him," I said.

The doctor sat silent for a spell, then said, "This may sound arrogant, but I am deadly serious. I have been sent out here to do a job, namely, to clean up this drug mess, and I am going to do it—warden or no warden."

There was another long period of silence, which Shannon broke. "Doctor, you are my boss and I do as you direct, but the Public Health staff here has been getting along with the correctional staff very well. Sure would be nice if we could continue working together comfortably." Shannon's speech was followed by yet another long pause.

"Well, of course we want to work together. The medical staff will certainly try in every way to cooperate with the correctional staff. What do you guys think I should do?"

"Would you talk with the warden?" I asked.

"Hmm, come to think of it, we have had very few words with each other so far and he has done most of the talking. When would be a good time for me to see him? What is the procedure for seeing him? I'm still feeling my way, with this working in prisons." He paused. "Never mind." The doctor reached for the phone and dialed. "Warden, this is Dr. Belcher. When can we get together?" He finished the call and turned to Shannon and me. "He'll see me now," he said, his voice showing a bit of surprise.

The doctor stood up. "Mr. Gregory, I can put this institution under quarantine and be in absolute control of it." His face was grim and his voice did sound arrogant. He slapped me on the back and said, "I'm going down right now to see your boss and we are going to get along whether he likes it or not."

I stared at the doctor, shaking my head slowly from side to side. Who could ever understand the politics of governmental institutions?

15

Dr. Melvin Ralston

It was not an easy climate in which to work during the next few weeks. Tension was building. I was eating more antacid pills and smoking more cigarettes, but I wasn't the only one under increasing nervous strain.

We were all amazed at Officer Shields one day. He had the responsibility of all the gates in the West End—gates to the yard and points beyond—clothing room, dining hall, and hospital. Only one gate could be opened at a time. There was often a wait. The officer never had more than one set of keys at a time. He had to return a set to the West Gun Gallery officer on the line before another set would be sent down.

On this day, Shields, who was shy and seldom spoke, was working his keister off when Warden Swope came down to the West End.

"Mr. Shields, I never see you smiling. What's the matter, don't you like us?" the warden asked.

"Warden, this is a very serious job. There's nothing to smile about," Shields said in a strong, firm voice without hesitation or a break in his routine.

Those of us within hearing looked around to see who had talked to the warden in such a way. Seeing that it was Shields, we couldn't keep the smiles from our faces. We had never seen Shields stand up to anybody, and certainly never expected to hear him speak to the warden so forcefully.

Mr. Cecil, the personnel director, called me at the West End and said, "I want to see you immediately." Cecil had been palmed off on Alcatraz from another prison as a correctional officer. At Alcatraz he somehow became a fixture in the front office with the title of "personnel director." This was called being kicked upstairs.

"I'm busy. I haven't time to see you now." I was serving as Cell House One.

"Didn't you hear me, Mr. Gregory? I said right now."

"You can take your 'right now' and shove it you-know-where." I hung up the phone, growling a few more bits of Marine profanity. I knew that Cecil had called me because it was about time for "that class" to start, but I didn't want to be anywhere near it.

The class had been proclaimed by the bureau to be essential to those who wanted to be successful prison officers. Having met Dr. Melvin Ralston, the teacher from the bureau, I wanted no part of it. After almost fifteen years in the prison service, I didn't think an industrialist-advisor-turned-government-bureaucrat could possibly tell me how to work with the inmates on Alcatraz. He had never worked inside the walls of a prison.

The occasion of my meeting Dr. Ralston was a boat trip during the transfer of a particularly dangerous inmate from the mainland to the island. The captain had sent me over to assist in the supervision of the inmate on the boat and on through the entry into our system. Once on the boat, I escorted the inmate and the officer who had brought him from Leavenworth up to the wheelhouse. We were all comfortable there and it kept the inmate from being stared at by the other passengers.

I had worked with the Leavenworth officer, Concanon, years before. We were getting caught up on gossip when the door suddenly opened and in walked a tall, scrawny man of about forty whom I didn't recognize.

Holding up my hand to indicate he should stop, I said, "You shouldn't be up here. Please stay in the main cabin."

"I'm from the bureau and I'm here to talk to this man," he said, and proceeded to address the inmate with the fervor of a fundamentalist preacher. He told the inmate he didn't have to stay at Alcatraz very long—that he could get a transfer back to Leavenworth or one of the other prisons in the system. The inmate looked from Concanon to me as if to say, Get this nut away from me. When we docked, we had to tell Dr. Ralston to leave the boat so we could get the inmate off and take him up top.

This is why I felt justified in my reluctance to subject myself to further contact with the bureau's Dr. Ralston.

A few minutes later, the phone rang again. This time it was Captain Rychner. "Greg, can't you get out here for a little while?"

"Captain, you know damned well we have a troop movement going on. We're letting the inmates out for afternoon yard. They're restless and we have already had two scuffles." After a brief pause, the captain hung up. I thought, Now I've got the captain mad at me.

We were letting the last tier of inmates out to go to the yard when I saw the captain coming down Broadway. A rare occasion, indeed. In the last year or so, you could have counted on one hand the times he had been in the cell house. He came down and stood by my desk. I went about my duties, assigning officers to chores, getting ready to hear inmate complaints, and purposely ignoring the captain. I knew it wasn't the proper thing to do but I felt a primeval, savage delight in doing it.

When I finally acknowledged his presence, he was making a real effort to control himself. Through a fine spray of spittle and seeming about to cry, he almost shrieked, "Mr. Gregory, why didn't you come out to see Mr. Cecil?"

"Captain, I haven't got time for that man's silly foolishness."

Just then Lieutenant Tompkins showed up and the captain asked him, "Lieutenant, could Mr. Gregory be relieved for a while?"

I looked at Bunch with a pleading "no" head shake. But he turned so the captain couldn't hear him and whispered, "To hell with you, Greg." To the captain he said, "Yes sir, Captain, we can get along for a while without him." I think Bunch was afraid *he* might have to take that class if he didn't release me.

There was nothing I could do but follow the captain out of the cell house. Just outside the main gate, he stopped, looked at me, and said, "Greg, I hate this as much as you do but you better not screw up, dammit."

"Oh, there you are, Mr. Gregory," Cecil said in a sugary, sarcastic voice. "You made us wait, didn't you? Now that we are all here . . . "

Looking around the room, I was surprised to see several of the best officers on the Alcatraz staff plus a couple of kooks who were not so good.

"We will now proceed to the warden's office," Cecil said with a phony, pained look on his face as though all the responsibilities of Alcatraz were on his shoulders. He flashed a wicked grin of triumph as he walked by me.

I fell in line with Ernie Yates, a top prison officer, and was about to make a complaint when he held up his finger in warning.

"We get to go to school to improve as prison officers. Aren't you glad?" Yates whispered.

I opened my mouth to speak but he held up his finger in warning again. He put on a wondrous show of serious compliance, even as his eyes danced with humor, laughing at this charade. He hated this sort of thing too but was better at keeping his mouth shut than I was.

The warden's office had been set up to serve as the classroom. Warden Swope was standing at the front of the room with the scrawny man from the wheelhouse.

"Gentleman," said the warden as we settled into our chairs, "I want you to meet Dr. Melvin Ralston. He is here from the bureau to hold a seminar, the aim of which is to make us better prison officers. Also, we will discuss improvements that have been made in the prison service in the last ten years."

I couldn't help myself—just couldn't help it. "Are we to assume," I cynically asked, "that there have been improvements in the past ten years?"

Suddenly it became very quiet in the warden's office. The warden stood there with his mouth hanging open. Dr. Ralston stared in utter disbelief, which rapidly turned into anger.

"What is your name, young man?" Dr. Ralston asked.

"Mr. George Gregory," I said.

"Mr. Gregory, I see you have a lot to learn about prison service."

"I have to agree to that," I said, "and I guess you are going to teach me. Right?"

Dr. Ralston went through various facial contortions and then with a sickly, patronizing tone, said, "Well, we can all learn, can't we, Mr. Gregory?"

"Yes, *all* of us can learn." I can't say that I felt any better after that exchange, but neither did I feel any worse.

During that first session, we learned that Ralston had a beautiful wife and two darling daughters and that it really was a great sacrifice on his part to leave them and come way out to the West Coast to present this seminar.

"Oh, I forgot something," said Dr. Ralston. Turning to a stack of legal pads, he handed one to each of his "students." "Now, I want you to take notes at each of our sessions. Sorry I didn't remember to give them to you at the beginning so you could take notes on this session. At the end of the seminar, we will have a test. The mark you get on the examination may have quite an effect on your future as a prison officer. So let us be very attentive. I'll see you tomorrow."

On the way back to the cell house, I stepped into the captain's office and said, "I want no part of this at all. If you force me to do this, I will go on a long sick leave."

"Damn you," said the captain. He sank back in his chair and his shoulders drooped. "I was given direct orders to get a group of experienced officers together for this program. Dammit, Gregory, I had trouble finding ten people with enough experience and basic education who were not about to retire. Greg, you have got to do it. I'd say do it for me . . . " Then, after a pause, "Greg, someday you'll be sitting in this chair. It used to be a good job but it isn't anymore. Thank God I've only got two years to go before retirement."

"Oh, no, you're not going to cry are you, Captain? All right, I'll take the class. But you owe me."

"Yes, I guess I do owe you," said the captain, extending his hand to me.

On the second day of the study program, Dr. Ralston was not at all bashful about pushing the sale of a book he had written on penology. He strongly suggested that all members of the class could benefit from reading his enlightened views on prison reform.

Lomin, a new officer, eagerly said, "I'll buy one."

Studdle, another new officer, also bought a book. None of the rest of the class showed the slightest interest in the book and certainly no inclination to buy it.

Outside the classroom, these two officers began constantly talking about the contents of the book and quoting it in loud, admiring voices so others would be sure to hear them. The torture of going to the class was all that we trained and experienced officers could take. To have to listen to the discussions of these two weirdos, which were carried on from tier to tier in the cell house or wherever they might be, was getting on the nerves of the rest of us.

One day, Dr. Ralston took the class into the cell house to, in his own words, "Teach you how to search a cell." This was, to say the least, humiliating, patronizing, and insulting to experienced officers.

"What we hope to accomplish here," said Dr. Ralston, "is to learn how to inspect a cell quickly and in such a way that we do not disturb the cell nor let the inmate know that his cell has been searched. Now we will have one of you go through the exercise of inspecting this cell.

"Now, Mr. Gregory, you are elected, ha ha, to do the searching."

I didn't move an inch.

"Mr. Gregory? Mr. Gregory?" Dr. Ralston was looking right into my eyes. I was looking right back into his eyes, in disbelief at having to do what he ordered.

Gritting my teeth and holding in my irritation as best I could, I entered and shook down the cell according to institution-approved procedure. First I checked the ceiling, air vent, bars, toilet, and washbasin. Finding no discrepancies or contraband, I proceeded to the inmate's possessions, including toothpaste, toothbrush, shaving materials, books, and musical instruments. Then came the bunk. I removed the blankets and sheets one at a time and searched each one. I removed the pillowcase and examined it and the pillow carefully. I checked the mattress for tears, rips, lumps, or any variation in surface or contour. I ended the search by neatly folding the blankets and sheets and placing them on the foot of the bed.

"Mission accomplished, sir," I said with a slight bow.

"Well now, Mr. Gregory. Our purpose here was to develop a routine of speedy search without the inmate knowing that his cell had been bothered." Dr. Ralston looked around the group. "Mr. Studdle, what do you think of Mr. Gregory's work here?"

"First of all, he took far too much time," said Studdle, "and he did not make up the bunk. The inmate certainly would know his cell had been searched."

Dr. Ralston laid a big approving smile on Studdle.

"Just a minute, Dr. Ralston, could I say a word?" asked Ernie Yates. "First of all, I cannot see any reason in the world why anyone should be in a hurry to search a cell. If the cell is under suspicion for any reason, we can keep the inmate out of there for a week if we need to. We could put him in another cell so we could do a thorough search. Secondly, there is not an officer in the entire prison service good enough or clever enough to search any one of the Alcatraz inmates' cells without that inmate knowing it. The inmates know their cells are going to be searched regularly. We fold the blankets to show the inmates there are no hard feelings, we're just doing our job."

Dr. Ralston stared at Ernie, bursting with anger. He made a couple of attempts to say something but then turned and walked rapidly to the gate, and on out of the cell house. His class shuffled along behind him, snickering a bit, and wondering just what was up with this man.

16

Sick Call

In the cell house, Shannon arranged his *materia medica* on the table, looked over to Lieutenant Tompkins, and said, "I'm ready when you are."

"Open up for sick call," announced Bunch. The new system Dr. Belcher had started—holding the preliminary or general sick call in the cell house instead of in the hospital—was working out very well.

Immediately the levers on B-1 tier clanged open and the inmates who wanted to go to sick call marched down to the West End, where they stood in a single-file line some distance away from the table. A space was maintained between the line and the table so that the inmate speaking with Shannon would not be overheard by inmates waiting for their turn. Nearly all of the inmates were there for only one reason: to get on the drug list for that night. For the most part, Shannon put their names down without comment, until one rather simple, inoffensive inmate came up.

"End of the line for you, Cornell," said Shannon.

"What do you mean?" Cornell tried to look tough.

"You are just selling this stuff and I am putting you out of business right now." Cornell stared at Shannon and then smiled slightly, shrugged his shoulders, turned, and walked back to his cell.

A day or so later as Shannon was packing his medical kit for sick call in the cell house, he said, "I hope you can come down for the preliminary sick call again today. This business of stopping the drugs is getting more and more serious."

"Sure. I can come down," I said.

In the cell house, Shannon set up his table. The officer assigned to sick call happened to be Lomin. He was spouting up to Studdle, who was on the second tier, more wondrous praise of that damned book and Dr. Ralston. It made me want to puke.

Bunch walked over to Lomin and said, "Look, mister, you belong with your belly right up to that table. Now get there and stay there."

Just then, Dr. Ralston came around the corner wearing a white smock. Bunch's face turned pale with anger as he stared at Dr. Ralston. "What in the hell are you doing here?"

"I've come in to observe your sick call. I understand it is not being run very well. Maybe we can find some ways to improve it," Dr. Ralston replied.

"Dr. Ralston, I don't have enough officers here to protect you. We are about to let inmates out of their cells for sick call. Wearing that white coat, they are going to think you're the medical doctor and jump all over you."

"But I . . . "

"Get out of here before I have to throw you out."

"You can't order me around. I was sent here by the bureau!"

"Dr. Ralston . . . " Turning, Bunch said to himself, "Ah, to hell with it."

As Bunch walked back toward the MTA's table he noticed that Lomin had again positioned himself some distance away. Grabbing the inexperienced officer by the arm, Bunch ushered him right up to the table and said, "Now you stay here. Your job is to protect this MTA."

"But Dr. Ralston told us that the sick call was a private matter between the inmate and the medic and we should not invade that privacy," said Lomin defiantly.

"Lomin, I'm tired of your Ralston bullshit. Now get up to that table in a position to protect the MTA if he needs it," Bunch ordered. With fists doubled and teeth clenched, he looked around to make sure all was in readiness for sick call.

In the meantime, Dr. Ralston, having refused Bunch's advice to leave, had stepped up to within a few steps from the MTA's table. From there he observed all. The looks he gave Bunch were arrogant.

"What in the hell are you doing down here, Greg? Not that I'm not awfully glad you're here. Here we go." Bunch gave the order to the officers controlling the cell doors. "Open 'em up."

It was the black inmates' turn to be let out first for sick call. Kinson came charging down Broadway with a crazed look in his eyes. He was serving time for two murders. He came around the corner and did not stop at the designated mark on the floor to wait for a call from the MTA. Instead he stormed right up to the table, leaned over toward Shannon, and said, "Listen, you bastard, do I get my pills tonight or don't I?"

"Kinson, you know you have been taken off that list," said Shannon without flinching.

Kinson leaped over the table. Lomin ran. Shannon didn't have quite enough time to get his hands up, and Kinson got him by the throat. The force of his impact turned over the table and knocked both of them to the floor. I was the closest officer but I was several yards away. I took off like a missile and landed right in the middle of Kinson's back. I threw my arm around him, hoping to get his throat. I missed and hit his mouth. Taking advantage of the opportunity, Kinson sunk his teeth deep into the base of my thumb. In another second, Bunch was there and jammed his hands into Kinson's eyes and pulled back. Kinson was a powerful man and by now was completely out of control. With my free hand, I put everything I had into a blow behind his ear. This stunned him a bit and Bunch was able to pull his head back enough to loosen his hold on Shannon's throat. Shannon pushed Kinson with all his might. We were finally able to break his powerful grip. By this time, other officers arrived and began to pummel Kinson roughly.

"No, no, don't hurt him," said Bunch. "Get him over to TU."

I lifted Shannon's head. He was having a terrible time breathing. As I tried to help him into a better position, I yelled to an officer, "Get on the phone and get the doctor down here right now!" It seemed like an eternity, watching Shannon struggle to breathe. Dr. Belcher was there in a very short time with another MTA. He checked Shannon and told the MTA to call for an ambulance immediately.

One of the officers heard this, rushed to the phone, and called the boat officer. "Get the boat ready. Officer hurt," he said.

As it turned out, Shannon had some badly damaged tracheal cartilage. Years later at his retirement dinner, he still talked in a hoarse voice that was the result of the trauma sustained in the attack by Kinson.

The last we saw of Dr. Ralston, he was banging on the main gate to be let out of the cell house. The "seminar" came to an abrupt halt without the promised final examination. Ralston left the island never to return. No reason given. Not that anybody needed one. However, his enlightened pamphlets continued to flow from the bureau.

Dr. Ralston had come to believe his own ideas on how to deal with inmates, although he had never worked in a cell house. He could not imagine that any inmate would do bodily harm to another person. But the cons at Alcatraz played by a set of rules that was completely foreign to the likes of Dr. Ralston.

Although we missed the examination, we were still graded on the seminar. Following the arrival of the bureau mail pouch one day, the grapevine was abuzz with the news. Dr. Ralston had given me an "A," which led to another nickname—Teacher's Pet—and much razzing from my colleagues.

Lomin, believe it or not, continued to work at Alcatraz for some time. His devotion to Dr. Ralston never wavered.

Shannon returned to work after a few days and continued to shorten the mighty drug list. Returning to the hospital one day after the cell house sick call, he said to the doctor, "Now is where we are going to have our first serious session." He showed the doctor a list and said, "This is a list of those that you might cut off drugs today. Quite a few of them are very capable of causing us some trouble."

"Physically?" said the doctor, but he already knew the answer.

"Yes, I mean physically."

"What can we do about that?" Dr. Belcher asked me.

"What do you want to do, doctor?"

"What I am going to do is tell these inmates they will no longer be on medication, unless there is a good reason for it."

"Doctor," I said, "are you giving us—the correctional staff—permission to use whatever force is necessary on these inmates?"

"That's right. You people know how to maintain the safety of the staff and the inmates. That is what I expect you to do. Mr. Shannon, I am ready to hold sick call."

Thinking we might need some help, I said, "Let me get hold of the lieutenant." I called the West End. "Bunch, can you come up here to the hospital? Important. Oh, and if you have an extra officer around there, bring him up with you."

When Lieutenant Tompkins and Officer Ambers came in, I explained what was happening. For several long moments, Bunch rocked gently from heel to toe, apparently considering the responsibilities of the two government bureaus—the Public Health Service and the Federal Prison Service. "You know, I really should call the captain," he said. Then he asked, "Doctor, do we have your word . . . "

"You have my word that whatever happens, I'll take full responsibility."

Bunch picked up the phone and called the West End. "Start sick call, but send up only one con at a time. Get it? *One con at a time.*"

Hickens was a muscular, sullen-faced, cauliflower-eared con with a record of several known brutal murders. He came up to Dr. Belcher's desk.

"What can I do for you, Hickens?" Dr. Belcher asked in a quiet voice.

"You know damned well what you can do for me. You can give me my yellow ball."

Bunch and I slowly eased up on either side and slightly behind Hickens while Ambers came up directly behind him. Shannon, who was sitting next to Dr. Belcher, casually put his hands palm down on the desk and said, "Hickens, you will get no sleeping pills or any other drug tonight."

"You mean you are cutting me off, Doc?"

"You are cut off."

With a mad lunge, Hickens started over the table. Shannon jumped to his feet and shoved his hands into Hickens's face, while Bunch and I grabbed his arms and Ambers put a lock on his neck. Hickens struggled for a few seconds, but the more he struggled, the tighter the holds became and the harder it was to breathe.

"Down to TU with him?" asked Bunch.

"Is there a strip cell available?" the doctor asked. The strip cells, which were located in the hospital, were constructed of a heavy wire mesh instead of solid walls. This was for maximum observation. There was no furniture or fixtures in the cells. This was for the safety of the inmate, not for punishment.

"Yes, we can put him in there. Okay, Hickens, let's move it. You can do this the easy way or the hard way," I said. We hustled him down to the strip cell and took off all his clothes except his shorts and left him there screaming in an insane rage, threatening us with all kinds of horrible death.

Back in the examining room, Shannon looked at the list and said, "The next one is Gillis." For a moment there was absolute silence.

Gillis had a constant air of cold cynicism about him. He rarely made eye contact, but when he did it was with a faint smile of patronizing disdain. He was a five foot ten inch, brawny lad. He was quiet and seldom spoke to an officer. Two of the four homicides to his credit were fellow inmates. The inmate population reacted to him with much fear. Needless to say, the correctional force handled him with kid gloves.

"Gillis, huh?" said Bunch. "We got to watch this bird."

Gillis came into the room in a bit of a crouch, slightly up on his toes. There was no doubt that he smelled trouble. Bunch took him by his left wrist.

"Don't touch me," snarled Gillis and tried to pull his arm away. Bunch held on and I immediately grabbed the other arm. We guided him, with only the necessary force, to a position directly facing Dr. Belcher.

"What can I do for you, Gillis?" the doctor asked.

"Never mind your bullshit, man. I want to be on that list. I want pills. And I want them tonight. And I want the same for my friends."

"Your friends, huh? Now I am understanding."

"What do you understand?" Then it dawned on Gillis that he had just let it be known that his friends were collecting pills for him. Suddenly, with a wild, animal-like scream, Gillis started over the table toward the doctor. It was a feinting move. When he seemed to have relented and we relaxed our hold on him, Gillis broke loose and sprang to the corner of the room where there was a table with several large glass jars of cotton swabs, tongue depressors, and the like. Grabbing one of the jars, Gillis smashed it against the wall, knocking out the bottom and spilling the contents. Now he had a sharp, jagged, ugly weapon.

"Don't come near me," he screamed.

Bunch and I took a few steps toward Gillis and then hesitated. We could sense that he was about to spring at us, undoubtedly thinking only of killing. Knowing full well that I would probably get cut, I came up on my toes and sprang at him first. But suddenly he wasn't there, and I missed him, falling rather clumsily to the floor. As I got to my hands and knees, there was Gillis lying next to me on the floor. He was on his back with the business end of a broom shoved into his face. It was only seconds before officers were all over Gillis, who was now yelping in pain. When I got to my feet, I saw Ambers on the other end of the broom. A potentially deadly situation had ended up almost funny. Just a guard's simple old trick, to use a broom. Ambers had done some fast thinking and acting.

At a later date, when things had calmed down, everybody involved in this incident chipped in and bought the broom handler a dinner at a fancy restaurant in the city. Along with the dinner, we put in Ambers's name for an award for exceptional duty above and beyond. But the Alcatraz Awards Board, true to its past history, did not consider his actions worthy of an award.

Gillis, now under complete control, his anger spent but not his hatred, suddenly began to quiver—a strange type of shaking from head to foot. His lips drew back in a horrible sneer and he began to sweat. His face showed a gray pallor.

"Let's get him out of here," said Bunch.

"Just a minute," said Dr. Belcher, "Put him on the treatment table." Without question the officers took Gillis, who was now giving no resistance, and put him on the treatment table. The doctor whispered something to Shannon, who left the room. Returning, he showed the doctor a syringe.

"That's fine," Dr. Belcher said. "Let him have it in the arm, a full syringe."

"Now you can put him in a strip cell," said the doctor when the syringe was empty.

When we came back to the examining room, Dr. Belcher said, "You may wonder why I gave a shot to that man. He has become addicted. Although we could allow him to go 'cold turkey,' as vicious and homicidal as he is it will be better to clean him slowly."

Then Dr. Belcher said with a little smile, "Come on, who's next? Let's get through with this."

We went through the rest of sick call. There was some mild scuffling and lots of profanity, and occasionally the doctor ordered an inmate to be checked into the ward, until the ward was full. Two of the inmates, at the doctor's suggestion, were put in the Hole. On the way through the cell house to the Hole, they both did a lot of hollering, yelling, and struggling. This apprised the population that something unusual was going on and caused most of the rest of the inmates on sick call to just accept what the doctor said. They were playing it cool, until they could find out what it was all about.

But although some of the inmates caused little trouble at sick call, when they got back to their cells their hollering and complaining made it clear to the rest of the cell house that there had been a change in the dispensing of drugs. At the same time, up in the hospital the officers were congratulating each other and generally letting off steam now that sick call was over.

The phone rang. Shannon answered. When he put down the phone he said, "We have a big chain coming in." Immediately there was silence.

The silence was broken by Bunch. "A chain? When?"

"Sometime this evening."

"Well, you can look for some overtime tonight, so don't run away," Bunch said as he looked around the group. "I had better go down to the front office and see what's going on."

"Just what is a chain?" Dr. Belcher asked. He said "chain" as if totally unfamiliar with the word.

"It'll be a group of about forty inmates and we're already overcrowded,"* I said with a grimace. "We're going to have to put some of them on the inside of C Block."

"Why is that such a problem?" Dr. Belcher asked.

"The inside of B is where the blacks are celled. If we put whites on the inside of C, which is just across Broadway, there will be trouble. There's no privacy because the fronts of the cells have only bars." I shrugged my shoulders.

Alcatraz had begged the bureau to keep the count down so we would not have to cell people facing each other. But the bureau, seemingly indifferent to the possible problems, or just not understanding the situation, simply said, We've got to find places for inmates and you are the only institution that has any vacant cells.

"What do we do in the hospital tonight?" asked the doctor.

"Probably nothing, because none of the inmates will have come directly off the street," I said. A physical examination was done on inmates who were first entering the Federal Prison System, but few came to Alcatraz directly from sentencing. "They have been institutionalized before. But eventually they'll come in with the usual variety of stories, trying to get drugs."

---

*The inmate population at Alcatraz averaged two hundred sixty. When the population climbed to around three hundred, there was more trouble with the inmates.

Back in the doctor's office, I was treated to a new development. The doctor had discovered a small electric kettle that could be used on direct current. (All the electricity on Alcatraz was supplied by direct current.) He made instant coffee for Shannon and me.

"See, I can cook, too," Dr. Belcher said with his little smile.

Before we had finished our coffee, the inmate orderly yelled from the ward, "They've started cutting themselves!"

"My God, what with?" I said, going for the ward door with the doctor right behind me. We stood at the door looking in. Three of the inmates laid on their bunks with their legs exposed, bleeding from self-inflicted cuts. Dr. Belcher looked at them and said, "Just superficial—let them lie there for a while," turned, and walked back to his office.

I gave the appearance of doing the same, but instead ducked into a closet from which I could observe and hear the inmates without being seen by them. I was hoping to discover the instrument they were using.

"What is that doctor going to do? Just let us bleed to death?"

"He's got to come in and give us some shots and sew us up." This was said in anger but also in fear and uncertainty.

Then I saw something being passed from one of the bleeding inmates to a real kooky inmate, and the kook screamed out hysterically, "He'll come in here and give me a shot and sew me up, by God," as he slashed his thigh. But he went too deep and he really began to bleed.

I yelled for the doctor and grabbed the phone to call the acting captain. "Lieutenant Parant, we need some help up here right away. A man in the ward has cut himself. He's bleeding badly. We have to get in there." It was the rule that the door to the ward could not be opened without at least two correctional officers present.

"Oh, those bugs are always cutting themselves," sneered Parant.

"No, really, this one is bad."

After a pause, Parant said, "Well, observe and report," and, with a chuckle, hung up.

"I've got to get in there, Greg," said Dr. Belcher standing at the door. "This guy won't last."

I tried to give the key to Shannon and said, "Here, you hold the key and I'll go in with the doctor."

"Like hell you will. That's my job. Open the door."

"Okay," and I opened the door. Dr. Belcher and Shannon rushed into the ward. I closed the door behind them but did not lock it. I watched Dr. Belcher sew up the wound while Shannon held the inmate as still as he could. The doctor worked rapidly and finished within a few moments. To me, standing on the outside, it seemed to be an endless time. Millions of things that could go wrong raced through my mind. That doctor and MTA were very brave men.

"You are not getting any drugs of any kind," said Dr. Belcher. "I know this didn't hurt very much. I'll tell you this, if you try to pull these stitches out, we'll put you in restraints and you'll stay in them until your system is completely free of drugs." With a professional swish of his white coat, the doctor turned and started for the door. Recalling that incident still sends cold chills up my back.

I told the associate warden about the cutting and that there was an implement somewhere in the ward. A search was instituted and half of a safety razor blade was found. There was exceedingly close custody on razor blades. Where this half came from was never determined. Come to think of it, where was the other half?

17

The Chain

The carload of hard-to-handle inmates from Leavenworth arrived at the Oakland Mole late in the evening.

I observed their arrival at Alcatraz from the clothing room, where I was temporarily assigned as officer-in-charge. The sally port into the clothing room was quite small. It would hold about ten people at a time. As I watched the first group being put into the sally port, I couldn't help but notice that the officers who brought the inmates from Leavenworth looked tired, strained, and cross.

The inmates looked much the same as the officers, with their sullen faces and downcast eyes. However, they began to show a bit of curiosity as they stared through the bars at their new home.

The whole place had taken on an eerie, spooky kind of feeling. Having all the lights on created more shadows than there usually were at night. Everyone seemed to move in slow motion. It was like watching a silent movie. The only sounds were the clanking of the inmates' chains and the grating of steel as the sally port was opened and closed. It would be opened on one side, filled up, and the door locked; then the other door would be opened and the sally port emptied. We silently guided the prisoners to the benches in the shower room. This process was repeated until we had the entire chain inside and the sally port was secured.

The inmates sat and waited for the officers to remove their irons. For the trip, they had been shackled in twos. The first thing they did was rub their ankles. No matter how careful you were, ankle chains rubbed and hurt.

I noticed that Officer Hughes had skipped a couple of pairs and moved on to unshackle another twosome. The inmate he was eager to get to was a repeat to Alcatraz, a large black man. No sooner did Hughes have the man freed than he grabbed him by the front of his shirt and backed him against the wall, bounced him against it a time or two, and said, "Now, dammit, we're on Alcatraz and I'm not going to take any more of your big talk."

Captain Rychner walked over to Hughes and said, "This man been giving you trouble?"

"Yeah, he was a bigmouth the whole five days we were on the train."

The escort officers had had quite a rough time of it on the train. The inmates were noisy and tried to act tough all the way—probably because they were so nervous about being imprisoned on Alcatraz.

"Get in there and get your shower. Get it quick and keep your mouth shut," ordered the captain.

Give credit to the con—he caught on quickly. His defiant expression became sullen but there was no resistance from him at all.

With the excellent help of Officer Jerry Ward, we had the inmates showered, clothed, and out in good time. The inmates were also checked against the incoming roster and given their Alcatraz (AZ) numbers.

After the clothing room, the inmates went to the dining hall for fried eggs, fried potatoes, bread and butter, and coffee. Following the meal, they were shown to their new cells. They were dead tired. There would be no trouble from them at least for the rest of this night. But in the morning, things would be different.

The new arrivals were put in cells on the inside of C Block. The bureau's reasons for transferring all these cons was now irrelevant. It was now our problem.

One of the inmates who was helping out in the clothing room, a prison-wise good ol' southern boy, walked by me and said out of the side of his mouth, "Man, there's going to be trouble."

The next morning, it was as if all the new inmates had undergone a complete personality change. They were entering a new world as they marched into the dining hall for breakfast. Each one was trying to establish a place for himself within the population, all the time pretending there wasn't anyone else present. There were furtive looks at others, but no direct eye contact. They were probably looking to see whether there were any old enemies among their new neighbors.

At the same time, they were getting wily looks from the Alcatraz inmates, who were trying to figure out who would be a likely prey for an aggressive homosexual, who was the toughest, and so on. The officers were also observing. The faster you got to know a new inmate, the more likely you were to be able to keep order.

18

The Sleeping Potion

"Greg, you doing anything this evening?" Shannon asked.

"No. Why?"

"How would you like to make some overtime?"

"Fine with me, I guess."

"The doctor wants the two of us to make the rounds putting out the medications tonight."

"Oh?"

"Come here, I want to show you something." Back in the pharmacy, the good doctor was wearing an apron and mixing some rather nasty-smelling ingredients in a large beaker.

"Ugh. What in hell is that?" I asked.

"That," Dr. Belcher said with his little smile, "is the sleeping potion for our dear boys tonight."

I must have looked puzzled. The inmates who demanded drugs at night were always given pills to help them sleep.

"Greg, I want you and Shannon to take charge of this program. What you will do is go along to the cell of each inmate on this list, put a pill cup on the bar of the cell door, and pour some of this mixture into it. About two-thirds full equals one sleeping capsule. Tell them they have to drink it right then and see that they do. If they refuse and you can't get it back, simply mark the list and they will get no more until they are willing to drink it in your presence. Why am I doing this? If there are any inmates saving drugs for someone, this will help us identify them and put them out of the drug business."

Prior to this, the medical staff put the pills in individual packages, indicated the inmates for whom they were intended, and gave them to the officer in charge of the cell house on the evening watch. The officer delivered the packages to the inmates before the lights-out signal. There was no supervision of the inmates taking the pills.

"I love it," I said. "I will gladly be of assistance. And if they won't pay me overtime, I'll do it anyway."

It made me sick to realize that the inmates had managed to gain control of the institution during the years of reform. And where had this reform led? It had led to goofballs.* To quote the armchair penologist Dr. Ralston, "These poor inmates are nervous and frustrated. They need drugs to get their proper rest at night." I don't think Ralston knew what a high trade value sleeping pills, tranquilizers, and uppers had. He didn't know they were stockpiled and used to purchase favors. He didn't know that a large percentage of the prison population had been drug abusers on the outside and had been able to continue their drug use here at Alcatraz.

He did know that discipline was a laugh. He had been told that officers were being slugged and beaten all too often. But he said, "What are the officers complaining about? That's part of their job." Ralston's theory on rehabilitation was that inmates should be made to feel they are in control. He believed that if inmates were allowed to express themselves fully, rehabilitation would be accomplished.

One inmate "expressed himself" by lunging at Officer Joe Burlingame with a shiv. Joe's fast move saved his life—his cheek was sliced instead of his jugular vein.

At the end of my shift, I went into the officers' mess and ate a typical evening meal—in other words, the usual tasteless food. The only good thing I could say about it was that it sustained life, if just barely.

Down in the Mule Barn, I listened to the news and took a snooze. At nine o'clock, I was back in the cell house. This was quite a surprise to Fenton, the cell house officer on the evening watch. The cell house was not the usual place for an officer to be during his time off.

I wandered up and down the aisles. This made Fenton, who was new at Alcatraz, more than a little curious. Finally he let his curiosity get the better of him and said, "What gives, Mr. Gregory?"

I smiled. "You'll find out pretty soon. I can tell you this much, it will be something you haven't seen before."

Meandering down the aisle, I saluted the West Gun Gallery officer and thought of all the boring hours I had spent in gun galleries and towers.

• • •

*Barbiturate sleeping pills.

The West Gun Gallery was about as boring as the Road Tower. We had an officer who had great difficulty staying awake on the morning watch. When assigned to the West Gun Gallery, he managed to wake up and call the Control Center every half hour, but slept in between calls. Hoping to force him to stay awake, the lieutenant added the duty of using a flashlight to signal the Road Tower between the half-hourly calls.

One quarter, I was assigned to the West Gun Gallery and Ernie Yates was assigned to the Road Tower. I called Yates on the phone and told him I wasn't going to follow the new rule and he shouldn't expect any flashes from me. I didn't have any trouble staying awake.

"Okay, Greg."

"But," I said, "if you see Lieutenant Kent coming out to check up on me, call and let the phone ring once and then hang up."

It didn't take long. My phone rang. Once. I flashed my light.

After this happened for a couple of nights, I decided to liven things up a bit. A minute after Yates called, I bellowed over the microphone, "I've been standing here flashing my light at you for ten minutes. Why don't you answer me?"

"Well, Greg, the lieutenant and I were talking and I just didn't have time."

"Don't let it happen again. When I signal you, I expect to get an answer."

"Okay, I'll answer you." There was a hint of laughter in Yates's voice.

"I don't see anything funny. I take my job very seriously and try to follow all the orders of my post." Every time the lieutenant came out, we went through the same routine. The lieutenant knew we were teasing him but he was so determined to catch me failing to observe the rules that he had to keep trying.

One night, Yates didn't have time to signal me on the phone so he more or less danced around the lieutenant until he was in a position to flash his light at me. I saw the flash and returned the signal. The Control Center and Dock Tower officers were sorry when the lieutenant finally gave up trying to catch me. They missed my conversations with Yates.

It's interesting to me that during all the hours I spent in towers and gun galleries at Alcatraz, there was never anything exciting like an escape attempt. *Colliers* magazine took my picture one day when I was assigned to the Dock Tower. I didn't find that exciting either. At the time, I had a good chiropractic practice over in the city and wasn't at all eager for my patients to learn where I spent my time when not in the office.

When the last of the inmates who worked in the kitchen were back in their cells, I took a trip around the cell house again to get a feel for the inmates' mood. Then I phoned Shannon. "All clear down here. Whenever you're ready, come on down."

"See you in about ten minutes."

Shannon came down to the cell house with a large beaker full of the liquid sedative, an empty half-pint beaker, and a stack of pill cups.

"We'll use the half-pint beaker to pour the liquid into the cups. We wouldn't want anyone hitting the big beaker and spilling all the doctor's handiwork," said Shannon.

"Well, ain't you the clever one," I said.

Shannon looked at the list and said, "Let's start on the top tier on the outside of B Block."

By the time we got up to the third tier, in spite of the fact that we had made no unusual noises, we could tell by the utter quiet in the cell house that the plumbing line had been busy. The first stop was at the cell of a longtime Alcatraz inmate. He was middle-aged and usually very quiet.

"Roberts, would you like something to help you go to sleep tonight?" Shannon asked.

"Yes," said Roberts questioningly.

Shannon placed a pill cup on the bar and carefully poured some of the liquid into it.

Roberts said with a nervous snort, "What is this supposed to be?"

"It's a liquid sleeping medicine. If you want it, drink it down right now."

"But I'm not sleepy right now."

"Come on and drink it. You either drink it now or go without."

Roberts, being an old prison-wise inmate, considered the situation briefly while looking from Shannon to me and decided argument would be useless. He drank it.

Other inmates could hear what was happening. So, as Shannon and I went from cell to cell pouring the potion for those on the list, they accepted it. There was a certain amount of yakking and cursing, but no refusals until we got down on the second tier to MacDonald's cell.

MacDonald was one of the inmates who had served the most time in Alcatraz and was a very intelligent man. When Shannon offered him the potion, he shook his head with a smile and waved us on to the next cell.

It took nearly half an hour to complete the list. Eleven inmates had refused the sleeping potion.

"Okay," Shannon said, "so much for that. Are you ready for TU?"

"As ready as I'll ever be."

We had hardly got inside TU when an inmate hollered, "Is that the Doc?"

"Yeah," came the answer from an inmate who was celled near the door.

Immediately, the usual babble of conversation stopped and the three tiers of TU became quiet.

"Same routine?" I asked. "From the third tier down?"

"Yes, that will be fine."

"Good, our first customer is a real nice con."

"Irwin?" asked Shannon. Irwin had occupied the first cell on the third tier for a long time, except for visits to the Hole. He was about twenty-three years old but looked much older. In many ways he was already an old man, but he was still not fully developed emotionally. A small person, he was constantly fighting to keep the big studs away. In Washington, D.C., he had had a pretty good career, brief though it was, as a baseball player.

Shannon said in an innocent voice, "Got your sleeping potion here, Irwin."

Irwin was lying on his bunk, staring up at the ceiling. "Just leave it there on the bar. And I don't need any of your goddamned yakking."

"No, Irwin, I don't think you understand. You see, we are pouring this cup full of a medicine that will help you to sleep."

"What?" said Irwin, quickly sitting up.

"See this little cup of liquid? If you want this sleeping potion, you have to get up here and drink it right now."

Irwin shot a mean look at Shannon and then at the cup. "Where in the hell is my sleeping pill?"

"No more sleeping pills, Irwin. You want this or not?"

"What do you mean? I drink it instead of a pill?"

"Yes, that's the idea."

"Well, I'm not sleepy now, so I'll just save it."

"No saving. Drink it now or else."

"Or else what?" Irwin said, with rage beginning to tinge his voice. He had a reputation for resisting authority and here he was in a take-it-or-leave-it situation. Suddenly he burst into a screaming tirade of vile obscenities, grabbed the cup, and threw the liquid into Shannon's face.

"Ooooh," said Shannon, yawning deeply. "Help me, help me. I'm falling asleep."

Irwin finally began to run down. He realized that all he was doing was blowing smoke and that he had thrown away his drug. He stopped his diatribe and said, "All right, Doc, if that's the way it is, give me the cup."

"Irwin, you've already had a cup. Only one to a customer."

The yelling and screaming started again. We could no longer understand the words.

The rest of the inmates in TU learned fast. When they were offered the potion, they drank it with very little fuss.

Having returned to the hospital, I stood watching Shannon put things away. "Well, Doc, what's the verdict?"

"Good, to the extent that we cut a few more off the drug list. I'm sure some of those who drank the sedative didn't really want it. They would have saved it for a friend or an enemy with a hold on them if we had let them."

Some days later, I was witness to a staring match between the doctor and a member of the administrative staff. The administrator came up to the hospital, handed Dr. Belcher a piece of paper, and said, "These men stay on." There was no doubt in my mind that he was referring to inmates receiving drugs.

The doctor took the list and put it with the other notes on his table. The two men stared at each other. I had never seen the administrator display such determination or such cold eyes.

I felt uncomfortable. I never saw the list—neither did I want to see it, considering the emotion it had generated. However, I suspect the administrator won that round.

19

The Chief Steward

The chief steward—the head of the bureau's culinary department—was coming to Alcatraz. This was a special event: We had never before had a visit from the chief steward. People from the bureau liked to come to Alcatraz, just to take in San Francisco and what it had to offer—at least this was my opinion. But the chief steward's responsibilities seemed to keep him in Washington.

It wouldn't be long before everyone on the island was calling him "Mr. Chief Steward, Sir." But when he first got off the boat, he was directed to the dock office where the lieutenant had him sign in and then told him rather curtly to get on the bus that would take him to the bachelors' quarters in A Building.

As the story was told to me some time later, the chief steward took one look at his room in the bachelors' quarters—which was a miserable, dirty mess—and the next thing anybody knew he was up top and on his way into the warden's office. Those who saw him, of course, saw a stranger—a very angry-looking stranger. Although Bertrand made a feeble effort to stop him, the steward brushed by him and charged on into the office, the secretary following. Warden Swope was surprised at this invasion, to put it mildly. The chief steward grabbed a chair and dragged it up to the warden's desk. The warden, staring in bewilderment, started to stand up.

"Don't get up, Warden," the stranger said as he motioned the warden back into his chair. As the warden sat down, the stranger grabbed the telephone and said, "Is it all right if I use your phone?"

By now Bertrand was beginning to think this man was someone important. In a few more moments, the secretary *knew* he was someone important, because he was talking directly to the bureau in Washington, D.C. After exchanging a few words, the stranger turned the phone over to the warden, who went through several facial expressions and colors. The warden finally put down the phone and said to Bertrand, "Get the personnel officer in here right now, and see to it that Mr. Whittower is given every courtesy we can offer while he is on the island." The warden begged the chief steward to stay in his house, an offer that was quickly refused—Whittower chose instead to stay in the city.

I was officially introduced to the chief steward on the *Warden Johnston* during its 5:40 p.m. run to the mainland. As I shook hands with him, I noted a wide smile that was almost hypnotizing, big blue eyes, curly brown hair, a heavy set to his shoulders, and an appearance of being even taller up close than from a distance—a very handsome man.

"Greg," said Milan, the Alcatraz steward who had introduced us, "you're just the man to help the chief. You know a lot more about the city than I do."

"Be glad to try," I said. "What do you want to know?"

"First of all," said Whittower, "I would like to take in a genuine Italian restaurant. I understand there are a lot of them in town."

"I'm headed for one right now. It isn't very fancy, but it's famous for its food. Could I ask you to have dinner with me?"

"I'd really appreciate that. And you know what? The bureau is buying."

From the dock at the foot of Van Ness Avenue, we walked through Fisherman's Wharf—I had trouble getting Bill Whittower out of there—and on to the Gold Spike Restaurant on Columbus Avenue. We enjoyed a delectable Italian meal of several courses—from antipasto to dessert. Whittower's training in foods and seasonings had not prepared him for the various dishes that were served to us.

When the waiter brought the check, I pointed to the chief steward and it was put in front of him. I watched him as he studied the check and his expression became one of disbelief. "What's this? Only ninety cents for a meal like this and only twenty-five cents for a drink? And they forgot to put the wine on here. How much was that?"

"The wine comes with the meal. Come on, Chief. Pay up."

The next morning, after Bunch completed roll call and job assignments, he took me by the arm and said, "You and I have an urgent appointment in the warden's office."

Whittower was already in there with the warden. Judging by their expressions, it was apparent that something serious was brewing.

"Why don't you tell them, Mr. Whittower?" Warden Swope said.

"Not much to tell. But we are going to take a very important step as far as the culinary department is concerned." The chief steward told us briefly what he was going to do: There were to be no more second helpings and no more special meals for the kitchen crew or anyone else. In addition, inmates on kitchen duty would start from the bottom and be promoted to the better jobs according to their work record and seniority. The chief steward told us that he fully expected the kitchen crew to go on strike.

The warden leaned back in his chair and looked at Bunch. "Lieutenant, I want you to call an emergency, voluntary meeting of the custodial force for this evening. Put some people on the phone and notify everybody who can come— on or off duty. I want it to be known that we are a hundred percent behind Mr. Whittower."

"Warden," said Whittower, "I will get in touch with the bureau and we will have people from all the western penitentiaries, at least by tomorrow evening." He turned to me. "Greg, I would like to have you with me in the kitchen when I tell the crew about the changes we are going to make."

Later, I found Whittower in the kitchen making an inspection. He was opening cupboard doors and garbage cans and inspecting the food storage. There were two stewards on duty and they seemed to be ignoring the chief. But the inmates weren't; they were keeping their eyes on him, watching his every move.

Mr. Whittower walked up to Briggam, the kitchen officer, and asked, "Is all the kitchen help in here now?"

"No, there are a few in their cells," said Briggam.

"Can you get them? I want all of them here."

I said, "I'll go get them." When we returned, Whittower took over.

"Men, gather around. We are going to make some changes in the kitchen."

I listened intently as Whittower explained the program in detail. I liked what I heard. I also watched the inmates as they listened to how things would be.

When Whittower had laid down all the changes that would be made, he said, "Now, I expect that if you don't like it, you are going to protest, probably go on strike. But this is the way it is going to be, no matter what you do."

I sat on the edge of a dining hall table, scanning the faces of the twenty-five or so inmates. For a long moment there was utter silence. I looked at Alvin "Creepy" Karpis. I could tell by his insolent smile and cold, steely eyes that he wanted a strike. I also knew that the other inmates got the same message. I looked around the group, but no one wanted to look directly at me.

I got Bunch on the phone and reported, "They're going on strike."

"We'll be in shortly. Hold them until we get there."

In good time, Bunch came in with several officers. He looked at the kitchen crew and said, "This is your last chance. Are you all going on strike?"

There was silence.

"Okay, men," Bunch said to the officers, "put them over in A Block."

A Block was not ordinarily used for celling inmates because it still had the old, soft iron bars for the cell fronts. This made it necessary to create a new post— on each shift, an officer was assigned to guard the striking inmates. They were confined to their new cells. Their meals were brought in to them.

A few of the older inmates volunteered to work in the kitchen. They were due to be transferred to other institutions because of their good records—otherwise they might not have been so willing to go against the inmate bosses. We knew they were taking a grave risk and would need all the protection we could give.

As the morning went on, two more stewards who lived on the island came up to help. Word went out that officers were needed to work in the culinary department during their time off. They volunteered readily, out of curiosity if nothing else.

At Alcatraz, where the inmates had few privileges, going to the dining hall three times a day for a good meal was important to the population. The interruption of the regular schedule of meals could cause their small concerns to escalate out of proportion. This is why Whittower requested help from other institutions.

Within twenty-four hours, help began to trickle in and the kitchen was being run mostly by stewards—our own and those from other institutions—along with the few inmates willing to work. This relieved some of the officers who had been working in the kitchen during their time off.

By the noon meal on that first day of the kitchen strike, I had to admit that I was apprehensive when the inmates began to file in. I had never known the dining hall to be so quiet. The inmates finished their meal in record time—not that they were hurried; they just didn't waste any time gossiping.

About two o'clock, I was called into Warden Swope's office.

"Ever hear of a man named Eastland?" the warden asked.

"No, sir."

"He is being sent here by the bureau. He has a reputation of being a tough correctional supervisor. If he can get a plane of some kind out of Washington, he should be here early this evening. I want you, Mr. Gregory, to get this out to the staff and make it loud and clear to everybody, no matter what their rank: Mr. Eastland will be in absolute charge of the correctional staff until further notice and he is to be given, without question, all possible cooperation. All officers will carry out his orders explicitly."

"Yes, sir."

As I walked back into the cell house, I had a strong feeling that the proverbial feces was about to hit the fan. It made me feel even more apprehensive, but also filled me with a strange kind of excitement. I popped a couple more Tums in my mouth and carried out the warden's orders, sharing my Tums with those who needed them.

20

Mr. Eastland

The sun was setting over the Golden Gate Bridge. It was one of the most glorious sunsets I had ever seen. Amazing how a few clouds can change a beautiful sunset into a spectacular one.

Down on the dock, I watched the approach of the *Warden Johnston*. It had made a special trip to the mainland to bring the already famous Mr. Eastland to the island. When the boat was secured, up the gangplank came several officers and a stranger. They were all laughing and hooting as though something was a big joke. As the stranger came up the gangplank, I made a summary of what I saw. Eastland was a medium-sized man with reddish-brown hair, piercing blue eyes, and a smile from ear to ear.

The officers gathered around and moved with him as he headed toward the dock office to sign in. It wasn't exactly the Second Coming, but the officers were greeting him like no bureau official had ever before been received.

"I understand," Eastland said as he put down the pen after signing in, "that all you Alcatraz prison screws have been walking around with your tails between your legs like a bunch of beaten mongrels. Well, guys, that is going to change right now." There was a moment of silence and then a spontaneous burst of cheering, yelling, laughing, and backslapping. This was the best news we had heard in a long time.

Bunch stepped up. "Mr. Eastland, I'm Lieutenant Bunch Tompkins. We are going to have a meeting in the social hall so everyone can meet you and get acquainted."

"This isn't a formal kind of meeting, is it? I don't much go for that."

"That's entirely up to you, Mr. Eastland," Bunch said with a straight face and a twinkle in his eye.

"Call me John, but my official title is associate warden."

We moved along toward the social hall and John began telling jokes and stories. Not exactly Sunday-school stories, and they were pretty funny. When we got to the social hall, Warden Swope, some of the office staff, and several officers were already there. Normally, a group of officers entering the warden's presence would become quiet immediately. However, Eastland prevented that by continuing his stories until he looked around and in a loud voice said, "Where is the warden? Oh, there you are. How are you, Warden?"

"Just fine. How was your trip?"

"Actually, it was kind of boring. I understand you're having some problems here. You're not the only one, Warden. It seems to be hitting all the prisons."

"Hmm, yes, we seem to be having our share. Wouldn't you like to go to your quarters and freshen up? We can talk business tomorrow morning."

"No hurry about my quarters, Warden. Let's start talking business right now. But how about something to eat? Is there any place around here to eat?" Looking around the group, he spotted the chief steward. "Hi, Bill. The chief steward right here and I can't get anything to eat. Something should be done about this."

"Well, if it's okay with the warden, we'll have something to eat here in a very short time," said Bill, looking at Warden Swope.

"We can do better than that. We'll go up to my house."

"Who's 'we'?" asked Eastland.

"Why, uh . . . ," said the warden. It was obvious that he meant just a few of the top brass, certainly not the whole group of peons.

"No, no, nothing like that," said Eastland, "We can meet right here."

The warden gulped, cleared his throat, looked at one of the stewards, and said, "Can you get something to eat down here?"

"All I need is your permission, Warden, and we can have coffee, sandwiches—the works."

"Let's get the tables set up," said Bunch. In record time, the tables and chairs were ready and the food was brought in from the kitchen and the Alcatraz Store.

"Hey, this looks great," said Eastland. "Now, I'm not much for formal talk, but I'm glad that you guys were kind enough to come out on your own time to meet me. All I want to say is this—you are going to have this prison back under your control again." A big cheer went up from the officers. "No, no, I'm not giving you a bunch of B.S. I'll tell you right now that it will be rough in places. But if we all work together, it will come out okay. Incidentally, did you hear the one about . . . "

That is the way the rest of the evening went. Others joined Eastland in the storytelling. Never before during my tenure at Alcatraz had I seen such spontaneous camaraderie among the officers and a big shot from the bureau. Was this guy for real? He had to be. Unbelievable!

I was drinking my third cup of coffee when Bertrand eased up to me and said, "Guess what?"

"Don't you dare spoil this good feeling I have with some bad news."

From the corner of his mouth, the secretary said, "I'm sure for you it is good news."

"So, what is it? I can take it."

"Parant left this afternoon. He's been transferred to another institution with a promotion."

"What? I don't get it." I was about to ask some questions.

"No questions. You'll have to figure it out for yourself."

When I left the social hall and started down to the Mule Barn, I couldn't keep a smile off my face. No, I wouldn't miss Parant. But I remembered a time when he actually gave me an assignment at my request.

Parant had assigned me to the Dock Tower morning watch for an extended period of time for punishment—or so he thought. I don't remember the incident that incurred the acting captain's wrath, but it was no doubt a case of my not showing the proper respect to a lieutenant for whom I felt no respect.

Although I generally preferred assignments that involved interaction with the inmates, at that time I wanted the Dock Tower morning watch. Now that I am beyond the reach of recrimination for infraction of the rules, I will tell why.

I was attending the San Francisco College of Chiropractic during the day, in preparation for leaving the prison service. Working the morning watch in a tower was perfect. I put my notes on three-by-five cards and carried them in my pocket. During the watch I took out a card, flashed my light on it just long enough to read it, and then memorized it by saying it over and over. On occasion, I would mumble a little too loudly and the Control Center officer would quietly say over the microphone, "Greg, are you all right?" He knew what I was doing and didn't want my nemesis, the lieutenant who wanted to be warden, to hear me.

One of my friends overheard Parant say he thought I had been in that tower long enough to learn my lesson and that he was going to give me a different assignment for the next quarter.

I sincerely wanted to stay in the tower. But I will admit to being in kind of a mischievous mood when I went into the acting captain's office.

"Captain," I said, "I know we are supposed to be rotated every three months. But I wonder if I could stay on in the Dock Tower morning watch?"

Without looking up at me, Parant turned red in the face, took off his cap, and smacked the desk with it. I walked out without waiting for a reply. I was reassigned to the Dock Tower morning watch.

As for showing respect for lieutenants, there was an incident at Sandstone that caused me to view lieutenants with wariness and perhaps to display my lack of regard for them more than I should have. Junior and senior officers were rated annually by the lieutenants, who also made recommendations for promotions. A friend of mine overheard a meeting of the lieutenants in which they discussed the possibility of my being promoted to senior officer. One of the lieutenants said, "We can't promote that man. If we do, the next thing we know we'll be working for him." There were murmurs of agreement.

I was not promoted.

During my tenure at Alcatraz, I worked under some of those same lieutenants. There was a lot of transferring from one institution to another. When an officer was promoted above the rank of senior, bureau policy required that he transfer to another institution. But being promoted and leaving the island on required transfer did not necessarily mean we had seen the last of these officers. In some cases, they were back within a year or two, working on another promotion. It was the transfer policy that kept me from going after a promotion. I did not want to leave the Bay Area: It was home by now, and for several years after graduating from the College of Chiropractic, I had a good practice that I did not want to give up.

Some lieutenants were aggravatingly ambitious. They had to be promoted to captain, then associate warden before they could get to the top. Lieutenants who were acting captains were the worst kind. They seemed to think that gaining attention for some special feat—such as catching an officer in dereliction of duty—would mean a promotion. To a lesser degree, the same was true of senior officers as acting lieutenants. A captain who was acting associate warden was also in a position to cause problems—he had greater responsibilities and more power than a captain.

As much as I had appreciated Mr. Miller's opinion of me, it set me up as a target for these ambitious acting lieutenants and captains. A lot of men in those positions seemed to feel that catching my failure to observe some idiotic rule would be their ticket to the top.

I made a contribution to their trip by not observing rules that were tailored to only one officer or Mickey Mouse rules that had nothing to do with safety, custody, or security. We had a few of these at almost every post, written by aspiring officers who wanted to get their names on a piece of paper. That was another thing they thought would get them promoted.

But the kinds of papers these officers signed all too often were their own letters detailing my failure to obey some silly rule. I speared the first one of these that I received on the hook in my locker and forgot about it. A couple of days later, the acting captain who had written the letter came to me, angrily demanding to know why I had not answered his accusation. He became quite confused when I informed him that according to the laws of the United States, as a wounded war veteran, I had thirty days to answer any complaint concerning my employment. Even a legitimate complaint.

By the end of my career, the hook in my locker couldn't take any more complaints. It was full to overflowing. The pages of criticisms impaled on that hook became one of the standing jokes on the island. On one occasion, an officer with years of experience on Alcatraz was asked by a new officer, "What's it like to work on The Rock?"

"You want to know what it's like to work here? Go down to the locker room and read all the letters on Gregory's locker door. That's what it's like," said the older officer.

In my presence once, an officer in an acting position above my rank failed to obey some rule of which he did not approve. Tongue in cheek, I sternly rebuked him and said I would have to write a letter to the captain concerning his dereliction of duty.

The captain was somewhat amused when he received a written response to the complaint I had not written. And I was amused when the captain's clerk gave me a detailed explanation of why the rule had not been honored.

On the surface, it seemed that things were going along normally; but just underneath, tension was continuing to build. We officers were quite taken with Mr. Eastland and his calm demeanor, almost nonchalance: It inspired us to try to look and act the same, keeping our own tension under control. But I couldn't help wondering where it was all leading.

A kite from the striking kitchen crew came out of A Block, offering to bargain with the new associate warden. Eastland sent Captain Rychner in to tell them there would be no bargaining. If they wanted to get out of A Block, they would have to accept the new kitchen policy and the administration would decide what to do with them.

When a particularly loud and fairly tough inmate got testy in the dining hall, Officer Akins decided to put him on report to see how Eastland would handle it. Indeed, we were all waiting to see the result of Akins's action—would the inmate be tried or would Akins be tried?

"Okay, let's try this guy," said Eastland. Court was held in a remodeled cell in A Block. Bunch was there in his capacity as cell house lieutenant; he told me the story later. Officer Krenshaw brought in the inmate, Koupnick.

Eastland began the proceedings. "We have here, Koupnick, a report by Officer Akins that you were shooting off your mouth while in the mess hall. Do you have anything to say?"

"Why, that sonofabitch, I never did no such a thing."

"Are you calling the officer a liar?"

"I'm calling him a liar and I heard about you. You're supposed to be tough." Koupnick rose from his chair. "You mess with me, man, and I will break your goddamned neck." Turning from the court, he swaggered out the door and started toward his cell. Krenshaw stood uncertainly, wondering what he should do.

"Bring that man back here!" shouted the associate warden, "I'm not through with him yet."

"You heard Mr. Eastland," said Bunch gleefully as he grabbed Krenshaw by the arm. "Come on, let's go get him."

"Bring him back here, even if you have to drag him back," Eastland continued. "And if he happens to bump his head a few times, that will be just too bad."

Of course, Koupnick could hear all this. It was a complete surprise to him. Before he knew it, Bunch and Krenshaw were roughly dragging him back into court.

"Now you listen to me, you no-good punk," Eastland said. "I was going to let you go with a reprimand, but seeing that you're so tough, I'm going to put you in the cooler and I don't know when you're going to get out." Looking at Bunch, he added, "If he gives you any resistance, let him have it with both barrels."

This action hit the grapevine and went through the prison like wildfire. Both the prison population and the correctional staff wondered just what it meant. We officers hoped it was a harbinger of better discipline to come.

In TU, Koupnick made another bad mistake. When the inmates shouted down to him, asking how the court went, he said, "Ah, just a bunch of bullshit. These screws are trying to act tough."

"Shut up," said Bunch.

"Whaddayamean, shut up? I won't shut up for you or any other goddamn screw." This was said loudly so everybody in TU could hear as he tried to strut out in front of the other inmates. But before he had taken more than two steps, Bunch had him.

"Still acting ornery, huh?" said Bunch. "Take off your clothes."

"What?" Koupnick sounded a little panicky. "I'm not taking my clothes off for anybody." Before he could say anything else, Bunch and Krenshaw had his clothes off and piled on the floor.

Bunch had Koupnick's head in a reverse hammerlock. "Get a Hole cell open," he said to Lewis.

No one had had the nerve to put an inmate in a Hole cell for such a long time that Lewis was bewildered. But he quickly recovered and had the door open by the time Bunch and Krenshaw got there with the naked Koupnick, whom they had dragged down the aisle well out in front of the other cells so that the inmates could see him. He was then deposited in the cell, none too gently, and the door was shut with a bang.

Absolute quiet reigned in TU. It was going to take some time for the inmates to figure it all out, that was for sure. It even took Koupnick several minutes to react. When he did, he began the same old shouting, screaming, and profanity.

"Let him holler for a while," said Bunch as he was leaving. "I'll be back later."

There were many similar incidents. Officers began to write shots just like in the old days of Johnston and Miller. Court was held and the culprits were duly punished by the revoking of privileges, by being put in TU, or by losing good time.

With Dr. Belcher in the hospital, Mr. Whittower in the kitchen, and Mr. East-land in the cell house, many changes were being made in the operation of Alca-traz. There was a kind of desperate attitude on the part of many of the inmates, and violence was escalating. In rare cases, the brutality ended in a death and a federal court trial in San Francisco.

21

The Clothing Room

The stairs going down to the clothing room were in the West End opposite B Block. The area we called the clothing room consisted of two rooms used for band practice, storerooms, the clothing room proper, and the shower room, which had a long row of back-to-back shower stalls. On shower days—Tuesday, Thursday, and Saturday—several officers were required to maintain order and safety in the partitioned showers. On other days, there was just one officer to supervise all the enclosed areas, and it was difficult. You were constantly on the move to make sure you didn't miss somebody who had sneaked down the stairs.

The clothing room was used as a meeting place for friends and enemies alike. Inmates would get permission under false pretenses to go down for a clandestine meeting. Over the years, it was the scene of many bloody knifings and fights.

Kevin, a young black kid, was involved in some clothing-room fights. He was in prison because he did a favor for a person he didn't know. Kevin had worked in a theater in a southern state. A man came in, handed him a small package, and told him to give it to a person who would come in and ask for it. Kevin didn't know what was in the package. He was arrested and convicted of handling dope.

Kevin told me the story of his arrest and the thirty days he spent in quarantine. The kid was put in a dormitory with a group of aggressive studs. Unable to defend himself, he was raped five times the first night.

Kevin seldom initiated fights at Alcatraz, but he did try to defend himself. We were always finding knives or razor blades on him. One time we had him remove his jacket and shirt but still couldn't get him past the snitch box. He finally passed through without his shoes—there was a razor blade in one of them.

One day Kevin went down to take a shower, wearing his robe and carrying his dirty clothes to drop into the laundry hampers. With his hands occupied, no one thought anything about his toothbrush being in his mouth. He had made a shiv and inserted it into the handle of the toothbrush.

In the clothing room, Kevin went after a con who had been pestering him for sexual favors. He was stopped before he was able to use his weapon, but we never knew where he got the razor blade.

We tried as best we could to protect Kevin and others from the wolves. We also tried as best we could to ignore the activities of mutually consenting inmates.

On another occasion in the showers, a big guy, Tivorney, went after Kevin with a knife. The alarm went off and I ran down the stairs, where I saw the chase and some very scared officers. Being scared is your best protection without training—these guys had been hired off the street and didn't know what to do. I met Tivorney with his knife head on and grabbed his wrist. He dropped the knife and it was all over. I took the kid up to the hospital and got him patched up. He had two superficial gashes on his abdomen. It was close, but the knife didn't get down under the peritoneum. Kevin's ability to dodge and run fast had saved his life.

Kevin also used his youthful, desirable looks as a weapon to protect himself. That is, by half promising one wolf favors, he got him to fight another wolf to whom he had also half-promised favors. As long as they fought each other and were put in the Hole, Kevin felt relatively safe.

I kept talking to the supervisors and the parole officer about getting Kevin out of Alcatraz. Finally, when he was called into disciplinary court on some infraction of the rules, I asked him to tell his story of how he got into prison and what happened to him during the thirty days of quarantine. Paul Madigan was on the court that day (he was associate warden at the time) and I made a point of seeing him afterward to tell him how badly I felt about Kevin's being in Alcatraz. I told Madigan that Kevin really needed someone to show a little interest in him. This made an impression and we were eventually able to get Kevin out of there.

While Kevin was with us, he found something he liked—the saxophone. He fell in love with that instrument. Not knowing one note from another did not interfere with his enjoyment of making sounds on the saxophone. He played quietly and in his own way.

Kevin learned something else while he was with us. I had noticed that his cell was always in a mess—bunk not made, clothing on the floor, and shelves in disarray. One day while giving assignments to officers, I said, "Sarge, how would you like to be a D.I. again? Take this guy down to his cell and teach him how to make a bunk and how to organize his belongings and put them away." Sarge had recently retired from the army. He must have been a good teacher and Kevin a fast learner. From that time on, Kevin's cell was in perfect order.

• • •

During one stint of duty I did in the clothing room, a new inmate was assigned to work for me. Chuck Parks was a tall, lanky, black kid with a lot of muscle stretched along his bones. The first time I asked him to do something, he loudly refused and called me a few choice names.

"Get out of here and go back upstairs," I began, but I didn't get to finish. Chuck burst into tears—the tough-talking kid was just an overgrown baby. I rang the bell to indicate I was sending someone upstairs. Chuck went back to his cell and the rest of my crew quietly went back to work.

After Chuck went to disciplinary court, he was reassigned to me. I explained to him that there were jobs to be done and I would be the one who told him what to do. He never gave me any more trouble. As time went on and I got to know him, I found that Chuck was not very bright. Sometimes it was hard to find things for him to do—janitorial work was about all he could handle. He got to be known as "Gregory's boy."

Chuck became the target in a clothing-room knifing. We had several young men who had been in prison since they were teenagers. The older cons had tolerated them and even enjoyed some of their pranks. But when these young men found themselves in their mid-twenties and were no longer cute kids, they thought the only way to make a name for themselves was to prove how tough they were. They decided that one of them would kill Chuck.

They drew straws to see who would do the knifing. Koupnick got the short straw (the drawing was probably rigged). That was the end of Koupnick's pretending to be tough. He refused the assignment, knowing he would be looking over his shoulder for the rest of his stay in Alcatraz.

On the second drawing, a loud-mouthed con named Elwood drew the short straw. Elwood was happy to accept the assignment. He simply walked up to the poor innocent kid and pulled a knife. Chuck made a quick turn so that the knife thrust went into his back instead of his front. It went deep into the lumbar portion of his spine, cutting a nerve to the bladder. He became incontinent as a result of the injury.

Shortly after Chuck was knifed, one of the young, smart group came down to the clothing room and said to me, "Well, I see they got your stool pigeon." I couldn't believe they thought the poor kid was my stool pigeon. With his mental capacity, he wouldn't have been a reliable source of information.

Elwood was tried in federal court but found not guilty. He continued his big-mouth profanity and bragging.

The story behind Chuck's knifing came out when another inmate was marked for extinction. The designated hit man tried to reason with his associates, but finding that impossible, he decided to testify in federal court. After describing the cold and calculated drawing of straws to see who would murder a fellow inmate, he was turned over to the U.S. marshals for immediate transfer out of Alcatraz.

During the early 1950s, the administration allowed the inmates to alter the prison-issued clothing in whatever way they wished. Inmates who could sew were suddenly in great demand. There were pegged pants and Eisenhower jackets everywhere, causing a constant hassle in the clothing room. "These ain't my pants," was a complaint often heard on shower days. We did the best we could to return the desired clothing to the inmate.

Another problem we had was the shortage of towels. This was one of the more ridiculous situations I was involved in at Alcatraz. Inmates had installed unauthorized showers in some of the shops down in the industries and in the kitchen basement. The administration ignored the extra stalls and the fact that many inmates were taking showers daily. But they could not ignore my supply orders for additional towels to eliminate the shortage created by laundry workers passing towels directly to the inmates who used the illegal showers.

It doesn't take much to set a riot in motion among a group of men as volatile as the occupants of Alcatraz. I didn't want that to happen as a result of not having clean towels to give them on their regular shower days. But the administration was afraid to use a little simple logic and rip out the illegal showers. Instead, the acting captain, my nemesis Parant, had me called up for a full-dress disciplinary action with all the top brass taking part. He came very close to calling me a goddamned liar. All of this over a few towels.

As ordered, I counted the towels going to the laundry, but I never got the same number back. My continuing orders for towels gave the front office something to complain about until Mr. Eastland, who was not scared to death of the cons, took over and had the illegal showers ripped out. Then we had more towels than storage space.

I had an exceptional group of orderlies working for me in the clothing room during one quarter. They worked well together and got along with the other inmates when they came down for showers and clean clothing.

One end of the clothing room had a long counter that partitioned off the area where we kept the clothing and other items to be issued to the inmates. Steel mesh extending from the counter upward completed the partition. A window in the mesh was used to pass out the clothing and other items.

The pine countertop had a knothole deep enough to hold the sharpened end of a pencil. For weeks, the guys always seemed to be messing around that part of the counter. I noticed they kept a pencil standing there at the ready all the time.

I didn't bother them—they weren't hurting themselves or anyone else and were getting the work done.

Then one day, with the work finished early, the boys started a game. They stood on a mark on the floor, stretched a rubber band between their fingers, and using a paper clip as a projectile, shot at a spitball on top of the ever-present upright pencil. They were having a good time.

"Let's have four tries at a time. Let's see who can hit four out of four," said Wrey, who had been a marksman in the army.

There was total agreement: "Okay." "That sounds good to me." "You first."

"All right, you guys, stand back because the army is coming through," said Wrey as he let go and the spitball fell. There was cheering all around as the target was put back on top of the pencil.

"That was a regular Matt Dillon shot!" That was their name for me, but I ignored the reference.*

"I bet Matt Dillon couldn't do that."

On the next three shots, Wrey made the spitball fall each time while the cheers and references to me got louder and more demanding of attention.

"Matt Dillon ought to be able to hit four out of four. I hear he qualifies at the range every time with no problem. Besides, he was a rifle coach in the Marines."

"Ah, that don't mean a thing. Marines can't shoot straight."

I was sitting in the office, feet propped up, checking the towel and clothing lists. The game proceeded and the spitball fell with amazing regularity. There were some misses, but the men were hitting their target most of the time. Finally, they started addressing me by name.

"Mr. Gregory, come try this."

"What's that?" I innocently asked.

"Hit the spitball with a paper clip."

"No, I'm not going to play your game. Anybody could hit that target," and I continued my pretense of paying no attention to them.

"Oh, come on, Boss. Let's see you try it."

As the game and comments continued, I began to wonder if I *could* hit that spitball. That did it. I found myself standing on the mark with a rubber band pulled back and a paper clip aimed at the spitball perched on top of the pencil. Except for the sad strains of a guitar coming from the music room, there was absolute silence. My crew stood and watched as I fired the first paper clip and the spitball remained on top of the pencil.

*Gregory did not know who Matt Dillon was when he first heard the inmates call him by that name. But after watching the television show *Gunsmoke,* he said, "I couldn't help but feel a bit tickled about my nickname."

"That was close, Mr. Gregory, and on your first try! Try another one." I did, and the spitball was still sitting there.

"That's pretty good shooting for a Marine," said the army marksman.

By this time, I was mentally kicking myself for getting roped into something like this. After the fourth miss, I said, "I give up. You guys are better at this game than I am."

There was a snort and a snicker and as I turned to look at my audience, they all burst into hearty, good-natured laughter.

I walked over to the counter and tried to take the pencil out of the hole, but found it difficult. A hefty tug brought it up suddenly, along with a string that was tied to the part of the pencil that was concealed.

"Where's the other end of this string?" I asked, trying without much success to look somber. The string operator crawled out from under the opposite end of the counter and they all took great pride in showing me what had taken them weeks to work out.

The circumference of the last inch or so of the pencil had been reduced by sanding it and a groove was made for the string. The knothole had also been treated so that when the pencil was inserted it rested easily in an upright position without falling through. The string went along under the counter to the end, where the operator could watch the shot being fired and respond by jerking the string to make the spitball fall—or by not jerking the string.

I stood there shaking my head in wonderment at the ingenuity, time, patience, and cooperation that had gone into setting up this prank. I was glad I had not disappointed them. At the same time, I was flabbergasted at their knowledge of me. They knew exactly how to get my feet off the desk and my toe on that mark.

Periodically, I would have to replace some of the inmate workers for one reason or another. I had a couple of guys, Vince and Doug, who were very good workers. If I hinted to them that something needed to be done, it was done. But they were forever going behind the showers and getting into a fight.

"They're at it again" got to be a common refrain. I never knew what the fighting was about, probably one trying to punk the other.

"By gosh, I've had enough of this," I said one day. "You're going to finish this fight with an audience." I called the other inmates. "Come out here and have a seat. We're going to watch a fight." The other inmates gladly came from whatever jobs they were doing and sat on the benches.

"All right, you guys, let's get this over with."

Neither of them really wanted to fight, but Vince, who was bigger than Doug, started in as if he were very serious. He kept an eye on me—hoping I would stop them—while he kept taunting Doug. The truth was, Doug was getting the best of the big guy.

Soon I noticed that my orderlies were quietly fading away. They were sort of melting off the benches and doing a disappearing act, going back to work. I looked around to see what was causing this strange behavior. The acting captain stood there with that "gotcha" look. He had sneaked down the back stairs, which he did several times when I was the clothing-room officer.

I let the guys exchange several more blows and called a halt to it. I expected to find a written reprimand in my box or at the very least be required to account for the fight to the brass. I never heard a word. Not even "They're at it again." My orderlies had lost their taste for fighting.

Following showers, the music rooms came alive with sounds that were sometimes actually musical. In fairness to the inmates, I have to say that the greatest musicians in the world would not have sounded good in that concrete-and-steel setting. The inmates set up one room with chairs and music stands for the various groups to use for practice. They were very serious about their music, their practice periods, and how the room was set up. It had to be just right. There were several trumpets and saxophones, a piano, bass, and drums. These sessions were also accompanied by a lot of hollering and yelling at each other.

When the director raised his baton and the playing started, you could not tell one note from another or one tune from another. All of this was a kind of play-acting. Many inmates had a way of making themselves believe they could do things they really could not do. I guess it was a way of maintaining their sanity—but their music just about drove me nuts.

One day I noticed the inmate called Smitty stop at the piano and punch a few keys—one at a time, then two and three together. He was entranced with the sounds he made. When it was time for the evening meal, he left reluctantly. I wondered where his interest would take him, but I never saw Smitty around the piano during music practice. Carlin, a wizened little character who was forever running for his life, was the only one who played the piano.

"You better get in there," one of my orderlies mumbled one day as he walked by me and nodded toward the music room. He didn't break stride, which emphasized the importance of what he said and the need for him to stay anonymous. Reporting an incident to an officer could be dangerous.

From the doorway, I saw five black men angrily huddled by the upright piano where Carlin sat and played ragtime as if he were the only one in the room.

"What's the problem here?" I asked.

"Smitty wants a turn to play the piano," one of the men answered.

I walked over to Carlin and said, "That's enough for you today, somebody else wants a turn." He ignored me and kept on playing. I reached over, got a good hold on the back of his collar, stood him up, and walked him away from the piano.

"Okay, Smitty," I said, "it's your turn." Following that incident, I made a schedule for those who wanted to play the piano.

Several of the blacks made a point of thanking me for giving Smitty a turn at the piano. One of them was a man who played blues on the clarinet quite well. He said, "I know that deep down you are prejudiced just like the rest of them, but I want to thank you for being fair."

When there was a vacancy on my crew, I requested Smitty. This gave him more opportunities to enjoy the piano. When we finished work early, I always knew where Smitty would be.

One day, Smitty was handing out clothing and I was, as usual, standing nearby. Needing to check on something in the office, I walked away from the window and sauntered back out after two or three minutes.

"Mr. Gregory, you're supposed to be right here all the time when I'm handing out clothes. They try to make me do things I don't want to do, and they may say I didn't give them something when I did," Smitty said rather angrily.

I apologized to Smitty. He was right. I should have been there. Afterwards, I always made a point of doing so—especially when Smitty was working the window.

When Mr. Eastland came along, he outlawed altered clothing and we had some trouble with inmates who were unwilling to give up their customized jackets and pegged pants. One day, while inmates were taking showers and the clothing room was full of people, a big black guy came up to me, mad as hell.

"These ain't my pants," he said, and threw them on the floor right in front of me.

"Pick up those pants," I said, meeting his direct stare. The chatter in the room stopped suddenly. I was the only officer in that area of the clothing room. The harder the inmate stared, the harder I stared. Then he leaned over, picked up the pants, and handed them to me.

I checked the size of the pants against the size listed on his cubbyhole and handed them back to him, saying, "These pants are your size. You are not going to have your own specially tailored pants anymore." He believed me. He took the pants and went back upstairs to the cell house. You could feel the release of tension in the cons all around. I relaxed a bit myself.

This incident occurred shortly after I had removed a white man from the piano bench so a black man could play. The result was a good measure of respect directed toward me from the black inmates. My black orderlies began to take great pride in working for me. That is, as long as I did my part.

22

Trouble Coming

"Boss," Johnson said without looking up from the paperwork in front of him, "noon today."

I gave no indication I had heard Johnson, my clothing-room clerk. He had just told me that the prison was going to bust wide open sometime around the midday meal. I felt the sweat trickling down my back.

"Some of those guys are southerners, like me, you know," said Johnson with righteous resentment in his voice. "It just ain't right to cell white men right across the aisle from niggers. The things they say"—his face was twisted with disgust and embarrassment—"and you have to listen to it. They can look right in your cell and you just have to undress right in front of them and listen to their dirty cracks." Johnson's emotion was genuine. There were other inmates who felt as he did and believed they were victims of a great wrong.

I understood Johnson's reaction, but I said nothing. It was none of my business where the brass housed the inmates or whether or not the inmates liked it.

It was clear that the new administration would not allow inmates to make decisions around the joint, as they had been doing pretty much ever since Mr. Miller left. As part of Dr. Ralston's enlightened reform, the brass had been all too eager to settle every little complaint to the satisfaction of the inmates. It did not lead to rehabilitation as predicted. But it did lead to officers being slugged and beaten; inmates being attacked and in some cases killed; stockpiling and sale of drugs by inmates; and mounting tension felt by all concerned.

Dr. Ralston left me one pleasant memory—the sight of his white coattails flying through the main gate when an inmate tried to use the power and latitude given him by enlightened reform.

Now I wondered what Karpis and Klint, another inmate who always had a leadership role in planned disruptions, had up their sleeves. I knew they were behind the impending trouble but I also knew it would be hard to catch them at anything. It would be the punks who would raise all the hell, doing what they were told by the leaders. They'd think they were being real tough hoodlums instead of the damn-fool stooges they plainly were.

With new administrators in key positions, I knew there would be interesting, maybe even profound, changes in the operation of Alcatraz. I could feel the excitement building among both officers and inmates. I could read it in their faces. Like animals sniffing at the wind, they felt a primitive sense of danger. As Shannon would say, "Stand by for a ram."

And now trouble was coming. I figured it would involve the two major complaints: the housing arrangements on the inside of the B and C blocks and the doctor's conservatism in giving out medications.

I stared out at the inmates in the clothing room. They were all busy working. Everything was so damn quiet and peaceful that I knew Johnson was leveling with me. I knew because of the sickening stillness that tied up my guts and nagged at the back of my neck. I had been through strikes and riots before and I knew the signs.

I blew the whistle. The inmates stopped working and made sure everything was in place before leaving for lunch. It was all done very deliberately. Swallowing at the bile rising from my stomach, I lined up the inmates at the door and counted them out for the lunch break. Not a muscle changed in my face to acknowledge Johnson's mumble of "Good luck to you, Mr. Gregory" as he walked by.

Row after row of inmates filed into the cell house from the industries buildings without one word or action to betray the impending crisis.

Lomin called to another rookie officer, "Did you read that latest pamphlet by Dr. Ralston, Joe?"

"Wasn't he sharp?" answered Joe, as though he had been genuinely thrilled by the article.

I swallowed at the sourness in my stomach again. Those sad, damn fools, I thought to myself. I gave my detail count to Lieutenant Tompkins.

"Check," said Bunch.

"Noon," I said under my breath.

The lieutenant's eyes narrowed just a bit. "Check," he said again.

I stood at my post in the dining hall, trying to appear casual and at ease while striving to ignore the tension in my stomach and the trembling in the calves of my legs, which were itching for action. It was action I didn't want but knew I was going to get. It was beginning to look as if this caper had been well planned to catch the officers off guard.

My gaze roved over the inmates as they quietly ate their meal. The striking kitchen crew was now being fed in the dining hall instead of in A Block, and I paid special attention to the main agitators, Karpis and Klint.

The inmates ate their meal peacefully. They filed out of the mess hall. There was absolutely no trouble. But trouble was there! I knew it was there! I smelled it, tasted it, felt it all around me.

What was going on? Why hadn't it already happened, here in the dining hall? Tables overturned, food and trays and pots and pans and utensils thrown everywhere? Yelling, screaming, cursing? Officers knocked down and kicked and beaten? This was where it *should* start. This was where it *always* started.

I looked down the long dining hall to where Bunch was standing. Our eyes met, and it was obvious he was puzzled too. An officer nodded to Bunch, indicating that all the eating utensils had been counted and correctly tallied. Bunch jabbed upwards with his thumb and then followed the last table of inmates as they filed out of the dining hall. Following the noon meal, the inmates always went directly to their cells to be locked in.

Bunch came out with his whistle in his hand. Normally, he would blow it and officers would proceed around each tier of each cell block, making one of the frequent official cell house counts of the day.

He didn't blow his whistle. Some inmates were still out in the aisle. The count could not be made until all were locked in their cells.

"Get those men in their cells," he said.

A minute later, a scared, embarrassed Lomin looked down from the second tier. "They won't go in," he said in a strained voice.

"They" were the white inmates celled across Broadway from the black inmates. So this is what they were up to. I finally relaxed. Now I knew what we faced. Uncertainty and tension melted away.

Bunch's mouth tightened. He picked up the phone on his desk and jabbed at the dial, still holding the whistle in his hand. "Need some help in here," he said grimly into the mouthpiece.

One of the inmates on the tier swaggered up to the railing and contemptuously elbowed the rookie Lomin aside. His hair was all clipped off, his shirt was unbuttoned down to his belt, and his sleeves were rolled up to his shoulders, exposing powerful biceps and obscene tattoos. His name was Benson, known to all as "Bull." He was doing life for rape and murder.

"We ain't going to be celled across from these goddamned niggers!" he shouted down to the lieutenant. "And we ain't going in these goddamned cells no more!"

The lieutenant straddled the corner of the desk and stared implacably up at Bull. The rookie officer was looking at Bull with bug-eyed fear.

Why doesn't he practice some enlightened reform on him? I thought to myself.

"Git on that phone," shouted Bull with years of stored-up insolence, "and tell the warden to git in here. We're goin' to have a talk with him." In his voice was the unquestioned belief that in the face of impending trouble the warden would be only too glad to talk with the inmates. It had been that way for the last several years. The administration would talk. They would placate, cajole, give in, and immediate trouble would, again, be deferred; but discipline would be just that much more undermined.

I heard the quick cadence of feet coming down Broadway. Eight officers came in, each carrying a riot club he could obviously handle. Mr. Eastland was with them. He flicked a glance up at the inmates on the second tier. He looked at the lieutenant.

"Put them in the Hole," he said, as though the order were already carried out.

"Don't any of you screws come up here," shrieked Bull in amazement when he heard the order. "We'll kill ya! We'll kill all of ya!"

The riot squad went up the stairs two abreast. The rookie officer was still in a bug-eyed trance. One of the riot squad officers poked his club teasingly at Bull. Bull grabbed it with both hands and wrestled mightily. His hands thus occupied, another officer locked an arm around his neck. A third one then rapped Bull's fingers smartly with a club. Bull released his grip as though he had grabbed something hot. The officer who had him around the neck then persuaded him roughly down the stairs.

Bull was on his way to the Hole and the tier was swarming with officers. In a matter of moments, all the defiant inmates were on their way to the Hole.

Lomin came down off the tier, trying to arrange his face back into a composed expression. "It was so unexpected, that is, I didn't know . . . " he said, looking at Lieutenant Tompkins imploringly. Then, as if mad at himself for being apologetic, he said, "Well, you didn't expect *me* to use force, did you?"

Bunch looked at him but waived his right to comment.

"Well, I'm certainly glad that it's over," said the rookie with genuine relief.

"Son," said the lieutenant not unkindly, "it's not over. It hasn't even started yet." The rookie looked at Bunch as though he were trying to convince both of them that the lieutenant was all wrong.

"You'll see the results of Dr. Ralston's years of enlightened prison reform in the next few days, bub," I said sarcastically, staring into Lomin's frightened eyes.

Then I looked away, disgusted with myself for my emotional outburst. Bunch smiled slightly while the rookie looked at me open-mouthed. He just didn't get it.

There was quite a racket now coming out of TU. Inmates were banging and shaking the bars and shouting and cursing. Their thoroughly unexpected defeat had made them humiliated and angry. They were venting their frustration by making a racket that was just as harmless as it was loud.

All right, I thought, that's good. But the cell house was unusually quiet. That wasn't so good.

The noon count was completed without further incident. As usual, Shannon held general sick call. It went smoothly. Working inmates were then released from their cells for the afternoon work schedule.

I stood in the clothing-room office looking out over the busy inmates without actually seeing them. Johnson was working a few feet away but was carefully avoiding me. During such times it just wasn't healthy for an inmate to seem too friendly with an officer. Johnson was not a stool pigeon but he did respect the "Boss," as he called me. He would not willingly cause me any trouble if he could help it.

Johnson was serving a life sentence. He had told me he wasn't getting involved in any prison ruckus because he was beginning to realize his only way of getting out of jail was to compile a long record of good behavior. I knew Johnson would go along with the other inmates' plans but would not be a leader in a strike or riot.

Klint was one of the inmates assigned to the clothing room. He was feared by the other inmates. Klint was a slightly built man with black, deadly, unblinking eyes, not unlike the eyes of a snake. Aside from this, there was little about him to command attention. He had been in prison for fourteen years, doing life for kidnapping. He was wanted for the cold-blooded killing of a deputy sheriff in Kentucky, but there was little chance Kentucky would get the opportunity to try him. Such a trial would have to follow his release from federal prison, and that was not likely to occur.

Klint's prison record was almost without blemish. He did everything asked of him. He requested no special favors. Dr. Ralston had had several interviews with Klint and felt there was much good in the man. Periodically, Klint was the spokesman for the general population during some complaint or other. On such occasions he was always polite and smiled a lot. In spite of this I knew, as did all of the experienced personnel, that Klint was one of the brains behind any devilry stirred up in the prison.

I watched Klint as he went calmly about his duties. I wondered what was going on in his cold killer's brain. I knew he was planning whatever trouble was to come during the succeeding days in the joint.

The day's work ended and supper was served as usual. All went according to routine. Some of the inmates were certain they would get an unusually good meal: For the past several years, each altercation had been followed by what might be called a "Sunday supper." However, the inmates were served the menu that had been planned a week earlier. They ate without complaint and let themselves be locked in their cells for the night as if resigned to their fate.

Back in the officers' mess, the steward was making cold-cut sandwiches for the night shift. I helped myself to one, washed it down with a glass of milk, and started on my way to the Mule Barn. I paused to check out the bulletin board across the hall from Mr. Eastland's office.

"Got anything special on tonight, Mr. Gregory?" Eastland asked.

"Not a thing."

"Well, you take a break and then you might wander back up here. We might be able to use some extra help tonight."

"Sure thing," I said.

Dr. Ralston's favorite student had been standing nearby and overheard this conversation. "What's going to happen tonight, sir?"

"We might have to 'rehabilitate' some of these inmates. And right sudden, too," was the associate warden's grim reply. Lomin's eyes bugged out again. I noticed he didn't offer to be on hand for the rehabilitation, and neither was he asked to be present.

When I got back to the cell house about eight o'clock, I was advised that quiet still prevailed. It was the kind of quiet that precedes activity. I grew up in the Midwest, where frequent violent storms were foretold by just such a calm. I glanced at the other occupants of the ready room.* Some had returned, as I had, by request of Mr. Eastland and others were reporting for their scheduled working hours. I lowered myself into the chair behind the desk and leaned back to prop up my feet. Suddenly the phone on the desk rang, shattering both the quiet and the pretended composure of the officers. I snatched the receiver out of its cradle.

"Gregory here." I listened briefly and replaced the receiver. "It's Burroughs in the cell house," I said, looking across the hall at the associate warden. "He says Wagon Wheels is going to cut himself if he doesn't get some goofballs."

*The ready room, or officers' lounge, was in the administrative wing of the building.

"Call the doctor and get him in here, will you, Greg?" said Eastland.

I dialed the doctor and requested his presence in the associate warden's office. The ready room settled back into an unnatural silence.

I thought about the time a few years ago that Wagon Wheels first came to my attention. He was one of my favorite inmates. The moniker applied to him by his fellow inmates was very appropriate. His ears had been cut and bruised in beatings when he was growing up. The repeated scarring had enlarged and re-shaped them into "cauliflower ears." He was undoubtedly one of the ugliest men who ever lived. He had no teeth, his nose had been broken, one eye was slightly askew, and then there were those wagon-wheel ears. He was neither liked nor dis-liked by most people. He was harmless. But he was a nuisance. From his youth, Wagon Wheels had been an addict and had learned all kinds of ways of getting drugs.

One Sunday, after all the inmates had gone to the yard for exercise or to the movie for entertainment, I was headed for my post in the kitchen. On the way, I noticed Wagon Wheels sitting in his cell.

"You don't like the movie?" I asked.

"Nah, Boss, I don't like any of that kind of stuff."

"Well, would you like to do a little work?"

"Yes, Boss, I'd sure be glad to do something, anything to get out of my cell," Wagon Wheels said with unmasked pleasure.

Back in the kitchen, I showed him a bag of potatoes and asked if he would like to wash and peel them. Wagon Wheels responded by going to work on them. During the afternoon, Wagon Wheels would smile as I went by as if he really ap-preciated the activity. As a result, this got to be a Sunday afternoon habit.

When I was not otherwise occupied, I would visit with Wagon Wheels in the afternoon. I heard many interesting stories about what it had been like to grow up in the hills of Tennessee. At the end of these visits, I would arrange with the steward for Wagon Wheels to cook a steak for himself. He would sit in the offi-cers' mess to eat it. On one such occasion, I came by when Wagon Wheels had just sat down with his steak. He cut off a piece, put it in his toothless mouth, gummed it, and swallowed. He was in heaven—sitting at a table in the officers' mess, gumming on a piece of steak. His damaged face crinkled into a grin. "Boss," he said, "I wonder what the po' people is doing outside today."

The doctor came in and Eastland reported Wagon Wheels's threat. Dr. Belch-er would have to handle this aspect of the strike. The associate warden was ob-viously wondering how the doctor would meet this responsibility.

"Well," said the doctor, "we could put him in a strip cell to protect him from himself, but we can't keep him there forever, and if he really wants to mutilate himself he will do it sooner or later regardless of where he is. I guess there's no time like the present to teach these characters they are not going to get what they want by, as it were, pounding their heads on the floor and bawling like spoiled brats."

Eastland looked at Dr. Belcher with complete satisfaction. "Gregory," he said, "call Burroughs and tell him there will be no goofballs for Wagon Wheels."

"Right," said Burroughs when I conveyed the message. Burroughs had been in prison service longer than I had. He needed no explanation of the full import of the associate warden's order.

Dr. Belcher made himself comfortable in a creaky old captain's chair in the associate warden's office and settled down to wait. In the ready room, we smoked quietly. We didn't know when, but sooner or later something was bound to happen.

The phone rang again, sounding like an alarm in the hushed room. I jumped and snatched the receiver from the cradle. "He did it," was my report.

The doctor started toward the cell house with his little black bag. He didn't ask anybody to go with him but several of us tagged along. It was our job.

Burroughs met us inside the cell house and led us without comment to Wagon Wheels's cell. He was sitting on the edge of his bunk, unclothed. He had made a long, messy gash on his thigh. I was surprised, as I always was, that these self-inflicted wounds did not bleed very much. Wagon Wheels stared hostilely through the bars at the doctor, but said nothing.

"I'll want some of you fellows to hold him while I sew him up," said the doctor in a quiet voice.

"What? You going to sew me up *here?*" asked Wagon Wheels in complete disbelief.

The doctor ignored the question and went into the cell. Two other officers and I crowded in after him. Wagon Wheels watched apprehensively as the doctor threaded a wicked little curved needle.

"Lay down on your bunk," ordered the doctor.

Wagon Wheels licked his lips and stared at the grim-faced officers standing over him. "Doc, ain't you even going to give me something to kill the pain?" he asked hopelessly.

"There won't be much pain," said the doctor as though he were stating a scientific fact to a forum of his colleagues.

"By God, you ain't goin' to do it!" shouted Wagon Wheels.

I took Wagon Wheels by the shoulders and pushed him down on the bunk.

"Come on, Wagon Wheels, lie down like the doctor said. We don't want to hurt you." The other officers quickly assisted in spread-eagling the hapless Wagon Wheels, and the doctor dexterously took sixteen stitches.

When Dr. Belcher finished, he looked at us and said, "I think this is a clear case of misconduct so if you will take him over to the Hole, I will accept all responsibility."

"Yes sir," I said, being careful to exhibit no emotion. "Let's go, Wagon Wheels."

Wagon Wheels could have gotten out of our grip easily but he went willingly enough, knowing that he would be asking for more trouble by resisting. However, all the way to TU he hollered with all his might as though we were hurting him. Understanding the necessity of saving face, we ignored the yelling. In reality, the fight left Wagon Wheels when he realized he was not going to score with the doctor for narcotics. It is doubtful that any of the inmates who heard the yelling were fooled.

Wagon Wheels was greeted loudly by those already in TU. As soon as he was safely in a cell, he started moaning and groaning about the brutality he had suffered at the hands of the doctor. He was explicit in his description of how we had held him down on the bunk. The inmates, for *our* benefit, were loud in their sympathy. Actually it just wasn't in their personalities to feel sympathy for anyone but themselves.

We walked through the cell house on our way back to the ready room, hoping we would have time for a smoke before the next round. But that was not to be.

"Doc is up on the second tier with another patient. Guess he'd be glad to see you guys," reported Burroughs.

This time it was Hickens. Dr. Belcher sewed him up as we replayed our part in the Wagon Wheels scene and escorted Hickens to the Hole.

When we had Hickens safely stored in the Hole and had returned to the ready room, I asked, "Doctor, how come there isn't more bleeding from these cuts?"

"They've had a lot of practice at this," said Dr. Belcher. "Did you notice the scars on their thighs? They have used this self-mutilation act many times to get drugs and they have learned just where and just how deep to cut. They barely penetrate the skin and are very careful to avoid the large blood vessels," he explained. "It's the inexperienced ones, the new users like the fellow in the hospital a week or so ago, that worry me."

After putting several more cutters in the Hole, I analyzed my feelings. I was still tense, but it was no longer the sick tension of waiting for action. Now we were getting action. That I could handle. I sat down at the desk and struck a match, but it never got to the end of the cigarette between my lips.

There was a crash and a loud piercing yell: "Don't let 'em take it away!" The cry was taken up by hundreds of other maniacal voices until it echoed throughout the institution, becoming one insane, rumbling roar.

There were more and more crashes, then a ragged cacophony: ripping, tearing, breaking, pounding, and the sound of objects being thrown out of cells as the inmates indulged in their favorite response to denial. This was what we had been waiting for. We could visualize what was going on in the cell house. Ink and human refuse would be running down Warden Swope's newly painted pink-and-yellow cell house walls, lights would be broken, clothing would be torn up, and everything loose that could fit through the bars would be thrown out into the aisles.

Mr. Eastland came into the ready room. His face was stern and resolute.

"I want you men to go into the cell house and get the names and numbers of inmates you actually see throwing things out of their cells or engaging in any kind of destruction. But," he pointed his finger for emphasis, "I don't want any bum raps against any of them. Don't list them for hollering to save face. Get the ones who are actually destroying something or throwing stuff out. I don't need to warn you to be careful of some of the stuff they throw."

The cell house was being demolished. Planks, bunks, tables, chests, blankets, mattresses, pillows, clothing, everything possible was being torn or broken and thrown out of the cells. The shouting and cursing was slamming off the walls with a force as great as that of the solid objects. The outpouring of language—loathsome, vile, and vicious—welled up from layers of hatred that had been repressed for years. The decibel level and degree of maliciousness in the inmates' screams escalated as they responded to each other. They were unleashing emotions that they were powerless to control. In a word, they were wild.

As they screamed and hollered their deep rage at their incarceration, certain words became more and more intelligible. First one, then several, then nearly all began yelling, "Shithead, Shithead," in deep tones that rumbled through the cell house.

Everyone knew who "Shithead" was. As a matter of fact, he had just appeared, tiptoeing around the corner of C Block, and he was not amused. He was Senior Officer Hank Courtwright. Hank was a very good prison officer and had been promoted to lieutenant a couple of times but had been demoted each time because of off-duty escapades. The thing that gave him his dubious fame or notoriety was the fact that he referred to all inmates as "shitheads." Eventually, the inmates began to refer to Hank as "Shithead" behind his back.

I chose a tier and prowled along it gingerly, ignoring the invectives directed at me. The inmates felt immune to individual punishment and made no pretense of hiding their angry destruction of property. I walked along with my notebook in hand watching for missiles thrown from the cells. By the time I got to the end of the tier, I had a fair list of names and specific offenses committed.

On the way back, an inmate named Curly Young abruptly stopped his foul yelling when he saw me. I decided to tease him a little. I passed his cell, waited for a moment, and then rushed back just as he threw back his head, closed his eyes, and screamed an unprintable obscenity. Opening his eyes, he found himself staring me right in the face. Young's utter surprise and embarrassment was as uncontrolled as my roar of laughter. He ducked his head, laughed, and muttered, "Damn, damn, damn." Quite a comedown from the obscenities designed to make sure his fellow inmates knew he was doing his part. For weeks after the strike when Young would happen to meet me face to face, he couldn't help but smile sheepishly.

I looked down to the first floor and noticed Burroughs had his pants rolled up and was wearing rubber boots. That was proof the inmates were using another of their favorite tricks. Anything loose that hadn't been thrown out of the cells was being stuffed into the toilets so that, with continual flushing, the cells and aisles could be flooded. Water from the second and third tiers was running into the cells below. The inmates in the lower cells weren't very happy about this and were making it known by cursing heartily at their upstairs neighbors. The good neighbors showed their concern by responding in kind and continuing to flush.

I threaded my way cautiously over to the black section. Not one black inmate was engaged in the riot in any manner. They were well aware that the celling of whites directly across from them was one of the major causes of the riot. It was an open and direct slap at them. A larger percentage of blacks than whites had become users of prison-supplied drugs, and they didn't want to give them up any more than the whites did. But they were too proud to enter into a riot that was initiated by racist whites.

This will be a big break for us, I predicted to myself. We will be able to fill some of the positions left open by the rioting whites.

I sniffed, then sniffed again. There was a fire somewhere. I skipped rapidly down to the main floor, where Burroughs was also sniffing. The odor came from one side of the cell house. I went to B Block and peered around the corner. The whole aisle was full of smoke and flames coming from cotton mattresses, feather pillows, and other flammable materials. The fire had been set by the prison version of a Molotov cocktail—a medicine bottle, match heads, and a cotton fuse. The thick, black smoke and the stink from the burning cotton and feathers was almost unbearable.

Within minutes, several fires were burning big and dangerous and the inmates were feeding them by throwing more and more stuff on them. I looked up at the officer in the West Gun Gallery. His eyes were streaming with tears from the smoke.

As I stood there surveying the scene, to my amazement, Teena—an inexperienced officer—came out with a small fire extinguisher and ran toward the smoking mess. As he stood in front of the cells trying to adjust the extinguisher properly, the inmates got busy. With a target so close, they couldn't miss with some soft, smelly missiles. Thus hit, the officer misdirected his aim and sprayed several of the cells. There was another blast of the smelly stuff. Finally realizing what it was, Teena dropped the fire extinguisher and ran around the corner of the cell block to safety.

The last I saw of Teena, he was going out the main gate saying something unintelligible in a voice that was between a nervous laugh and a sob. I could only think to myself, Thank God he didn't have a tommy gun—some guys are just not cut out to be prison screws.

Lieutenant Tompkins came into the cell house. "Get out the fire hoses," he ordered.

The hose boxes were located at each end of the cell house and were therefore out of range of the inmates' trajectories. However, to put out the fires it would be necessary for us to stand directly in front of the cells.

I grabbed the nozzle of one of the hoses and several other officers held the cord-stitched fiber hose. We had a firm grip, but even so we staggered and struggled a bit when the powerful force of the water caused the hose to whip around.

Trying to swallow the sourness in my stomach, I began to march the hose directly down the aisle toward the nearest fire. For a moment, the inmates just watched as though they couldn't believe the screws could be so stupid as to walk right out and be sitting ducks for them. We pulled the hose straight ahead without looking at the inmates. We knew we couldn't keep all the cells under surveillance.

I ducked instinctively when an ink bottle crashed against the wall just above my head. I heard the vicious laughter of the inmates. Something soft splattered against my neck and the side of my face. Even before I could smell it, I knew what it was. My stomach rolled with nausea and I began to shake with disgust and a terrible rage.

"You rotten, filthy sons of bitches," I cried under my breath. "You rotten, dirty, filthy sons of bitches."

I knew from the curses behind me that other officers on the hose were also being splattered with excrement. We kept our voices low so the inmates couldn't tell that they were making an impression on us. We just kept pulling the hose down the aisle.

Another hose was being pulled in from the other end of the aisle. More and more missiles were being thrown at us. Thankfully, it is hard to get good aim and force behind a throwing arm when it first has to be stuck out through bars. Still, the inmates connected all too often. I heard somebody behind me groan softly and felt dead weight on the hose, but I couldn't turn around or let go of the nozzle.

Finally, the fires were out. The water was turned off and we were back at the end of the cell block, out of range of the inmates' foul or potentially lethal projectiles.

I wiped the filth from my eyelids, mouth, and the side of my neck, trying not to smell it, but I did and got sick. Two other officers were also sick. I went into the officers' bathroom and washed up the best I could. When I came out again, I asked, "Who got hurt?"

"Andersen," Bunch said. "Got him in the head with a metal cribbage board. We took him to the hospital. He was out like a light."

By now, water was ankle deep on the cell house floor. Rubbish, muck, ashes, pieces of shelf board, clothing, medicine bottles, and anything else that might be found in an inmate's cell and that would float was swirling in eddies throughout the first floor of the cell house.

The inmates were running out of stuff to throw. Their cells, rectums, and bladders were pretty well empty. The yelling continued, somewhat less frenzied but just as vicious. Through it ran the refrain of, "Don't let 'em take it away!"

"Did you get a list, Greg?" asked Bunch.

"Yes, sir, Lieutenant."

"Take it out to Mr. Eastland. He wants all of the lists."

I went out front to the associate warden's office, still trying to remove bits of filth from my uniform. I started to walk in, but seeing that Mr. Eastland was talking on the phone, I backed out.

"Come on in here!" the associate warden roared at me.

Turning back to the mouthpiece, Eastland said, "I want to thank you for offering to send Dr. Ralston out to help us. But I think he has helped quite enough already. We owe him thanks for this riot we are having right now. If he so much as shows his face in this institution, I will personally escort him out by the scruff of his neck and the seat of his pants!" Slamming down the phone, he growled, "I don't think the bureau appreciates the treatment their Dr. Ralston got here at Alcatraz."

He studied the list I handed him for a moment and then put it with several similar lists. His nose kept twitching irritably as though it smelled something extremely foul. It did. His eyes landed suspiciously on me, and I reddened under his gaze. Then he realized what the smell was and why.

"I'm sorry," he said simply.

This made me redden even more. "It isn't anything," I said lamely.

"Dammit, Greg, these inmates are going to learn to respect an officer before this fracas is over." Eastland glared at the wall for a few minutes. Then, coming back to the present, he looked at me and said, "Send in Lieutenant Tompkins, and then you get yourself a shower and some rest. I'll see you in the morning."

I gladly went to do his bidding.

23

Trouble Continues

The next morning, I walked into the cell house. What a mess! I had never seen anything so totally destroyed. Down at the West End, officers were already gathering. I could feel the tension in the air. What was going to happen next? There was one man who could tell us what was going to happen, and he was the man for whom we waited. I expected him to show up looking haggard, red-eyed, unshaven, and disheveled from his sleepless night. Someone said, "Here he comes!"

Mr. Eastland walked gingerly down Broadway, trying to keep from stepping in the worst of the puddles. He was clean-shaven and dressed in a natty blue suit, white shirt, red uniform tie, blue silk socks, and highly polished tan oxfords.

Taking several lists from his inside coat pocket, Eastland said, "These are the men I want put in TU this morning. You will notice Karpis and Klint are listed. I'm putting them in the Hole for administrative protection," he explained with a big, innocent smile.

I figured "administrative protection" was as good an excuse as any to get these two out of population, thereby seriously handicapping their influence and at the same time putting them where they could be closely watched.

"Mr. Eastland," said one officer cautiously and with some trepidation, "we have only forty-two cells in TU and they are nearly filled now."

Breaking into a grin, Eastland said, "Mr. Collins, have you ever loaded pigs for market?"

"No, Mr. Eastland, I never have."

"Well, first of all, you have to get all the pigs you possibly can in each boxcar. Because you pay by the car, not by the number of pigs. After you think the car is full, you take one more pig and shove his head in, smack him sharply on the butt, and he gets in. But remember, all those pigs have got to get to market in good shape. So let's put some more men in those cells, and we don't want any of them hurt."

Eastland looked around the circle of officers and added, "By the way, check the kites coming out of A Block from our striking kitchen crew, and if any of them want out, put them in TU as well."

My respect for Mr. Eastland was increasing by the moment. Every time he made a decision or gave an order, it contributed to better operation of the institution. He did not come across to me as a man of violence, but it was evident he would not hesitate to use whatever force was necessary to maintain control of the institution.

"We'll start at the top of each cell block and work down," instructed Lieutenant Tompkins. "I want plenty of men on each tier. Don't take any chances and don't use any more force than necessary."

I was sent over to TU to help Lewis. I briefed him on the score and then the inmates started to come in. Each was stripped, thoroughly searched, given a pair of coveralls, and assigned to a cell. There were no frills like underwear or shoes.

The inmates submitted meekly enough to the routine, and each man was greeted with great cheers from those already in the unit. It was plain they didn't know just what was going on, but they kept up the courage of the mob by yelling and cursing at us. They also thought that only forty-two men could be put in TU.

It took a few moments for the news to percolate through the cell house plumbing line, but when it did the inmates began to shout to each other, "They can't put us all in TU!"

The inmates knew that many of the forty-two cells in TU were already occupied. An uneasy note began to creep into their yells. Too many men were being taken from the cell house to the Treatment Unit. An inmate who was celled near the TU door kept a count of those brought in. As the count mounted, he began to yell out the numbers.

"Twenty-eight, twenty-nine, thirty, thirty-one . . . forty-one . . . "

"Gopher, you damn fool. Stop messing around with the count," yelled an inmate whose view of what was happening was limited.

"I'm not fooling. There goes number forty-three."

"Where'd you learn to count, Gopher? There ain't but forty-two cells in there," yelled another concerned citizen.

Gopher was almost hysterical. He knew that if the inmates thought he was kidding them, they would kill him without a moment's hesitation.

It wasn't long before each TU cell was occupied by four or more inmates. They began to feel the discomfort of the crowding. They had to take turns sitting on the bunk or the toilet.

In the cell house, the inmate leaders had sent out an order by the plumbing line: "Don't get caught. We're losing too many good men. We have to have enough left to carry on the fight." Following this message from the leaders, there was some sporadic hollering and screaming. Then the cell house was fairly quiet.

"Now that you have all those people in the Hole, we have got to give the ones left a chance to go to work," Eastland said. "I know they won't go, but I want all of you crew officers to go around and ask each one of your inmates if they want to work. If they do, let them out."

Officers went from tier to tier opening the cells. "Anybody who wants to go to work, come on out." A scattered few took a tentative step outside their cells, but when they saw no one else going to work they hopped back in.

"Okay, they will stay in their cells except for meals," said Eastland. And so the lock-down started. On succeeding days when the offer to work was made, the inmates began to return to work.

Late on the second day of the strike, I was given a sheet of paper with the names of seven inmates on it and told to let them out of TU. I noticed they were the oldest inmates at Alcatraz, both by time on The Rock and by age. (The age range of inmates at Alcatraz was from early twenties to sixties.)

I got these old gentlemen out of the TU cells. They found their shoes in TU storage and put them on; that is, all but one who couldn't manage that. Some of them had such bad feet they could hardly walk without shoes. I took them down into the clothing room for the usual shower and clean clothes.

Insull, the one who couldn't get his shoes on, had been in prison a long, long time. He had been one of the last of the train robbers. Some even claimed that as a kid he had taken part in the robbery of a stagecoach. That might have been stretching it a little bit.

At the beginning of the automobile era, Insull and some friends had traveled across a good part of the United States in a touring car, often having to build the road as they went. He had pictures of the car and the friends.

According to Insull, he had been cheated in what was supposed to be a fair gunfight. The result was a free-for-all in which he killed his opponent. Insull was arrested, tried, and sentenced to life in prison.

Eventually, Insull began to paint. One of his landscapes hung in his cell. It caught the attention of volunteer art teachers who came to the island occasionally and was highly praised by them.

It was with a great deal of difficulty that Insull walked down the stairs carrying his shoes in his hand. At the bottom, he sat down, looked up at me, and said mournfully, "Why do you want to do this to me?"

I felt compassion for the old man and yet I knew that if he had been allowed to remain in the comparative comfort and safety of his own cell he would have continued to do his part in the riot. To him it was just a big game. He was strictly a con for the cons. He thought it would be the usual kind of riot in which the administration quickly gave in to the wishes of the inmates and everything would be settled without much discomfort.

With the interruption of the inmates' work schedule came many adjustments in the officers' assignments. We were shifted from post to post as needed. Sometimes I had an inmate crew and sometimes not.

On the third day of the strike, I had the clothing room and the crew list included MacDonald, one of the old-timers. As he had always been right behind the leaders—holding out until the very end—in every ruckus we had at Alcatraz, I assumed things would be the same this time and I didn't bother to ask him to work. However, when MacDonald came down for his shower and clean clothes, I learned differently.

"Mr. Gregory," MacDonald said, "I heard them tell you people with crews to go around and ask your men if they wanted to work. You didn't come ask me if I wanted to work. If you had, I would have come to work."

I was surprised and somewhat embarrassed. I just didn't believe he would come out and go to work. I tried to say I was sorry, but then let the old man vent his spleen for a while.

"Don't get me wrong, I'm not for you screws at all. I'm for the strike. But now I have a chance to be transferred out of this place and I had sooner risk the cons pushing me around than lose that opportunity. I'm getting old and I'm not going to get many more chances to get out of here. This time, they'll have to fight their battles without me." After he had calmed down a bit, he lost the grim expression on his face, stripped, and went into the shower.

I was glad MacDonald wanted to work. In his free life, he had been a carpenter, apparently a very good one. Along with his menial tasks in the clothing room, he had a job he loved—refinishing the long dining hall tables when they got stained or scarred. The tables seated five on each side and were well-built, made of first-grade lumber. They were works of art in their own right. MacDonald would take them down to the clothing room, carefully remove the varnish, sand, and apply new varnish. When he finished with a table, it was beautiful. Most of the inmates knew the tables were something special and were to be treated with care. They did not willfully mark or scar them.

When the showers were over and the clothing room locked, I went up to TU. An officer was going from cell to cell saying, "Who wants to write a letter?" and leaving stationery on the shelf of each cell door for those who wanted it. This puzzled me because the administration was not usually that concerned about the letter-writing privileges of inmates in TU. Then I realized it was Eastland's way of seeing whether or not any kites would come out.

It wasn't long before a pencil was being passed around and the inmates were writing brief letters. When they finished, they placed their letters on the cell doors and an officer went around collecting them.

Wonder of wonders, the first letter opened was not a letter home. It was a kite to Mr. Eastland, begging to be let out of TU along with promises to be good and to have nothing more to do with the strike. And who wrote this message? None other than Bull. Up to this point, Bull had tried to give the impression that he was the leader of this hullabaloo. Fat chance of his getting out of here, I thought to myself.

Not much later, Eastland came into TU to make a routine inspection. He saw the letter addressed to him and stared at it for some time. I had got to know Mr. Eastland pretty well by observing his reactions to various situations. I had come to recognize a certain look and a certain pose, and I saw that something important was about to happen. And it did.

"How has Bull Benson been doing?" Eastland asked Lewis.

"He was the first one to write a kite to get out of here, believe it or not. And he's been giving me the eye ever since, almost pleading to get out. But at the same time, he's doing his part of the hollering and yelling," said Lewis.

For a moment, Eastland was deep in thought. Then he looked at Lewis and said, "Let Bull out."

Lewis was surprised, but hesitated only briefly before going off to release Bull. "All right, Bull, you're going out."

"No, I'm not going out."

"Yeah, you are." Bull made mild protestations to save face, but took great care not to touch an officer. Down the stairs he went as I escorted him to the clothing room.

In the clothing room, he took off his clothes and took a shower as ordered and walked up to the issuing window expecting to be given his own customized clothing. Instead, he was handed a green bathrobe with his inmate number on it and a stack of standard prison clothes.

"Put on the robe," said Lord, the clothing-room officer. Bull just stood there, confused, trying to figure out what this was all about.

"Just put it on and take your clothing. Be sure to check the stack and see that you have pants, shirt, underwear, socks, and a handkerchief. If it checks out, take them with you to your cell to dress."

"These are not my clothes."

"Just take them and go."

Bull was about to remonstrate further but reconsidered. He put on the bathrobe, took the clothes, and went up the stairs ahead of me. When we reached Broadway, Bull continued on toward the outside of C Block, where he wanted to be celled.

"Far enough, Bull. Down Broadway for you."

"What do you mean?" Bull said, stopping dead in his tracks.

"Down Broadway, inside C, tier two. Your same old cell."

"You mean I'm going to have to cell across from these . . . " Hard eyes stared out of impassive black faces pressed against the bars of their cells. Bull choked for a moment.

"I'm not going in one of those cells. You've got plenty of cells open on the outside. I know you have."

"You're also learning," I said evenly, "that you cell where we tell you to cell and not where you decide you want to cell. Now, are you going to get in your cell or aren't you?"

Bull threw his clothes on the floor. He pulled at his bathrobe, but thought better of taking it off, and let out a thunderous scream of absolute frustration. "I'm not going up there to that cell!"

"You do have a choice. There or TU."

With his hands balled into tight fists and his teeth clenched, Bull stalked off to the TU door, determined to regain emotional control.

It was only seconds before all the inmates in TU knew that Bull was back again. The bathrobe he was wearing was something completely new to them—another innovation by Mr. Eastland.

Everybody hollered, "What happened, Bull? What happened?"

Bull waited until he had put on his coveralls and was back in the cell he had left such a short time ago before answering.

"You know what they did?" Bull said. "They took me out there and purposely tried to put me back on Broadway. Just to see if I'd take it. Well, they know now I won't take it!" His explanation ended with renewed yells and screamed obscenities.

24

Dinner Is Served

While making assignments one morning during the early days of the strike, Mr. Eastland said, "Gregory, I want you to run the kitchen for the next couple of days. We transferred the head steward last week and Mr. Whittower was called back to Washington late yesterday. The visiting stewards have gone back to wherever they came from and we don't have many officers to spare with all this activity going on. Now it's up to Medford, the assistant steward. So I want you in there as culinary officer for the next two days."

"Yes, sir, Warden. Do we have any inmates willing to work in there?"

"Yes, here's a list of the ones that'll work. They are mostly from the black population. I think they will be a good crew."

The head steward had been a notorious conniver with the inmates. In order to get the work of meal preparation and serving accomplished, the head steward was forced to become part of Karpis's operation. This made it possible for Karpis to receive and dispense special favors. The kitchen crew, which was mostly white, had remained fairly stable for several years. Karpis and his cohorts made it very difficult for inmates who joined the kitchen crew without their approval. These inmates would give up the coveted position of kitchen worker rather than risk a fight with Karpis and his gang.

With Karpis's help, the inmates working in the kitchen had eaten very well while the main line hadn't. Cream was skimmed from the milk and choice cuts of meat withheld for the kitchen crew, their friends, and anyone who could pay. Extra servings were also available to the chosen few. Those who were not part of the inner circle took what they were given and knew better than to complain. It was from the crew's illegal cache of beef that I was able to confiscate a steak for Wagon Wheels on Sundays.

The basement of the kitchen was a popular place of assignation. It was a scandalous situation. The inmates had a shower installed down there and had a good alarm system so they knew in advance when an officer started down the basement steps. Without the backing of the administration, no officer or steward felt empowered to break up this cozy playhouse. As a result, the inmates used the basement as they desired. Whether they were naturally homosexual or had been forced into it didn't matter. It was a way to stay alive. An inmate didn't have much choice when faced with an aggressive wolf.

Karpis, the self-appointed head of the crew, was feared by the other inmates. He kept everything in line—the work got done. Thus, on the surface, the kitchen had seemed to be running smoothly.

Neither the kitchen nor the dining hall had been damaged in any way by the riot. When I walked in, the assistant steward was making huge piles of sandwiches for lunch. No one had asked Medford to make sandwiches. But he knew it would be impossible to serve a regular meal to all the inmates in TU.

Medford was a good chef. He had cooked in some of the best hotels in the world, but his feet had given out and he had to settle for institutional jobs where he could do more directing and less of the actual work.

"Hear the latest?" I asked as I poured a cup of coffee.

I took a sip from the heavy tin cup as Medford grunted something noncommittal and kept on making jelly sandwiches on homemade bread with lots of butter.

"It's going to be you and me back here for a while," I said as I took another sip of the strong, hot coffee. Still no intelligible comment from Medford. "Looks like you are going to be the head steward now."

"You can save that line of crap," said Medford with emphasis. "I ain't running no kitchen where the inmates tell me what to do instead of my telling them what to do."

"Karpis and Klint are in the Hole."

"Huh, that's a switch." Medford thought about the new responsibilities he would have as head steward and said, "Okay, Greg, I'm going to lay this on you. We can get away with a few of these jelly-sandwich meals in TU, but the law clearly states that we must feed the inmates a balanced diet each day. That includes a specified number of calories, grams of protein, carbohydrates, and so on. Sooner or later, we're going to have to serve them full meals."

"Mr. Eastland gave me a list of inmates who want to work in here. Are you ready for them?" I asked.

"Yeah, we'd better get at it so we can serve a decent supper."

Putting down my coffee cup, I left the kitchen. On my way out, I locked the door to the basement. The new rule required an officer or steward to escort inmates who went to the basement.

Having rounded up the volunteer crew, I took them to the kitchen. None of them had ever worked in the Alcatraz kitchen before. It was new scenery to them and, like all men who have been incarcerated for a long time, they were happy for a change. They did not try to hide their interest in their new surroundings, at first just looking and then beginning to open drawers and cabinets.

Medford had never before worked directly with blacks. He was looking at them with much doubt. They were looking back at him with much uncertainty.

"Here are your men," I said. "You just tell them what you want done and leave the rest to me."

The kitchen problem was solved. From that day on, black inmates worked in the kitchen. More white men were added to the crew as they returned to work, including some of the original crew. But the old ways were gone forever.

Medford gave instructions and pretty soon the kitchen routine was almost back to normal. The new crew was so eager to please Medford that I had little to do but reflect on other times I had worked in the kitchen.

Cooper, a military prisoner with a big mouth, was one inmate who came to mind. Cooper was in prison because he got drunk and killed two women in Germany. He was assigned to my kitchen crew with the comment, "Well, let's see if Gregory can straighten out this kid." Although he wanted to work rather than stay in his cell all day, he couldn't keep a job. His big talk was always getting him in trouble.

Cooper persisted in adolescent behavior in spite of being in his mid-twenties. He either tried to be a cute little kid or public enemy number one. He used the presence of officers as protection while he talked big to inmates. Cooper was a white southern boy and had friends among the blacks; he played table games with them in the yard and talked with them in the cell house. They seemed to understand him and tolerated his erratic and sometimes overbearing behavior.

Cooper came to the kitchen on his first day with his mouth working. I took him aside and said, "It's time for you to start growing up. These people are getting tired of your big mouth."

"What do you mean? I can say anything I want to," Cooper said, all in a huff.

I walked up in front of him and, staring in his eyes, kicked his shins—hard enough to hurt. He mouthed off. I kicked him again. After the third exchange, Cooper said, "Hey, what's going on, man?"

"Before somebody calls your bluff, you'd better grow up. And I'm going to help you. Every time you shoot off your big mouth, I'm going to kick your shins. Now, go back to work and keep your mouth shut."

At the end of the shift, I called Cooper over and said, "Cooper, tomorrow morning, right off the bat, I want to see a breakfast set up right here for me." The officers' mess was in a corner of the kitchen at that time. (It was later moved to another location.) The next morning, when I got to my table, my breakfast of a homemade Danish, cereal with whole milk, and coffee was there waiting for me.

It got to be a game. Cooper looked around to see where I was before he shot off his mouth. He was tired of getting his shins kicked. Then I started giving him one-sentence lectures: "You had better stop this stuff or somebody is going to walk up behind you and leave a knife in your back."

One morning he was really angry when he came to work. He went around mumbling, "He can't talk to me like that."

I got the story from another inmate who didn't want to see the kid get into trouble. A white inmate celled next to Cooper had threatened him for keeping up a constant chatter with the black inmates celled across the aisle. Of course, Cooper had pulled his big-mouth routine. His neighbor was a cold-blooded murderer and would have no trouble carrying out his threat.

Again, I took Cooper aside and said, "I'm going to try to keep that guy away from you. But you have got to cut out this stuff." He was trying to get himself under control, but had a way to go.

Word got around that a volunteer was needed for a job in the industries. Making sure I was within hearing, Cooper said, "I'd like to have that job, but I don't guess they'll let me have it."

I went to bat for him. Industries didn't want him, but I was able to convince them to take him on a trial basis. He got the job and moved off kitchen row.

When the new inmate assigned to the kitchen moved into the cell vacated by Cooper, we had another problem. The inmate, Lyman, walked into the cell and came out immediately, nauseated by the stench. I investigated. Cooper had used his Bull Durham bulk cigarette tobacco as chewing tobacco and the corner of his cell as a spittoon. Cooper was very clean as a person and in his kitchen work, but he thought nothing of using his cell in this way. I called him in to clean up the mess.

Cooper declared he wouldn't do it. I told him he would either clean up the cell or he would go to the Hole. I rejected his first effort, which was less than satisfactory, and made him start over. He grumbled and I threatened him with the Hole until he finally got the cell clean.

When Alcatraz closed, Cooper was transferred to Leavenworth. As soon as he was checked in down there, he started his big talk again. Ted Renneberg, one of the Alcatraz officers who had accompanied the chain, was asked to talk to him.

Renneberg went in to see him and said, "What you need is a visit with Mr. Gregory right now." They both laughed.

"How is Mr. Gregory?" Cooper asked.

I had been injured on the dock several months before Alcatraz closed and did not return to work. I hope the kid made it okay when he got out into free society.

During the afternoon, Mr. Eastland appeared in the kitchen. Medford approached him concerning the inmates in TU. "We're going to have a hell of a time trying to serve all those people in there," said Medford.

"Yeah, I know. Do your instructions say in what form the food has to be served?" asked Eastland.

"No, we just have to see that they get the proper rations each day."

"I see you have a lot of paper cups that you use for ice cream."

"Yeah, we've got cases of them."

"Okay, that's how you are going to serve the men in TU. Take what would be their daily rations of meat, potatoes, bread, and whatever else you are serving, put it through the grinders with a lot of catsup, pour it in the paper cups, and you're ready to serve."

"Whaaat?" said Medford. But his eyes were already laughing. "Well, you know how the bureaucracy works. By the time they get around to understanding this, we'll probably be out of the woods."

The armed officers who manned the gun ports covering the dining hall during the evening meal were probably more alert than usual. The black population was let in first. Then the whites were brought in. There was absolute quiet. A lot of staring was done, blacks at whites and whites at blacks—especially at the new blacks on the kitchen crew. The white inmates had not expected this obstacle in their war with the administration. Their leaders were now in the Hole, and they didn't know what to do without orders. In fact, most of them didn't want to do anything. They just wanted peace again and to do their time. They went back to their cells from the dining hall in routine fashion.

Following the meal, I stood in the middle of the kitchen keeping a wary eye on the purposeful confusion going on around me. The new inmate helpers were a little awkward but were intent on doing a good job.

Above the clang and clatter of the dishwashers, the two big food grinders were going lickety-split and the steward was carefully measuring everything he put into them. I ambled over close enough to peer down into the grinders. I saw a thick, brownish, lumpy mixture. While I was standing there, Medford winked at me and started dumping large containers of catsup into the grinders. The mixture began to turn pink, and then it got darker and brighter until it was quite a nice shade of red.

"I hope everybody in TU likes red," I said.

When the food cart was rolled into TU, the usual question heard was "Who's that?" and those nearest the door supplied the others with the answer. This evening, the response was: "Food cart coming in. Some more of those goddamned jelly sandwiches, I suppose."

After a while, someone said, "No, it's not jelly sandwiches, they got something in ice-cream cups. They going to give us ice cream?" A sad, sour giggle went through the tiers. Desserts were not served in TU.

The officers wheeled the cart up to the top tier and started handing out the cups, placing them on the service windows of the cells. During the serving of the first couple of cells, there was a tentative silence.

"What in the hell is this?" one inmate ventured to ask, staring into the thick red mixture.

"This is your dinner," an unsmiling officer responded.

By the time the third cell was served, a number of inmates had tasted the contents of the cups. After all, they were hungry. The decision was that it didn't taste bad. Finally, someone down toward the end of the line yelled, "What is it?"

"Bloody Marys," was the answer from one of the first to have been served. Thus, the gooey liquid meals were christened Bloody Marys.

Several officers, including Mr. Eastland, were standing down on the flats observing the procedure. About half the inmates had been served when suddenly one of the cups came hurtling down, making a sudden splash on the flats in front of the officers.

"Did anybody see which cell this came from?" Eastland asked.

"Yes, it came from the third cell on the second tier," said one of the officers.

"Get one of the men from there and bring him down here to clean it up."

"But I don't know which one did it."

"Just grab one and bring him down here. It won't take long before we'll know who did it."

An inmate was brought down and Eastland said, "Okay, here's a scrub bucket. Clean it up."

"I didn't do it."

"How do we know that? Go ahead and clean it up."

The inmate cleaned the floor, but he wasn't very happy about it. When he got back to his cell, there was a bit of a commotion. By the time an officer walked slowly to the cell, the activity was all over. The inmate who had thrown the Bloody Mary had paid a painful price for it. Suffice to say, no more Bloody Marys were thrown out on the flats.

Those of us involved in the Bloody Mary episode, officers and inmates alike, remembered it for years to come—with humor and with a sort of left-handed compliment to Mr. Eastland for solving a difficult problem.

25

My New Clothing-Room Crew

Six or seven days into the strike, a number of the strikers had returned to work, and in some cases the crews were fairly complete. It was the all-white or mostly-white crews we were having difficulty getting back to work.

Mr. Eastland came down to the West End, where several of us had gathered to get our assignments for the day. "We're going to have to do something about getting these guys down for showers and clean clothes," he said. "There are too many of them to go down in small groups. We need an inmate crew down there to get the clothing sorted and ready to handle the whole population. How about the regular clothing-room crew?"

"With the exception of one, they're still in the Hole," I said.

"Do you think you can find a crew?"

"I think so." Mr. Eastland gave me a long inquiring look. "I was just thinking the black inmates we put in the kitchen are working out so well, I would like to try black inmates in the clothing room."

"Well, now, what's to lose? Let's put them in there and see what they can do." Eastland reached into my shirt pocket and helped himself to a cigarette. "When this is all over," he said with a broad smile, "remind me to recommend you for the good conduct ribbon."

I smiled dourly at this allusion to the way the military rewarded good conduct and said, "When this is over you can just give me a nice quiet tower job so I can stay out of these goddamned messes."

"Which inmates do you want down there?"

"May I pick my own crew?" I asked cautiously.

231

"Take anybody you want. The clothing room is all yours. Just give me a list of those you pick."

I went to the inside of B Block, where the blacks were celled. The first man I approached was so tall he looked as though he had to hunch over in his cell. He was fiddling with the mouthpiece of a trumpet. His face was covered with keloid tissue, the result of knife slashings. He was a man who paid strict attention to "doing his own time." He had proved to other inmates on occasion how foolish they were to try to tell him how to do his time. He was feared and followed by the rest of the black population. His name was George Washington Jones.

I looked through the bars at him. Jones looked back at me and continued to produce tuneless sounds on his mouthpiece.

"Hiya, Jones."

He removed the mouthpiece from his lips just long enough to say "Hiya, Boss."

"Ever work in the clothing-room, Jones?"

Jones leaned toward me. "Play it out some more, will you, Boss?"

"How would you like to work for me in the clothing room?"

"You the badge down there now, Boss?"

"That's me," I acknowledged.

Temptation showed in Jones's eyes. For a long time, he had wanted to work. But then the interest died away and his eyes became sullen, impenetrable black agates.

"You mean just until this ol' hanky-panky is done rolled up," he said, with the hurt that only a person who has been exploited many times would know.

"Now who the hell said anything like that? This is a permanent assignment to the clothing-room crew and it makes no matter how this strike turns out."

"How about the white boys?"

"Are you afraid of the white boys?"

"You ain't givin' ol' Jones a bum steer, are you, Boss?"

"Have I ever?" I challenged.

Jones began to smile. "Boss, you got yourself a worker."

I went from cell to cell until I had a total of eight men. They were the toughest of the black population but they were also the most reliable. I already had one white inmate from the former crew, MacDonald, who was not honoring the strike.

I was about to let the men out of their cells when I suddenly thought of another black inmate I wanted to try. I walked down the tier to the cell of an inmate named Colin, who was locked in his cell almost all the time because of his violent temper. Inmates and officers alike feared him. He was sitting on his bunk, staring blankly in front of him.

"Colin, you've been pretty quiet lately. What's wrong?" I asked.

Colin looked up at me, apparently without comprehension. Looking into his eyes, I said, "How would you like to go to work?"

He stood up and came to the cell bars without a word. I understood, and Colin became a member of my crew. He willingly took orders from me but not from any other officers. I tried to train Colin to accept other officers as people to be obeyed. Most officers who came down to work in the clothing room during showers accepted Colin without any big to-do. But others who had occasion to give commands to him were not at all satisfied.

"A con is a con and he takes orders from all officers, not just the ones he feels like obeying," was the hostile statement made by one officer.

I had a strong feeling there would be trouble sooner or later and was afraid I shouldn't have taken Colin out to work. He was a good worker but I couldn't always be there to smooth the ruffled feathers.

My experiment came to a sad and violent end. An officer who was taking a survey of the inmate population on movie preferences asked Colin what kind of movies he liked.

"I don't go to no movies and I don't answer none of your foolish questions," Colin said, and turned away. He was returning to his cell following a work period.

The officer caught Colin by the arm and said, "Listen, man, when I ask a question I want an answer."

Whatever you needed to say to an inmate could be said without touching him. In cases where an inmate resisted going from one place to another, a come-along hold got the job done. But grabbing a guy's arm to tell him something and then letting go was a dangerous move. It was a bullying tactic, and not well tolerated by inmates.

Colin jerked his arm away and ran up the stairs to his cell on the second tier.

The officer and others who observed the scene thought Colin had simply gone to his cell in a huff. But suddenly, down the stairs came Colin so quickly that all the officers were frozen in astonishment and then fear. Colin had a trumpet in his hand and before anybody could react, he smashed it down on the head of the officer who had questioned him. Three rapid, brutal strokes landed on the officer's head. His skull was fractured in five places.

There was no doubt that Colin was mentally unbalanced; therefore, no trial was held. He spent the remainder of his time at Alcatraz in TU.

Amazingly, the officer survived the attack with no apparent permanent damage. The trumpet also survived and continued to be used in band practice.

For some time following this incident, some officers made sly, unkind remarks about me as a would-be rehabilitator of inmates. In truth, I had to admit that I had let my compassion distort reality.

I took my new crew down to the clothing room, where they began to check out the things behind the counter. When I thought they had learned about all they could by themselves, I explained to each one what needed to be done before and after we opened for showers.

When we were ready, I called the West End and reported that we were open for business.

Following the showers, we issued a bathrobe and a stack of clean clothing to each inmate. This was the first shower day that the population returned to their cells to dress. It reduced the number of people in the clothing room at any given time and cut down on the confusion.

With George Washington Jones as the de facto inmate leader of my new crew, I had no problems. During the time Colin worked in the clothing room, the crew accepted him. They understood he was a sick person and made allowances for him.

On the rare occasion when a white inmate tried to give a member of my crew a hard time, I stepped up to the counter and stared at him. He would be happy to terminate his bullying and move along.

26

Cold Showers for
TU Inmates

After the evening meal, the hollering and yelling that went on all day long subsided to some extent. Except for one night. Since Bull Benson's unsuccessful attempt to choose his cell, he had been brooding about the change in attitude toward him by the striking inmates. They were mad at him for trying to leave TU, and Bull realized he was losing his position as leader.

Lieutenant Boatman had the evening watch. He came into TU and gave the day crew permission to leave. I was one of those who was leaving, thereby missing one of the big events in Alcatraz history. However, I heard all about it from several officers the next day.

It was getting on to eight o'clock. From the upper tiers of TU, you could look out on the wondrous panorama of San Francisco Bay and the city. The lights of the city, boats, ships, and ferries truly made a sight to behold. But there were precious few in TU, if any, who were getting much of a thrill out of anything, inside or outside, on this night.

Suddenly Bull, trying to regain his position as leader, screamed out, "Let's go!"

Instantly, the inmates renewed their screaming and hollering. In a couple of the cells, they tugged at the framework of the bunks, trying to remove the heavy iron slats to use as wrecking tools. When they succeeded, they ripped the toilets from the securing bolts and beat them into powder.

The officer in charge shouted up to the West Gun Gallery officer to call out front for help.

Within minutes, a squad of officers came in, led by Captain Rychner. He had been at Alcatraz since it became a federal prison and was a calm, stubborn fellow.

The captain unlocked the fire-hose cabinet and told the officers to grab hold and pull. With a number of officers stationed on either side of the hose, Rychner cautioned them to get a firm grip on it because it would kick. He turned on the water gradually, but even so, the hose straightened out so fast that some of the officers were knocked down. They got up quickly and got the hose under control. The first few gallons of water that came out were very muddy. The source of the water was the bay—salt water.

The captain's instructions were clear; no inmate was to be hurt, but they would be made to understand that the destruction and noise had to stop. He directed the officers to aim for the legs of the inmates in the last cell of the third tier. When the captain heard them holler that they had had enough, he had the hose moved to the next cell.

Inmates in the second cell stopped their destructive endeavors and began to yell and scream as the cold water reached them. By now, inmates in other cells had stopped their activities and were paying attention to the progress of the hose. It took only moments in each cell. The water treatment was continued under Rychner's supervision until a proper "We give up" had been heard from each cell.

On reaching the closed front cells—the ones where the solid steel doors had been shut and the occupants in darkness—Rychner ordered that they be opened, except the last one. In the last cell were two of the toughest guys in the institution. One was big and strong and the other was wiry and fragile-looking. Both possessed iron wills. Neither of them had made much noise, but they were dedicated to making this strike work. They were two southerners who had been taught from birth that there could be no equality or brotherhood between white and black people. They neither liked nor disliked blacks, particularly. They just patterned their lives after what they had been taught.

The officers were kind of surprised at the captain's orders. Some of them thought the two southerners ought to get the best bath of all. But Rychner knew that those two might well die under the pressure of the cold water rather than give up. Such was their blind, stubborn belief in the correctness of their moral code.

The officers laid the hose out along the wall to dry and left the unit. TU was quiet except for the sounds of water dripping from the upper tiers and a few moans from the now subdued inmates.

The next morning when I walked into the cell house, there was a different feeling. The tension seemed to be relaxing. The crucial part of the strike was over. The strike leaders realized they were not going to win any concessions this time.

The days went by and some sort of order was maintained in spite of the strike.

The usual routine of work call, sick call, and meal preparation and serving was being carried out. Each day, one or two more inmates went back to work. The inmates had to make their own decisions about returning to work—their leaders were fresh out of advice.

One morning when the cells were opened for work call, two lieutenants came into the cell house and grabbed a tough, well-built inmate, dragged him out of his cell, and wrestled him onto the floor.

"You're going to work whether you like it or not. We're going to throw you out in the yard and if you don't keep on going down to the industries to work you can just stay out there and freeze," one of the officers said.

I saw what was happening from my position on the second tier and rushed down to help the lieutenants.

"Oh! Jesus Christ," the inmate said, "Don't hurt me, Mr. Gregory."

"Get out of here, Greg, we have it under control," said one of the lieutenants.

I let go and stepped back, realizing what must be happening. The inmate had probably sent a kite to Mr. Eastland saying he wanted to go to work, but didn't want his fellow inmates to know of his request. Eastland had worked out a way to help him save face.

There was one attempt to "force" an inmate to go to work that backfired, or maybe the officers got the wrong inmate. The inmate fought viciously when he was taken from his cell. The officers got him out in the yard but he would not go down to the industries building to work. He sat in the yard all day long. He wouldn't give in. But when the strike was over and things settled back into a quiet daily routine, this inmate became one of the most cooperative—and most comical—inmates in Alcatraz.

By the time this inmate had served his sentence, two important changes had occurred. Some inmates were being released directly from Alcatraz and the bureau had started using the airlines for transporting prisoners and parolees. The comic was the first parolee from Alcatraz to return home by air. For a couple of years following his release, he often called the Control Center to chat with whoever was on duty. He said, and just possibly meant it, that he missed Alcatraz—it had been his home for such a long time.

27

Return from Vacation

I took a much-needed vacation. The warden had all but insisted we take at least some of our strike overtime in time off, rather than being paid for it. I was happy to do so.

Now I was back in the harness and mildly surprised that there were still so many inmates in TU. Bunch Tompkins explained that Mr. Eastland was not in a hurry to put them back in the population. He was releasing just one or two at a time, leaving the ones who might hope to revive the strike till last.

An unexpected result of the settlement of the strike was that the inmates approved of the new routines. Discipline and control of the bullies made it much easier for the majority of the population to do their time and collect good time without fear of the inmate bosses.

As I settled back into the daily routine, I thought what a pleasure it was to work in an institution where the staff was in full control.

Discipline had become so lax before the strike that the unexpected had turned into the expected. For instance, one would not expect to see an inmate casually walking out of the warden's house with a shotgun in one hand and a box of shells in the other. But it happened.

I was driving the bus up top to collect the last of Warden Swope's possessions—he was retiring. When I stopped in front of the warden's house, the inmate houseboy came out carrying a shotgun and a box of shells.

I was dumbfounded. Trying to hide a sly smile, the inmate handed the weapon and shells to me. There was an ironclad rule that all weapons were to be kept in the Control Center. My first impulse was to take the shotgun to the Control Center and check it in. On second thought, I said nothing and the shotgun and shells left the island in the custody of the retiring warden.

For days I wondered whether I should report this incident. Two or three other officers probably saw the shotgun. However, it was never discussed and I finally stopped worrying about it.

When I thought of the danger the shotgun could have put all of us in, it really made me mad. In the event of a breakout, we did not want weapons scattered around the island. The houseboy could have told other inmates about the shotgun.

A few weeks later, when Paul Madigan left a stint at another prison and returned to Alcatraz as warden, I told him about the incident. He wasted no time in getting the houseboy transferred to another institution.

The phone rang. It was Bunch, who was acting captain that day.

"Better get out here, Greg."

A few minutes later, I was looking across a desk at Bunch's austere face. Mr. Eastland sat impassively on the corner of the desk. My stomach began to put out alarm signals.

"I'm leaving," Eastland said bluntly.

"Leaving?" I felt as if I had sustained a hard body blow. Then I knew that what I had heard from the plumbing line was true—a new associate warden was on the way and Parant was returning as captain.

"You're sure leaving Bunch and me in a hell of a position," I said, remembering all the bitter frustrations I had refused to express during Parant's last tour of duty at Alcatraz.

"I know I am," said Eastland. "But the bureau put it to me this way: It would be better for me to retire on an associate warden's pay than to stay on working for the pay of a junior officer. I used you two guys more than anyone else and I want you to know I appreciate all you did to break up the strike. Right now the institution seems to be running pretty smoothly with Warden Madigan in charge."

The three of us just sat there silently.

Then Eastland abruptly stood up and walked out the main entrance.

I never saw him again.

I continued my daily work as clothing-room officer in addition to carrying kites requesting the release of various inmates from TU. Word was out that I was one of the officers whose recommendations for release were being honored by the new associate warden. Friends of many of the inmates who were still in TU, two to a cell, asked me to help get them out and back into the population. I made myself available as much as possible to those who wanted to request the release of a friend.

The new associate warden came to me, begging for help in dealing with the holdouts. They were refusing to leave TU because they were determined not to cell across the aisle from the black inmates.

I went into TU and picked out the inmates I thought might be tired of the restrictions there. My pitch to them went something like this: "Let me know when you are ready to get out. I can get you out of here if you agree to take the cell assigned to you and demand nothing. You can't build up any good time in here. The sooner you get out of here, the sooner you get out of Alcatraz." I spoke with them individually and considered it a promise to them. One by one, we got them back into the population.

I went to the front office with the name of one of the inmates who had said he was ready to come out. But somebody out front didn't want him released from TU, and Warden Madigan agreed. I left without argument.

In order to speak with the warden in private, I stopped at the first phone I came to and called him. "Warden, that inmate agreed to the requirements and I made him a promise he could come out," I said.

"If you gave your word, I will back it up," the warden said. The inmate was released from TU and kept his end of the bargain.

We finally got the number of inmates in TU reduced sufficiently to cell them individually. Then we began to empty some of the cells altogether. I went out front with the name of yet another inmate who had agreed to the terms of being released from TU.

"Can't take any more out of there. We've got to keep a certain percentage in TU so the bureau knows we need a TU," the associate warden said.

I had to do a lot of yelling that didn't show much respect for my supervisors, but I finally got the guy out of TU.

On another occasion, I was sitting on the disciplinary court when the associate warden told Laiten he could get out of TU if he would behave himself for a few weeks. Laiten complied and in a few weeks he sent a kite to the associate warden requesting to be let out of TU.

Laiten was in TU for killing Karney, a popular inmate. The inmates hated Laiten and letting him out would not necessarily be to his advantage.

"I was there when you promised Laiten he could get out," I reminded the associate warden.

"So what? He's never going to get out."

I went back and told Laiten he would be staying in TU.

"You heard him say I could get out of here," Laiten said.

"Yes, I heard him. But he's changed his mind. So that's that."

Actually, Laiten was relieved because he knew he wouldn't last long in population. He knew how the other inmates felt about him and knew they would get him.

28

The End of an Adventure

For two or three years, the institution ran fairly smoothly and quietly. Then the same old problems began to show up again.

The social changes in the country during the 1950s and early 1960s affected the rules and regulations governing incarcerated people, giving the inmates more and more power. It wasn't long before officers, who had started writing shots on inmates when Mr. Eastland came in, found it was not worth it. The officer was more likely to be criticized than the inmate. An offshoot of an officer getting this kind of reception at disciplinary court was a double measure of disrespect from the accused inmate. Within a short time, friends of the accused would join in the disdainful treatment of the officer. Some officers found it impossible to continue working and quit the job.

Warden Madigan was unsuccessful in his efforts to get the bureau to make building repairs and improvements for better custody and greater comfort. Associate wardens, captains, and lieutenants came and went. The last of the old-time correctional officers were retiring. Officer morale plunged with the lax observance of rules and the lack of support from the front office.

The increased power that the inmates acquired did not lead to contentment. There was much unrest in the population. There were escape attempts that could not have happened had the philosophy of Mr. Eastland and Warden Madigan prevailed.

During the years I worked at Alcatraz, there were two escape attempts.* In 1956, an inmate named Floyd Wilson escaped but was recaptured. Two years lat-

*Gregory was on sick leave when two other escapes occurred, on June 11 and December 16, 1962.

er, Clyde Johnson and Aaron Burgett attempted to free themselves from The Rock. Johnson was recaptured but Burgett was not seen again until his body washed up on the island almost two weeks later.

During the time Burgett was missing, he acquired a nickname. "Wouldn't a cold Burgie be good about now?" was the question with which the inmates taunted us until Burgett's body was found. San Francisco's Burgermeister Beer company probably never knew it got some free advertising from the inmates on Alcatraz.

Several men who came on the staff as correctional officers soon found they were afraid of the inmates. Some of them managed to find favor with one administrator or another and were able to land paper-shuffling positions for themselves in the front office. This meant fewer officers to deal with the inmates.

On one occasion when I was feeling particularly frustrated with the way things were going, I noticed some activity in the visitors' room. Going over to the window, I saw two white-faced officers standing inside the door, looking as if they wished they were on the outside. I looked toward the opposite end of the room to see what had caused such terror. Backed up against the wall was a small, skinny, black kid with fists raised in a fighting stance. The kid had been transferred from some other institution and two of the paper shufflers, who were being paid to work with inmates, had been assigned the task of entering him into the Alcatraz system.

It was one of those times when I didn't feel like controlling my disgust with the willingness of the administration to keep correctional officers who either could not or would not accept responsibility for the duties assigned to them. I went to the door of the visitors' room and asked Captain Rychner to let me in, which he did with reluctance.

Once inside, I walked right by the two big hulks, who were still standing there transfixed by fear. I caught hold of the front of the kid's shirt and gave it a jerk, popping off a few buttons. The kid dropped his hands and made an effort to look at me. His eyes looked empty. He didn't seem able to be of danger to anyone—especially a couple of husky fellows who were about twice his size.

It turned out that the kid—I never did learn his name—was mentally ill and should not have been sent to Alcatraz. He spent most of his time on the island in the hospital.

After he had been in the hospital for several days, an MTA told me that he did nothing but lie on his bunk. He hadn't even taken a shower since being put in the hospital.

I took another officer with me and went up to see that the kid got a shower. I was surprised to find him in a strip cell. It was true he liked to wave his hands around, but to my knowledge he had never hit or even spoken to anyone.

I opened the cell door, and my fellow officer started into the cell to slap the kid around, playing the big, tough prison guard.

"Don't use that kind of stuff with this kid. Just stand back," I said as I walked over to the kid. "Come on, buddy, we're going to let you have a nice warm shower."

The kid's empty eyes indicated he didn't know what I was talking about. I started taking off his clothes. My partner was so rough in his efforts to help that I asked him to go get the shower ready.

I guided the kid into the shower. I literally had to walk the poor fellow into the spray of warm water. Just before I got him under the water, he looked at me with eyes full of fear. But once he felt the water, he seemed to enjoy it. I gave him a bar of soap and he proceeded to give himself a good washing.

A few weeks went by before I saw the kid again. Somebody had put him back into the population—not a good place for him to be. He went to the dining hall to eat, but other than that he just cowered in his cell.

I heard a complaint about his refusing to stand up at the bars of his cell for the formal counts and that all efforts to communicate with him were met with a fighting stance. Officers were afraid to approach him.

I opened his cell and went in. He was huddled on the floor in the corner. I walked over to him and held out my hand. He took it and I led him out and back to the hospital.

Whatever the kid had done on the outside, he should never have been put in prison—certainly not in Alcatraz.

By the time Warden Madigan transferred to the prison at McNeil Island in 1961, the inmates had again achieved a number of changes in the rules and regulations governing the institution. When Olin Blackwell became warden, we had many inmates who refused to shave or to have their hair cut reasonably short. The two showers per week were not enough to keep these inmates, with their long hair and beards, looking clean.

On one occasion, Warden Blackwell was standing by me as the inmates filed into the dining hall for their noon meal. When the line at the steam table slowed down, I stopped the line at the door. It was better for them to wait outside the dining hall.

An inmate from the Minneapolis area happened to be right in front of me when I stopped the line. He was a very personable Italian fellow and I had gotten to know him fairly well. I often chatted with him about Minneapolis.

"Mr. Gregory, could I move down to the lower tier?" the Italian asked. He had joined the group of inmates who refused to shave. His beard had grown untrimmed for several weeks and had become a matted, scraggly, unkempt mess.

I just stared at him.

The Italian looked puzzled. I kept staring. The warden was getting uncomfortable, but I kept staring.

Then a light went on in the Italian's eyes and he broke out in a giggle.

"All right, Mr. Gregory, I'll shave."

"Okay. When you are ready, you can change your cell," I said.

As this exchange was completed, I caught a glimpse of the warden's face. He was impressed.

It was Sunday and my post was dock-in-charge. The dock activity consisted of people going to the city or beyond for church or leisure activities and people coming to visit resident officers or inmates. It was a pleasant place to be.

But I kept staring at the Dock Tower, where I had to go at noon to relieve an officer for lunch. I looked forward to that with trepidation. A section of the iron staircase had rusted away and a wooden ladder had been erected to connect the remaining steps. My lifelong fear of high places (and, in particular, climbing steep, unsafe stairs) was putting me in a bad mood.

When the time came, I fought back my fears and climbed the stairs to the Dock Tower. I sat down as the post officer left for his lunch. The phone rang.

"Gregory, you're needed in TU to get those men shaved. The warden said it had to be done today because that inspection is tomorrow," the lieutenant of the watch said in his most pleading voice.

"Lieutenant, I just came up here as lunch relief. I'm assigned to the dock today and that is where I am going to work," I said in a voice far more commanding than the lieutenant's.

I had heard the news from the grapevine that a bureau official was coming out and I had wondered what the brass would do about all the cons with long hair and beards. It was another one of those things that could have been handled easily at the beginning. The longer nothing was done, the more inmates there were with long hair and beards.

At this point in my career, about the only thing I was afraid of was the steep stairs below me. I felt no fear in refusing the lieutenant's meek request. I knew there was a full crew of officers in the cell house and knew that the lieutenant had been told to "go in there and shave those inmates."

The lieutenant's excuse of having to supervise the Sunday afternoon movie did not impress me. He finally hung up when he understood it would take a direct order from the warden to get me off my assigned post and up to TU.

Lunch was over and the regular officer returned to the Dock Tower. I made my way carefully down the treacherous stairs and continued my duties on the dock.

"Gregory, bring the truck up top. Officer ill," the intercom boomed.

"I'm on the way," I said, and headed for the truck.

In the warden's outer office, I found a very sick man. Jimmy Jimmerson was near retirement—and as sick as he looked, I wondered whether he would make it.

Jimmy was one of the officers the lieutenant had ordered to shave the inmates. In the middle of the tussle, Jimmy's heart had given out.

We put him on a stretcher and took him down the hill on the back of the truck. There was no surface long enough to put the stretcher down inside the cabin of the boat, so we put Jimmy in the outside passage alongside the cabin. Since he was a friend of mine and I knew his family, I was elected to escort him to the hospital.

The water was quite choppy and sprayed over the side. I stood beside Jimmy and tried to keep the spray off of him. He was soaking wet from sweat and I was soaking wet from the spray by the time we reached the mainland.

There were two or three officers waiting to make the return trip on the boat.

"Come down and help us. We've got a sick man here," I called up to them.

"Who is it?" was the response.

"Jimmy."

My fellow officers turned and sauntered away. The boat officer and I got Jimmy up the gangplank, where we waited for the ambulance.

We had reached a point where too much energy was directed toward trying to get a promotion and too little toward consideration for other people. Had the sick man been a captain or higher in rank, the gentlemen at the top of the gangplank would have run over each other getting down there to help.

I had now become one of the "old-timers." There weren't many of us left. It was getting harder and harder for me to put up with the changes I saw in officers and inmates. Rules had become a joke again and the inmates were making many of the decisions. The roster was almost totally made up of inexperienced officers who had been given very little training. There were few people left on the staff who were capable of training new officers.

In March of 1962, I went on vacation and returned to work on April 2. As the dock lieutenant, I was overseeing the unloading of a barge that had arrived late in the afternoon. It was getting close to time for the inmates to go in for the evening meal and lockup. I walked over to the edge of the dock and looked down on the barge to see how much more there was to be unloaded. Just as I turned back, I saw the huge rope slings of the crane swinging toward me. There wasn't time to get out of the way, so I grabbed one of the ropes. The inmate crane operator was new, and I didn't know what he might do in an emergency situation. As he swung me out over the barge, I saw a clear spot and dropped down fifteen feet to the deck.

The crash landing on the barge broke my left leg and caused a blood clot that kept me checking in and out of the hospital for months. April 2, 1962, was the last time I stood roll call at Alcatraz.

During one of my visits to the hospital, a fellow patient called over to me, "Hey, Warden, I just heard over the radio that some prisoners escaped from Alcatraz."

"You must mean San Quentin," I said with a smile.

"You got a Walter Bertrand working at Alcatraz?" he asked a few seconds later.

"Yes," I said with all kinds of awful thoughts running through my mind.

"Well," said the man with the radio, "he's just been interviewed and said three inmates escaped from Alcatraz."

I thought, Glad I'm here and not on The Rock. I knew somebody would be made the scapegoat for this fracas, although the responsibility lay somewhere between the legislators, the policymakers for the Bureau of Prisons, and society as a whole.

During the coming weeks, I had no desire at all to leave the hospital—all hell had broken loose on the island. Officers who came to visit told the inside story.

Fred Wilkinson, assistant director of the bureau, came out and held a press conference concerning the escape. Attorney General Robert Kennedy came out later and held a press conference on the same subject. To my knowledge, it was the only time during my tenure that an attorney general came to California because of a problem at Alcatraz.

Two officers were given suspensions and the administration came down hard on the captain, who had been there only a few months. He was transferred to another institution.

Six months after the June 11 escape of Frank Morris and the Anglin brothers, two more inmates were able to get beyond the bars and into the water. That appeared to be the death knell for Alcatraz as a part of the Federal Prison System.* The rumors that I had been hearing from the time of my arrival in 1947 were now coming true.

---

*Although neither the general public nor the correctional officers knew about it, the Bureau of Prisons was considering the closure of Alcatraz even before the June 1962 escape.

Over a period of several months, the inmates were shipped out to other institutions and the General Services Administration of the federal government took over The Rock. The U.S. Penitentiary at Alcatraz closed and my adventure there ended.

The realization that my injury would not allow me to return to work and the news that Alcatraz was closing came to me at about the same time. The parade of memories that went through my mind stirred up an assortment of emotions. I was surprised at how much I had enjoyed my work at Alcatraz. It had been hard, sometimes unpleasant, but it had been satisfying.

I had helped some young men become good officers. I had been advisor, advocate, mentor, and disciplinarian to inmates, challenging them to be responsible for their own behavior. I watched some of them become cooperative. It gave me hope that they would also be cooperative citizens when released from prison.

I relished remembering the fun moments, the good times: sharing a laugh with Curly Young during the strike; Machine Gun Kelly's stories; the kid with the fighting stance and his trust in me; the spitball game; Smitty's willingness to open the cupboard where I had unwittingly locked my keys; Wagon Wheels's enjoyment of Sunday afternoons in the kitchen . . .

Memories of fights, knifings, and murders also came up. It was these horrible memories I was thinking about when I said to my friend Jimmy Jimmerson, "I signed my retirement papers today. Now I can forget about Alcatraz." Jimmerson had retired three years earlier.

"You S.O.B., you will *never* forget Alcatraz!"

Jimmerson was right.

At the Alcatraz alumni annual reunions, we reminisce, glossing over the terrifying experiences we had but enjoying the friendships cemented by those experiences and the memory of the rewarding moments of our life on The Rock.

Index

Page numbers in bold refer to illustrations.